CW00553360

HISTORY
44

BATTLES OF THE CRIMEAN WAR

Also available in this Series

CONDITIONS OF SALE

This book shall not, by way of trade or otherwise, be lent,
re-sold, hired out or otherwise circulated without the
publisher's prior consent in any form of binding or cover
other than that in which it is published and without a
similar condition including this condition being imposed
on the subsequent purchaser

British Battles Series

BATTLES OF THE CRIMEAN WAR

W. BARING PEMBERTON

UNABRIDGED

PAN BOOKS LTD : LONDON

First published 1962 by B. T. Batsford Ltd.

This edition published 1968 by Pan Books Ltd.,
33 Tothill Street, London, S.W.1

330 02181 8

© W. Baring Pemberton, 1962

Printed in Great Britain by
Cox & Wyman Ltd., London, Reading and Fakenham

Preface

The Crimean War has been called 'the last great war to be fought without the help of modern resources of science'. It was also the last great war to be fought by the British army in all its splendour of scarlet and gold, using weapons and tactics which would not have astonished the Prince Rupert or the Duke of Marlborough. To those who today have vivid recollections of modern warfare, battles such as the Alma, with columns of infantry volleying into each other at close range, field officers galloping about conspicuous on horseback, company commanders out in front of their men waving their swords, ensigns bravely carrying the Colours, or Balaclava, with its two spectacular cavalry charges, are hardly less remote than Naseby or Malplaquet. Yet many who fought in the First, and not a few who fought in the Second, World War will have known personally those who took part in such battles and heard their accounts from their own lips. Sir Fitzroy Maclean, probably the last survivor, died as recently as 1936. So near and yet so distant is the Crimean campaign.

On the other hand no campaign should be more familiar, because none has been 'covered' more fully and more candidly. Not only did the aftermath of every battle result in a flood of uncensored letters (which incidentally were subjected to the full foreign postage rate of threepence per quarter-ounce), but that novel intruder, the war-correspondent, was able to send back the most elaborate accounts, complete with revealing details and outspoken comments, all without any official impediment whatsoever. The historian of the Crimean battles has then (it would appear) only to make a synthesis of the innumerable letters and reports and his story is complete. Unfortunately this is not so. With smoke from the black powder then used drifting across the battlefield, lying heavily over batteries, the combatant could often see and report little more than what had happened in his vicinity; and even in this he is not necessarily reliable as this sentence from a letter from Lenox Prendergast of the Scots Greys proves:

Anyone who has been in a serious action knows how impossible it is even after a few hours not to fancy that incidents told one by somebody else are not part of one's own experience.

Nor, for much the same reasons, was the spectator or war-correspondent more favourably advantaged.

The impressions conveyed to my mind [wrote the surgeon of the 93rd] even through mine eyes, it would appear, were not minutely accurate; and yet I thought so at the time and their inaccuracy only proves that even an onlooker may know little of what occurs in a battle and the same incident seen by several at the same time may be differently described by all, and yet each individual speak with the confidence of being exact.

As for those who recollected in tranquillity – and there were many – it is enough to record the remark of a contemporary Canadian military historian: 'Memory can play tricks upon an officer after some lapse of time, especially when the officer's own interest and prejudice are engaged.'

Beset by these difficulties the writer who surrounds every incident with reservations and qualifications will rapidly weary his readers. He must on matters of moment, such for example as Nolan's responsibility for the Light Brigade charge, use his judgement on the evidence available and make up his own mind. This I have tried to do. If my interpretation of any controversial point offends, I can only say that it was not hurriedly made.

Without the help of those who most kindly lent me manuscript material or books, who advised me and patiently answered my questions, I could have done very little. It is therefore with the greatest of pleasure that I thank Mrs Bradford for the Vaughan Lee letters; Colonel Henry Clowes for those of Cornet Clowes; Mr Dashwood for the letters of Lieutenant Fletcher, RN; Sir Arthur Elton, Bt, for the Elton letters from the Clevedon Court Archives; Mr Cuthbert Fitzherbert for the Diary of James Godfrey and also for allowing me to quote extensively from the published letters of Henry Clifford, VC; to Captain Haly, RN, for the letters of Colonel Haly;

Mrs Hamilton for the Journal of Lieutenant Patrick Robertson; Major-General Hibbert for the letters of Captain Hugh Hibbert; Sir James Hunter Blair, Bt, for the Diary of Colonel Hunter Blair; Lady Jones for the Journal and Letters of Ensign Boscawen Griffith; Air Vice-Marshal McClurkin for the letters of Michael Heneage; Brigadier Maude for the Diary, papers and privately printed letters of Captain George Maude; my friend Major John Maxse for permission to examine the Maxse Papers; Major Paton for the letters of James Paton; Mr A. G. Shireff for the letters of Colonel James Patullo; Lady Skipwith for the letters of her grandfather Captain Alfred Tipping; Mrs Somerset for the letters of William Pechell; Colonel W. A. Stirling for the letters of his father Sir William Stirling and his uncles Francis and Charles; Mr H. E. Sutton for the letters of Major Edward Phillips; Mrs Patricia Taylor for the letters of Dr John McNeece and Mrs Wombwell for the letters of Sir George Wombwell.

A large number of people have lent me single letters or small collections, maps and books (some of them privately printed) for which I am most grateful. These include Mrs P. J. Roberts, Miss Babbage, Mr John Brooks, Dorothea de Culwen, Mr R. J. Cooper, Mrs Clure, Miss Chute, Mrs Greenacre, Colonel F. C. Hitchcock, Miss Helen Landon, the Rev. W. H. Cormack, W. Hallgarth, Mr Sergeant, Mrs Riley and Mr H. Skelton (both for gifts of books).

I have to thank Mr H. F. Longmore for two volumes of cuttings compiled by his father Dr Thomas Longmore of the 19th Regiment and Mr Christopher Hibbert for putting at my disposal the results of some of his researches for his admirable life of Lord Raglan.

As I had anticipated regimental archives yielded a rewarding harvest. From the Grenadier Guards came the letters of Henry and Grey Neville, from the Coldstream those of Gerald Goodlake and Clarke Jervoise; from the Scots Guards the diaries of Colonel Haygarth and Corporal Dolton; from the Gloucestershire Regiment the letters of Major James Williams and Colonel Frank Adams; from the Dorset Regiment the letters of Colonel Tinley; from the Black Watch the Diary of Captain Montgomery; from the Middlesex Regiment eighty-one letters from Major A. M. Earle. The Lancashire

Fusiliers allowed me to examine a collection of letters dealing with Inkerman and the Royal Artillery Institution lent me the letters of Corporal Mitchell, Lieutenant Richards and Surgeon A. H. Taylor. Other regiments, the Green Howards, the Duke of Wellington's, the Sherwood Foresters, the King's Own, the Lancashire, the Border and the Manchester regiments lent me regimental histories or bound copies of their magazine, and to these I should like to express my thanks.

To the Curator of the Scottish United Services Museum I am indebted for the Diary of Private McAusland and the letters of Lenox Prendergast; to the Librarian of the Staff College for much useful information; to the United Services Institution for a Crimean 'Scrap' book and above all to Mr D. W. King of the War Office library for his untiring help and assistance in providing me with books. I have to acknowledge with thanks permission from Messrs Constable and Co. to quote from Viscount Wolseley's *Story of a Soldier's Life*, and G. Bell and Sons to quote from *Soldier's Glory*.

I have to thank the Soviet Ministry of Foreign Affairs for very kindly supplying me with a number of photographs some of which are here reproduced and for answering questions dealing with Russian military formations. And I have to thank my friend Sir Frederick Hoyer Millar for the trouble he has taken in this matter and the British Embassy in Moscow for translating the Russian replies.

To Professor Cyril Falls and Mr C. R. N. Routh, who read the proofs and gave me most valuable criticism and assistance, I must express my very great gratitude.

Finally I have to acknowledge my over-all debt to Alexander William Kinglake. Although I think that occasionally his language becomes a little too pompous and I cannot agree with his unqualified adulation of Lord Raglan, it would be impossible even to begin to write upon the Crimean War without having his magnificent work at one's elbow.

To substitute present titles for numbers where regiments are mentioned would not only be an anachronism but in some respects misleading. In an appendix I have set out the modern designations in use prior to recent amalgamations.

W. B. P.

Billinghurst, 1961

Contents

Illustrations in Photogravure

Lord Raglan
From a portrait by an anonymous artist
(Courtesy of the Parker Gallery)

Sir George De Lacy Evans
From a mezzotint after R. Buckner, 1856

Prince Gortschakoff
From an engraving by and after D. J. Pound
(Courtesy of the Mansell Collection)

Marshal St Arnaud
From a contemporary engraving
(Courtesy of the Mansell Collection)

General Todleben
From a contemporary engraving
(Courtesy of the Mansell Collection)

Lord Raglan's Room
From a sketch by Henry Clifford, VC
(Courtesy of *The Illustrated London News*)

Battle of the Alma, showing Kourgane on the left
and Telegraph Hill on the right
From an eye-witness sketch by Henry Clifford, VC
(Courtesy of Nicholas Fitzherbert, Esq., and Michael Joseph Ltd)

The Charge of the Light Brigade at Balaclava
From a lithograph by E. Walker after W. Simpson, 1855

The Night of Balaclava
From a watercolour by W. Simpson
(Courtesy of Major John Maxse)

The Second Charge of the Guards at Inkerman
From a lithograph by R. M. Bryson after a drawing by W. Simpson,
1855
(George Brakenbury, *The Campaign in the Crimea*, 1855)

'A Hot Day in the Batteries' (facing the Redan)
From a lithograph by E. Walker after a drawing by W. Simpson,
1855
(George Brakenbury, *The Campaign in the Crimea*, 1855)

An artist's impression of the Fall of Sebastopol, September 8th,
1855
From a lithograph by and after Thomas Packer
(Courtesy of the Parker Galleries)

Maps

'The first quality of the soldier is
constancy in enduring fatigue and privations.
Courage is only the second.'

NAPOLEON

1

Peace and War

'England is the only country in the world thoroughly and universally impressed with the constant desire for peace.'

— Sir John Burgoyne

'CONSTANTINOPLE? NEVER! It is the key of the world!' Whether or not the story is true which attributes this assertion to Napoleon, when at Tilsit Alexander had demanded the Ottoman capital as his share of a European settlement, it supplies the clue to the Crimean War.

In the hands of Russia, Constantinople would have given her navy egress into the Mediterranean while ensuring it a secure retreat from any pursuing enemy; it would have provided her with a backdoor into the Balkans and must have extended her influence eastward throughout the Levant and the Holy Land as far as Egypt. But by the middle of the century it had become clear to Nicholas, who had succeeded his brother in 1825, that the Concert of Europe would never permit such aggrandizement. Austro-Hungary because of her proximity to the Balkans, France because of her own Near East ambitions, Great Britain because of her concern for the 'Avenues to India', would none of them tolerate without a war a Russian annexation of Constantinople. All that Nicholas now aspired to was a large measure of influence in the governance of the Porte. This he believed he might achieve without the use of force from which he was by nature averse. The abortive Montenegran revolt in 1852 had given point to some hints he had thrown out eight years before when on a visit to England. In January 1853, in a notorious colloquy with the British ambassador, Sir Hamilton Seymour, he returned to the subject. 'Turkey is falling to pieces. The sick man is dying. We must come to some understanding.' It was a mere feeler, but it was put forward by one whose innermost wishes clearly coloured his vision, yet in a sincere endeavour to avert what he believed would be an ugly scramble following the abrupt disintegration of the Sultan's patchwork dominions. The executors of the deceased party, he hinted, need be no more than two: Great Britain and Russia. To the first, in return for services rendered, could go Egypt and, if need be, Crete. The second would take Constantinople not *en propriétaire* – he had (he said) entirely abandoned 'the plans and dreams of Catherine' – but *en dépositaire*, pending a settlement of the Balkans which would establish Rumania, Serbia, and Bulgaria as independent states under Russian protection.

The Foreign Office when informed was not impressed. The integrity of the Porte had long become one of its diplomatic shibboleths. Once anything like a break-up was permitted France, always hankering to revive Napoleon's Egyptian dreams, would hasten to stake her claims and the overland routes to India could be imperilled. The pith of the Foreign Secretary's reply was embedded in Lord John Russell's dry remark, 'Nations are not apt to die in such a hurry.' Nevertheless, Nicholas may have felt that by laying his cards on the table he had proved his honesty and could be assured, if not of England's goodwill, at least of her neutrality in an affair which had just aroused his ire while at the same time equipping him with the means of reaching his goal by a less direct route. He was not the first nor the last European ruler to think that in her preoccupation with trade and money-making England would decline to fight in a cause not directly affecting her purse.

The nature of this alternative route was such as to give Nicholas an advantage over every other sovereign. The Czar of Russia was *ex officio* head of the Orthodox Greek Church; he was, in current jargon, 'Big Brother' to fourteen million Christians out of the Sultan's thirty-six million subjects. This status was further enhanced by certain features of Ottoman rule. Where, as throughout this empire, all expression of public opinion was forbidden to Orthodox subjects it seeped out in consequence through the pulpit and the presbytery. A religious champion was automatically a political champion. Accordingly when, soon after his conversation with Seymour,

Nicholas took up the question of the Holy Places, he was making not only a spiritual but a political démarche. It was this quality which supplied the immediate cause of the Crimean War.

In supporting the claims of the Greek Church to various privileges connected with the Holy Places, Nicholas was bringing himself into conflict with a man whom he detested on principle. To the Czar of All the Russias Louis Napoleon represented everything that was detestable in popular government and to show his feelings he had addressed this parvenu prince disparagingly as *mon ami* when protocol had required *mon frère*. Their paths need not, however, have crossed but for the association of France with the Holy Land. Her right to act there as Protector of Christians dated from the Crusades and under her aegis the Latin or Roman Catholic monks had acquired over the centuries certain privileges from the Sultan. There was the right to have the custody of the key to the main door of the Church of the Holy Sepulchre as well as of the two doors leading therefrom into the Manger; there was the privilege of placing a silver star stamped with the royal arms of France in the Sanctuary of the Nativity. But, during the second half of the previous century, and especially during the period of the Revolution, the interest of France had flagged to the advantage of the Orthodox monks. There, however, the matter might have rested, productive only of an occasional monkish squabble, but for the circumstances of Louis Napoleon's rise to power. Indebted to the church and *parti prêtre* and conscious of the need for *la gloire,* if his régime was to survive, he approached the Sultan regarding the lapsed rights of the Latin monks, quoting in particular certain Capitulations dated 1740. The French case was conclusive and the Greeks were ordered to hand over the keys to the Latin monks just two weeks before the Czar unbuttoned himself to the British ambassador. It was an affront which Nicholas could not tolerate in silence. His reactions were unequivocal. Here again the Montenegran uprising gave him encouragement. By rattling sabres Austria had compelled Turkey to withdraw her army once the revolt was over. He would ape her example. Two army corps were ordered to the frontier between Russia and the Turkish Christian principalities of

Wallachia and Moldavia. To Constantinople was despatched Prince Menschikoff, a man on whom he could perfectly rely to talk to the Porte in the only language he believed it would understand.

Early in March 1853, Menschikoff arrived, breathing arrogance and defiance and behaving with calculated insolence. Ominously he was accompanied by a military retinue. His demands at once indicated that his master was determined to use the occasion for gaining that paramount influence to which he aspired. The keys and privileges were not only to be restored to the Greeks but the Sultan was to acknowledge the right of the Czar to be Protector of the Greek Church throughout his domains. In achieving this he would score a double victory over Napoleon. Counselled by Lord Stratford de Redcliffe, the British ambassador and the most influential man in Turkey, the Sultan gave way on the first demand and a compromise settlement more or less satisfactory to all parties was reached. The second demand, likened by Stratford de Redcliffe not to a plan for an amputation but for an injection of poison into the entire Turkish system, was rejected. Menschikoff thereupon withdrew in a rage. Six weeks later the two army corps crossed the Pruth and occupied the Principalities as 'material guarantees' (so the Czar proclaimed) for the fulfilment of his demands. A period of agitated diplomacy ensued while ambassadors of the Great Powers assembled at Vienna and produced in all 11 notes and declarations. None was acceptable to both sides and then the Porte lost patience. Confident in the ultimate support of England and France, she ordered the Russians to quit the Principalities within 15 days. This they declined to do and war was declared.

The Turks started well by putting up a good fight on the Danube, but on the last day of November their fleet was caught in Sinope harbour and sent to the bottom. Coming on top of nine months of Russian blustering and bullying this perfectly legitimate act of war aroused the greatest resentment both in England and France. From that moment the two countries marched in step. A joint demand that Russia withdraw from the Principalities by April 30th was refused, and on March 27th and 28th France and England respectively declared war.

'The view [wrote Harold Temperley] that wars are always fought for economic interests finds little support in the origins of the Crimean War. National ambition, rivalry, and fear are the motives which impelled the nations to what proved to be a severe struggle.' There was a drifting, not a propelling into war. The British Premier, Lord Aberdeen, had seen it at close quarters 40 years before at Leipzig and hated it. Neither the Queen nor the Prince Consort agitated for war. The influential *Times*, reviled by a belligerent contemporary as 'The Russian organ of Printing House Square', was against it. The country, although since Sinope 'furiously Turkish and anti-Russian', was not spoiling for a fight. In Paris, where so recently Napoleon had made his pronouncement, *'L'Empire, c'est la paix'*, no crowds filled the boulevards shouting *'À St Petersbourg'*. Even the Czar showed little enthusiasm. Aberdeen had been right when he exclaimed sadly: 'Some fatal influence seems to have been at work.' Fatal but indefinable.

After 40 years Britain was called upon once more to fight on European soil. Except along the outposts of Empire war was a prospect which no one could have seriously contemplated. When off and on there had been fighting in New Zealand, South Africa, and India, it was something remote from the high noon of Victorian prosperity. Few, who in 1851 had thronged the Great Exhibition in Hyde Park, could very well have imagined that within three years of this spectacular affirmation of the arts of peace their country would be party to a European war. Had not the almost simultaneous death of the old Duke been symbolical of the passing of the age of war? Did not the future of England lie in her machines rather than her muskets? It might be diverting to gallop (if one was in the cavalry) about Phoenix Park or if a foot soldier take part in those 'picnics' or field exercises on the Surrey hills, and in either case to swagger about in resplendent uniforms. But the business of war was over. The army had never been a profession for which an officer need prepare himself, nor once commissioned take seriously. It had consequently persisted throughout these years of peace without a hard core of specialists, without even an organization. It remained as it had been in the eighteenth century a collection of regiments, each a self-contained unit, efficient or not depending upon the qualities of its commanding officer and its non-commissioned officers. There was no system by which these units could be combined, provisioned, moved and brought to manoeuvre in the field, or even taught to attack or defend. There were no brigades or divisions. There was no Army Service Corps – its painfully-built-up equivalent in the Peninsular War having been abolished at the peace in response to the usual Parliamentary howl for military economies. The spirit of the dead Duke, critical of change in his lifetime, hung heavily over the Horse Guards, where were housed both Secretary-at-War and commander-in-chief. The army's nine departments, which comprised its organization, all jealously guarded each its own independence and were often in conflict one with another. Of these, by no means the least in importance, the Commissariat was staffed entirely by civilians and was under the direct control of the Treasury.

Used (in default of an efficient police force) to keep order or put down riots, the army at home was never a popular service. Nor did the system of recruitment assist to integrate it with the people. Enlisting, till 1847 for 21 years, which meant virtually for life and since then for 12, the soldier was not easily absorbed in old age into society. He remained a thing apart, untrained if not untrainable for civilian life. From this it followed that there could be no reserves except those provided by hurriedly trained recruits. To bring regiments chosen to serve overseas up to strength others were stripped of their best men and NCOs, leaving them only indifferently manned to deal with the influx of recruits. On the other hand this eclectric process did create an 'Expeditionary Army' the like of which had never left these shores. In the opinion of a military surgeon: 'The men that filled its ranks were the finest soldiers I ever saw in stature, physique, and appearance.'

The quality of the officers was less satisfactory. All except the Gunners and Engineers had entered the army by purchasing their commission and in general they left the training and instruction to the NCOs. And what they had bought they could and did sell at any time they felt bored, aggrieved or disposed to do so, even in the midst of war. No standard of education was required.*

There was no full-time staff. Very few officers were sufficiently dedicated to their profession to attend what then passed for a Staff College, the Senior Department of Camberley. If they did they found all teaching in the hands of civilians. Although a Royal Warrant prescribed instruction for service in the departments of the Quartermaster-General or the Adjutant-General, no staff or administrative work of any kind was taught. In the last 18 years only 216 had gone through the course and of these only 21 ever obtained employment in the departments where favouritism and interest counted, and continued to count, for more than enthusiasm or proficiency. At the time when war was declared there were only seven serving officers who held the Department's Certificate.

The command of the army was given to Lord Raglan. It was practically an automatic choice and it is a commentary on the military state of the country that it should have been so. As Lord Fitzroy Somerset, the youngest of the Duke of Beaufort's 11 sons, he had served under Wellington in the Peninsula and had lost his right arm by what was supposed to be the last shot fired at Waterloo. Later he had gone to the Horse Guards, where for a quarter of a century he had acted as Military Secretary to the Duke of Wellington, then commander-in-chief. Since Wellington's death he had been Master-General of the Ordnance. He was 67 and had never commanded even a company.

Five infantry divisions were formed and with one exception were given to Peninsular veterans. The exception was the Queen's cousin, the Duke of Cambridge, who was promoted to command the 1st Division at the age of 35. Otherwise all were between 60 and 70, with Sir John Burgoyne of the Engineers, who functioned as a sort of Elder Soldier, as much as 72. Naturally these ages invited such criticism as that made by the highly capable George Maude of the Artillery. 'There is an old commander-in-chief, an old Engineer, old

---

* If there had been, one wonders how Gerald Goodlake, shortly to win the Victoria Cross, would have fared. In an argument with Michael Heneage, another Coldstream officer, on the way to spell 'weather' he, insisted on its having two aitches.

brigadiers – in fact, everything old at the top. This makes everything sluggish.' Such comments, however, were not wholly justified. The country naturally expected its army to be led by those who had seen muskets fired elsewhere than on a range, even if it happened 40 years before. It was not their age but their competence which mattered – Sir De Lacy Evans with 47 years' service and Sir Colin Campbell with 46 had more knowledge of the business of war than all the other generals combined, but the first commanded a division and the second only a brigade.

Where the Horse Guards blundered more egregiously was in their cavalry appointments. It would have been as well if their choice had been as humdrum. While war was still over the horizon Lord Lucan, in his darting impulsive handwriting so revealing of character, had written offering his services in any capacity. Now there were assuredly in India cavalry officers far more experienced in war and of much greater capacity than Lucan: in particular there was John Jacob, perhaps the greatest British cavalry commander of the century. But to indict the Government for not choosing him or any other 'Indian' officer is to ignore time and distance factors. Even under the most favourable conditions it would have taken four months to bring him home. Who in the meantime was to act? And when he arrived would an imported general who had spent all his life dealing with native troops be a success, notwithstanding his abilities, in command of a number of exclusive, pampered, Society regiments, destitute of experience in the field? The selection of Lucan was on paper not unjustified. He was a superb horseman, his courage unquestioned. He had even experience not enjoyed by an 'Indian' officer which might be of inestimable worth – he had served as supernumerary on Prince Woronzoff's staff in the Russo-Turkish War of 1829. Where the Horse Guards went wrong was in placing under him in command of the Light Brigade his brother-in-law, Lord Cardigan.

The story of the mordant family quarrel between Lucan and Cardigan has been too well told in *The Reason Why* to need more than a passing reference. What perhaps Miss Woodham Smith has not sufficiently emphasized is that but for initial parental opposition Cardigan, three and a half years older, would have entered the army three and a half years earlier and been so much the senior to Lucan instead of being eight years his junior. As the principle of seniority, when combined with birth, had nearly the force of Holy Writ in the Horse Guards, Cardigan and not his detested relative Lucan would have received the cavalry division. Yet knowing their intense mutual dislike, deducing as they should the degree of aggravation caused by putting a jealous, ambitious Cardigan under an impulsive, imperious Lucan, the authorities nevertheless proceeded with the appointment. Had they chosen a commander of the Light Brigade as sensibly as they chose James Scarlett for that of the Heavies, Balaclava might have shown very different results.

To give the Government credit it should be said that some regiments had already been embarked for Malta before the declaration of war. Throughout April and May others were constantly to be seen in seaport towns, marching with difficulty through dense, cheering crowds to the tunes of *The British Grenadiers, Cheer Boys Cheer* and *We're Going Far Away*. Their incomparable army was setting out 'to vindicate the Public Law of Europe', although most people would not have expressed it so orotundly as the Prince Consort. At any rate it was going to give Nicholas, 'this fiend in human form', the thrashing his bullying of the poor Turks deserved. Few in their martial enthusiasm asked themselves how its losses were to be made good or what experience Whitehall had in maintaining and supplying such an army at such a distance from home. Fewer still are likely to have commented upon the unserviceability of the gay uniforms or upon the lack of equipment. The headgear of the Guards was the bearskin, of the line regiments a patent-leather shako which gave no protection from the sun. The neck was encased in a leather stock which gripped it as in a vice. There were no ambulances, no stores for the wounded, no medical orderlies beyond some aged pensioners drawn out of retirement. That there was no provision for a winter campaign may be explained by the finality which Christmas invariably has for the British public on the threshold of war. As in 1899, 1914, and even in 1939, all is to be over by Christmas. The enemy by then having been taught his lesson, the troops will be home or at least in comfortable quarters. If not, well! the bear-skins of the Guards would (as *Punch* observed) make excellent foot warmers.

By the end of April the first contingents were reaching Scutari opposite Constantinople, where some went into barracks, others under canvas. At the end of two months, by which time most of the army had arrived and any senti-mental regard for Turkey or the Turks had been destroyed, a move was made to Varna, a wretched Bulgarian port on the Black Sea. Here, should the Turks fail to hold the key-fortress of Silistria further north on the Danube, the Franco-British army would be well placed to repel a Russian advance on Constantinople. But inspired by a handful of young British officers the Turks resisted until June 23rd, when threatened by Austria and ravaged by cholera the Russians raised the siege and retired not only across the Danube but out of the Principalities.

Here, forsooth, was an anti-climax to months of war-fever and high-pitched oratory – a *status quo ante bellum*, the original cause of the war disposed of without a shot fired, the noble British expeditionary force become 'an army of occupation on passive service', its energies directed to fight-ing not Russians, but cholera, fever and diarrhoea, fleas, flies, and sunstroke. For than Varna, 'the dirt and filth of which [wrote a British officer] must be seen to be appreciated', it would have been found hard to find anywhere better quali-fied to debilitate an army and sap its morale. There was little to do except to drink and the nearest unveiled woman was reckoned to be no closer than Bucharest, though one anxious local Pasha complained to Henry Clifford that 'the veils of our women fall lower every day'. Was there now to be added to these many frustrations the indignity of quietly packing up and returning to England? On the other hand in the army itself by this time there was a generally-felt dislike to fighting on behalf of the miserable, effete, lazy, cowardly, cheating lot the Turks at Varna and Constantinople had shown them-selves to be. 'I hate the Turks [wrote Captain Montgomery of the 42nd] and would rather fight against them than for them.' Daniel Lysons of the 23rd, with a fine military record await-ing him, was more emphatic. 'Everyone would be glad to go over to the Russians and help them against this wretched nation.' 'As for fighting for the Turks [Edward Phillips of the 8th Hussars told his father], such humbug is long past. A lazy set of ruffians, who would rob us all if they could.'

At such moments none is more bellicose than the civilian well settled in his armchair at home. The idea that this wonderful army should return without having inflicted a drubbing on the Muscovite was intolerable. *The Times* insisted that Sebastopol, Russia's proud Queen of the Euxine, be attacked and occupied, and Palmerston, who in such matters spoke for the great mass of his countrymen, was of the same opinion, 'the eye-tooth of the Bear must be drawn'. At a Cabinet meeting at which, overcome by the heat of a June night and a good dinner, more than half the members are alleged to have been asleep, instructions were approved which bade Raglan invade the Crimea and capture Sebastopol. 'On Sebastopol [wrote the Prince] hangs the whole fate of European politics . . . the honour of England and her prestige in the East which tells upon India.' It may have been so, but as nearly every officer who was writing home from Varna was soon saying, it was late in the year to undertake such an expedition.

Admittedly Raglan's instructions were permissive rather than mandatory. Only if 'he should be decidedly of the opinion that it could not be undertaken with any reasonable prospect of success' was he to hold his hand. But how could he and the French commander-in-chief St Arnaud (who had instructions to walk in step with his colleague) have any opinion about something of which they were ignorant? They had no large-scale maps of the Crimea, they knew absolutely nothing of its fortifications except that they were supposed to be of exceptional strength; they had no knowledge of the size of its garrison, esimates varying between 120,000 and 45,000 (which turned out to be approximately the correct figure).

What would the Duke have done? That was the question which Raglan and Sir George Brown, in command of the Light Division, whom he consulted, naturally asked themselves. Both had no doubts at all but that 'that great man' would decline to accept responsiblity for such an invasion

without 'more certain information'. But equally they agreed
that if Raglan refused the Government, who had clearly
made up their minds, would replace Raglan by someone more
complaisant. Raglan gave way and was soon heard prophesy-
ing that Sebastopol would be taken within 12 days.

Although the army and even its generals were still officially
kept in the dark, practice trench-digging and the making of
3,000 gabions a day indicated that something was afoot and
spirits started to rise. How much was left undone which
ought to have been done in those precious weeks of July and
August was to be evident well before the first shot was fired
in the coming campaign.

Losses from cholera (which included 700 deaths) having
been made good by drafts, it was a cheerful and impatient
army, 28,000 strong, which started embarking on September 1st, leaving behind it Varna with all its boredom, stench
and frustrations. True, there were many so enfeebled by sickness that their knapsacks had to be carried down to the quay-
side by mules. But every day at sea – and there were to be
fourteen of them spent on fine East Indiamen – was to re-
charge them with health.

A mightier armada never rode the seas. In six parallel lines
it moved slowly but imposingly at four miles an hour. Transports were towed in pairs by steamers, the smoke from
which, lazily merging into an immense cloud, created for
many a Midlander a skyscape conforming more to the
Black Country than the Black Sea. After inexplicable delays
which accompanied every Crimean operation, it was not until
the 12th that the coast line of Sebastopol, looking 'cold and
black', was sighted and the next day the ships anchored off
Eupatoria. Its surrender was peacefully received, but it was
too far north to serve as a base. Alfred Tipping, of the
Grenadier Guards, describes the scene as the fleet lay at
anchor.

It was a lovely evening, calm as July and hardly a ripple upon
the water – as far as you could see on every side just one floating
mass surmounted with a forest of masts, the decks crowded with
soldiers. At 8 bells the whole of the bands of this vast armament
commenced playing the usual call in the army for that hour, 'The
Tattoo', after which God Save the Queen and finishing with

Partant pour la Syrie (by a standing order to be played always after our anthem). Fading away to the right in the distance the French fleet appeared more like a confused mass of pins on a pin-cushion than anything else.

At three o'clock on the following morning, on the in-auspicious anniversary of the French entry into Moscow, the allied fleet having coasted farther south anchored in Calamita Bay in the vicinity of an old Genoese fort. This was reached at nine and in a very short time the French troops went smartly ashore. The instant they landed they darted up the beach and to cries of *Vive L'Empéreur* planted the tricolor on Russian soil. The British approach was more dilatory and less dramatic. The first to land, about an hour after the French, were some of the 23rd accompanied by Sir George Brown, complete with stock, as immaculate as if about to attend a Levée.

There was no opposition. Prince Menschikoff, better qualified to command an army in defence of Sebastopol than a diplomatic delegation to Constantinople, felt no doubt that he could deal more effectively with the invaders once they were landed on a bleak coast with no port facilities in their reach. He despatched an officer with a few Cossacks who for a time stood silently watching the approach of the allies from the top of a low cliff. One of them, according to Tipping, seemed to deliver a symbolic discharge of his musket before they all wheeled round and vanished into the drab hinter-land; but as darkness came down the southern sky flickered with the light of burning farms and homesteads, ricks, and barns. The technique of 1812 was being repeated. Before then 25,000 men had been landed, but only a dozen guns. Each man carried 50 rounds, three days' rations and all his personal effects coiled round his back in a rolled blanket. As far as it went the landing was one of the more successful operations of the war, and this was largely due to the un-failing skill and good humour of the sailors. They cheer-fully manhandled nervous landmen down the ladders and greeted anxious Highlanders with cries of 'Come on, ladies'. But already the first consequences of incompetence were in evidence. No tents were disembarked.

The army had just settled itself on a front which extended

three miles inland and was preparing to bed down on 'a few weeds and a plaid' under the sky when it suffered the first caprices of the Crimean climate. For hours the wind blew and rain fell continuously on the chilled and exposed troops. That night for many the recuperative effects of the sea voyage were destroyed in a few hours. The only stroke of good fortune lay in the enemy's neglect to make a night attack upon these thousands of dispirited soldiers, huddled together for warmth or else ceaselessly walking up and down, slapping their hands cabman-fashion against their bodies. A suggestion that such an attack be made had been put forward by an enterprising artillery officer but had been rejected. The next night, although it did not rain, the dew was so heavy that men awoke in the morning 'just like a dead rabbit and as stiff as a poker'.

Even before that first rain-drenched night there had been signs of those shortcomings which were to mark the campaign in all its stages – a want of any system of priorities, a failure to provide for the most obvious and elementary needs of an army about to take the field. Varna had exposed certain deficiencies but because there had been no fighting there had been no calamitous results: the cholera victims had been quietly buried. Now, on Crimean soil, with an unavoidable battle ahead, these deficiencies assumed graver espects. No army comparable with the British has in modern history ever landed upon a foreign shore more inadequately equipped for invasion. With nothing but what each man could carry, with few bat-horses, no ambulances, no knowledge of the countryside, its roads or its resources, it had for its objective a fortress reputed to be one of the most powerful in Europe. It was an impertinence; but an impertinence so sublime as to deserve success. How swiftly that success might have come will now be considered.

2

The Alma

'Yes, gentlemen, you won a brilliant victory at the Alma,
and for it you may thank your manner of attack which we
did not understand. Our soldiers are somewhat slow to
learn; but only give them time, and you will see that the
game will be a little more difficult to play.'

– A Russian officer during a truce

WHILE THE BRITISH ARMY so unnecessarily suffered
on the shores of Calamita Bay, the French showed
how much better they understood the business of war. Each
man landed with a third section of their famous *tentes
à abri* and (wrote an envious George Wombwell) 'in an
incredible short space of time the whole ground was
covered with them and everything as comfortable as if they
were encamped close to Varna'. Even the 8,000 Turks
bedded down in 'large handsome bell-tents and had plenty
of baggage cattle and mules'. At length on the third day tents
were disembarked, many of them threadbare veterans of the
Peninsula, but after two nights' use had to be returned to the
ships for want of pack-horses to carry them on the march. So
early indeed in the Crimean campaign were the army called
upon to suffer for the disbanding of the Land Transport
Corps; so soon was the truth underlined of Sir John Burgoyne's averment that 'nine-tenths of the evils of the army
were attributable to want of transport'. Yet it was calculated
that only two more vessels subtracted from the country's vast
maritime resources would have sufficed to carry everything in
the way of transport and comforts which an army of this size
required. Once a landing had been made there was indeed a
most energetic attempt to buy up Tartar arabas and ponies,
but only 300 vehicles, or one-third of the numbers needed,
were secured. This meant that in addition to having to return

tents and to spend the next two weeks without any shelter, everyone had to carry his possessions upon his person. For officers called upon to do this for the first time in any war, and for men recovering from sickness, this burden was oppressive and frequently brought about a collapse.

In one branch of the service it would be imagined that after the experiences of the past months any shortages and imperfections would have been remedied. Yet medical supplies were no more ample than when the army had left England six months previously. If the experiences of the 23rd were not exceptional these were limited to one bell-tent per regiment, ten stretchers to be carried by the bandsmen and pensioners, a small roll of dressing, a tin or two of beef and a little brandy. Some medical officers were not even issued with the regulation forms on which to enter the names and particulars of the sick and wounded. For reasons of space Thomas Longmore, surgeon of the 19th, had to squeeze all his medical stores and equipment into 'two small panniers of a vicious brute of a pony.'* The equipment, furthermore, which so far as it concerned instruments a parsimonious government required every surgeon to supply as part of his contract, might be adequate or not according to that surgeon's whim or pocket.

The wantonness of these neglects was aggravated again by inevitable comparisons with the French army. With maritime resources far inferior to our own they had landed sufficient mules and horses for the transport of all baggage together with a complete hospital service, while we with our immense mercantile marine had not a single vessel equipped as a hospital ship. For this deplorable state of mismanagement responsibility rested primarily with the Treasury, the various government departments and their strangling red tape, but in the ultimate resort a commander-in-chief had it in his power to force a government's hands by threat of resignation. No such threat came from Lord Raglan. On the other hand it may be that such matters were deliberately concealed from

* While still in Bulgaria he had written 'such a letter about being without medical comforts for a hospital when it was full of cholera and diarrhoea was prevailing – backed by my colonel – that a general hubbub was created. My complaint, however, was proved to be "frivolous" by General Airey, the new Quarter-Master General.'

him in pursuance of the policy adopted by his Staff and cynically explained to Captain Adye on taking up his appointment: 'Never trouble Lord Raglan more than is absolutely necessary with details, listen carefully to his remarks, try to anticipate his wishes and at all times make as light as possible of difficulties.'

The allied march on Sebastopol began on September 19th after irksome delays which infuriated St Arnaud and caused him on the 18th to write: '*Il y a deux jours que j'ai aurai pu avoir battu les Russes qui m'attendent à Alma et je ne peux partir que demain grace à MM. les Anglais qui ne se gênent guère, mais qui me gênent bien.*' Even then there was no departure till four hours after the agreed time. The French claimed the post of honour on the right, which because they had the fleets on one side and the British on the other might have been called the post of safety. But as the British alone possessed any cavalry it was only just that to them should fall the post of danger. The order of march, which was roughly the order in which they were to go into battle, was as follows:

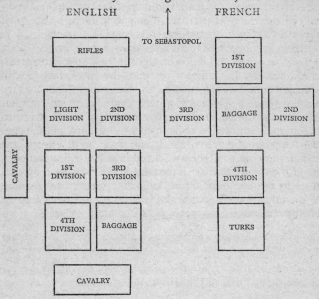

The French moving in lozenge formation were always about two miles ahead of the British left. The asymmetrical British line of march, three divisions on the left, two on the right, each in double companies from the centre, with cavalry behind and on the flank, was adopted to enable it by rapid deployment to deal with any attack on the left or rear. The combined allied force now on the move numbered roughly 60,000, of which 27,000 were British, 25,000 French and the remainder Turkish. Amidst these thousands there rode by himself a bearded figure in civilian clothes, whose presence was a novel feature of the campaign. In the months ahead some were to couple the names William Howard Russell with a malediction, but to others (and they the great majority) they denoted a man whose outspoken articles were preserving the army from complete annihilation. Backed by the potent influence of his great editor, John Delane, *The Times* correspondent was able to pitch his tent and to roam more or less where he willed. He entered into conversation with everybody, became the recipient of every camp 'shave' or rumour, of every grievance or scandal, described in detail the disposition of the troops, their hardships and sufferings and, in the complete absence of any sort of censorship, transmitted his outspoken reports back to his newspaper.

Hollywood in all its extravagance has never screened a grander spectacle than that presented by the Franco-British-Turkish army as it turned its face southwards towards Sebastopol on a surpassingly lovely morning of early autumn. The gently rolling, treeless, featureless downland, stretching for miles, permitted the deployment and advance of a land armada without parallel in military history. A few more years and progress in artillery would make such a concentration of troops on the march impossible. 'The effect [reported Russell] of these grand masses of soldiers descending the ridges of the hills, rank after rank, with the sun playing over forests of glittering steel, can never be forgotten by those who witnessed it.' With bands playing and colours uncased, in bearskin and bonnet, helmet and shako, its uniforms varying from those of the brilliant Light Brigade on the left, past the scarlet tunics of the infantry, to the *pantalons-rouges* of the Zouaves on the right, this giant host four miles in width and as many in depth marched almost noiselessly over the muffling grass of the undulating steppe, crushing beneath its feet a herb which emitted a peculiar fragrance. Larks sang overhead, partridges rose in coveys, terrified hares ran crazily through the ranks and provided that evening an agreeable alternative to the salt pork ration. It was a parade-ground exercise on a mammoth scale. 'A beautiful sight', notes Corporal Dolton of the Scots Fusilier Guards in his diary, 'to see the regiments marching like as if they were at some Review in close column, each Division parallel with each other.' But between this and a Hyde Park Review there was this difference: barely a third of those taking part would ever see their homes again.

For, with all its majestic appearance from afar, a closer scrutiny would have revealed some alarming features. The British army was marching to war *in forma pauperis,* its sick unprovided for, traces of cholera and fever to be seen in pale faces and lank forms, officers limping along under their unaccustomed burdens, those of the Guards with the additional weight of the bearskin, looking like 'animated lumps of undigested packages, all cloak, bundle and hairy caps'. It was not surprising that the gaiety and excitement of the march soon wore off. First the men ceased to talk, then the bands ceased to play and finally nothing was heard but the soporific swish of the grass underfoot as column after column moved across the waterless plain under a burning sky. Nor was it long, too, before those nights on damp sodden ground were exacting their price. Every so often a familiar and dreaded look would come over a soldier's face, a blue tinge would spread round his mouth, he would utter a choking cry for water and collapse. The ranks would open to pass on and the victim of cholera would be left to whatever attention the small overworked band of stretcher-bearers could provide. Even on the faces of the more robust who marched on there were drawn and haggard looks, as if the men were at the end rather than at the start of a campaign. Such a march under heavy equipment, in such heat and without water, was an ordeal almost beyond endurance and the 4th Regiment of Foot had half its men temporarily prostrated before the River Bulganak was reached in the early afternoon.

It was half-past three, soon after the men had relieved their thirst, when the first shots of the war were exchanged. The incident is of importance only as revealing one of Raglan's weaknesses as commander-in-chief and as the first occasion when the Russians disclosed that strange apathy of theirs at a time when resolute action might have produced a neat little success. The cavalry had been ordered to clear some Cossacks visible on the heights ahead. Four squadrons, two each from the 11th Hussars and 13th Light Dragoons, advanced to the brow of an intervening hill. In front of them was a dip and across it appeared some 2,000 Cossacks. The four squadrons advanced a short way down the incline, halted and formed a line. The Cossacks advanced, halted and formed a line. The Russians threw out skirmishers. The squadrons threw out skirmishers. The Russians opened fire at extreme range. The 11th and 13th replied. After 20 minutes of desultory exchanges, four horses had been killed and four men wounded – one a paymaster-sergeant who had no business to be there. Except for these casualties it could have been an exercise on Hounslow Heath. But while this more or less innocuous affair was going on some 6,000 Russian infantry, supported by a brigade of cavalry, were gathering in the rear of the hill, unseen to the men of the Light Brigade but visible to Raglan. To have risked his only mounted troops in a full-scale engagement so early in the campaign would have been an act of madness. Very properly Raglan determined on a withdrawal, and to cover this he ordered up the two leading divisions together with two troops of artillery, Brandling's and Maude's. It only remained to ensure the retirement of the cavalry, eager as he knew them to be for a fight. To do so no general with any experience of command would have failed to word his orders in exact and mandatory language. Not so Raglan. It was impossible for him to shed the ingrained Whitehall consideration for the feelings of subordinates. In the words of his hero-worshipper Kinglake, he was 'unwilling to embarrass Lord Lucan by an order too precise and imperative'. He accordingly deputed Airey, his Quartermaster-General, to make his wishes known. The retirement was in due course brought about, but had it not been that Airey was a tough and forthright man, the message he bore might have inflamed still further an argument in which he found Lucan and Cardigan engaged and have disastrously delayed the withdrawal. Five weeks later another message involving these two brothers-in-law, but not unfortunately carried by Airey, was to have infinitely graver consequences.

The Cossacks might jeer as they watched the cavalry draw back but their lack of enterprise had let an opportunity slip of administering a disconcerting, even serious rebuff to the invaders. Why, with a cavalry brigade in support not to mention infantry, the Cossacks were not ordered to charge the four squadrons ranged in front is hard to understand. The explanation suggested, that they were awed by the British steadiness and exact ceremonious formation, might be convincing if similar hesitation to act with decision and vigour in an emergency were not to recur time and again.

What in the circumstances might be called the successful skirmish of the Bulganak determined Raglan to bivouac for the night with his back to the river, and the march ended with several hours of daylight left for the men to collect dried grass which with some broken staves of meat and rum barrels provided the only fuel for cooking their evening meal and preparing their tea and cocoa. When night came the inadequate watch and camp fires glittered on the great plain like so many glow-worms. There was, too, a strange, almost eerie silence on this last night for over 350 British soldiers. Not a shot, an alarm or a Cossack vedette disturbed the sleeping army.

Unlike the British Staff, which seems to have given little thought for the morrow, the French had been hard at work and before retiring for the night St Arnaud had ridden over to Raglan's headquarters in a ruined post-house to discuss the plans for the battle. The council of war – if such a meeting deserves such a status – which followed was as singular as it was inauspicious.

It had been learnt soon after landing that the Russians were established on the Heights above the River Alma, seven miles beyond the Bulganak. From the mast head of the warships further details had been obtained. It was on what they believed these to show that the French based their plans, which St Arnaud now explained to Raglan, gesticulating vigorously in his excitement and breaking repeatedly into French. The

Russian left, being at the mercy of the naval guns, must be devoid of men. Menschikoff would, he reasoned, deploy his troops a mile or more inland along the heights overlooking the Alma river. It was against these, reckoned to be his main force, that St Arnaud proposed to send his own divisions, leaving the British (as he thought) the lesser but important task of sweeping round and rolling up the Russian right flank.

Although Raglan was excessively conscious of the need to keep Anglo-French relations frictionless, he could not pledge himself in advance to a manoeuvre which might lead to the annihilation of his army. Only closer reconnaissance in the morning would show whether the French information under-lying their plan was correct. So beyond assuring St Arnaud with his habitual courtesy that he could rely upon his full cooperation he refrained from committing himself. In fact, he hardly spoke throughout the interview. Now if caution had been his only motive, Raglan would have deserved unqualified praise for the manner in which he had conducted this delicate affair. But it is suggested by Kinglake, who came to know him intimately, that Raglan was inspired by something quite different. By 'putting forward no plan of his own and in short eluding discussion ... Lord Raglan dealt as though he held it to be a clear gain to be able to avoid entrusting the Marshal with a knowledge of what our army would be likely to under-take.' This guarded attitude, which he describes without a hint of disapproval, was in Kinglake's opinion, the result of 'his truly native English dislike of all premature planning'. Given an expert staff there might have been time the next morning between dawn and the firing of the first shot to do that planning; but the staff was not expert and the morrow was to show the risks and pitfalls of such a haphazard approach to battle.

Nor was it only that Raglan kept his counsel from the French, whom in unguarded moments he was still by force of habit heard to speak of as 'the enemy'. When next morning Prince Napoleon and General Canrobert, whose divisions were on De Lacy Evans's right, came to discuss with him details of the attack, the most experienced of all the British divisional generals had to inform them that he was without orders from headquarters.

By one of the very few security measures taken during the campaign the allied armies were aroused that morning by neither bugle nor trumpet. But, instead of breaking camp immediately, there followed exasperating delays while the British ammunition train was being brought up and the troops guarding the flank and rear were wheeled into line. However, it was during this wait that St Arnaud took the opportunity to pay a morning call on Raglan. As he passed through the British lines this 'little wily debauched looking man' received an ovation which touched him visibly. Thinking no doubt to make a fitting acknowledgement, he turned to the cheering men (they happened to be of the 55th) and taking off his cocked hat cried, 'English, today you will see the Russians. I hope you will fight well.' Aggressively an Irish voice replied from the ranks, 'Hope, your honour? Don't we always fight well?'

It was not until the army had been fretting some hours that the order to advance was at last given at about ten, and then it was not to move straight on the Russians but to incline to the right front and close a gap which incompetent staff work had allowed to develop during the previous day between the two armies. The Light Division on the left and the 2nd on the right moved forward, the first preceded by a set of fifes, the other by a small band, both playing only fitfully. The heat was overpowering and the halts were in consequence numerous. It was not till well after eleven that the gap had been filled up and then as both armies proceeded on their way, now in parallel lines, a curious phenomenon was noticed. Over the troops, marching as they knew into battle that very day, fell a strange hush. All music ceased and beyond the occasional neighing of a horse and the peculiar rocking sound of artillery wheels when passing over the dry tall grass, nothing broke the silence of the beautiful morning. The imminence of battle on such a day seemed to young Cardew of the 19th unbelievable. Others who knew their Thomas Campbell were reminded perhaps of the lines

> *There was a silence deep as death;*
> *And the boldest held their breath*
> *For a time. ...*

About noon (no two accounts exactly agree as to times)

a rise in the ground was topped and the Heights of the Alma were visible cutting across the Southern sky. A halt was called. The spell was broken. Raglan and St Arnaud rode forward to reconnoitre while the men were ordered to eat their midday meal. As they did so, sprawling amidst sheaves of corn which here thickly covered the ground, they could see two miles ahead down a gentle slope a river running between poplar trees to the sea. Behind this on the slope of the Heights there were to the naked eye what seemed large patches of dark undergrowth from which darted countless diamond-like flashes of light, which when studied through glasses proved to be massive bodies of infantry whose bayonets were glinting in the sun. These patches were thickest along the eastern end of the Heights beyond which a large force of cavalry was discernible. On the heights towards the sea no troops were to be seen. Here, then, was a complete justification of Raglan's overnight caution. To attempt to turn such a strongly-held position backed by at least five times the number of his own cavalry would be entirely irresponsible. To St Arnaud's direct question whether he would do so, he replied he would not. To St Arnaud's plan, however, that the French should nevertheless attack the Heights in three waves in echelon starting with Bosquet on the extreme right followed by Canrobert and Prince Napoleon, it would have been improper for Raglan to object; but he declined to be committed to any precise moment for throwing in his own army against the Russian right. Ideally no doubt this should come when the French divisions had established themselves on the Heights and the Russians were confused and distracted, but the exact time must be his responsibility. With this amicable but inconclusive agreement each to go his own way the two generals returned to their armies. Then were the British given the ominous order, 'with ball cartridge, load', whereat it was said many a soldier turned white and in the sombre silence that ensued nothing was heard but the noise of ramrods being driven home. After that came the command to resume the forward march.

The reason for Menschikoff's lop-sided deployment now became apparent on closer approach. The Heights of the Alma, which began abruptly from the other side of the river, rose to about 400 feet, reminding some of the South Downs

The Battle of the Alma

Skirmishers

Black Sea

Oulougoul Akles

Minsk (1Bn.)

Telegraph Tower

Moscow

Tarutin

Brest Bialostock

Borodino

Vladimir

Kourgane Hill

Uglitz

Sousdal

Lesser Redoubt

Great Redoubt

Sappers

Kasan

R. Alma

Vineyards

White Farm

Bourlouk

Almatamak

Canrobert   Bosquet   Turks

P. Napoleon

Forey

Raglan

2nd. Division   95 55 30 47 49 41

3rd. Division   4 44 28 38 50 1

Light Division   23 33 17   7 88 19

1st. Division   7 9 3 42 C.G. 5.F.G.G   79 9 3 42

I. Battery   C. Battery

Light Brigade

Cavalry

N

0   ½   1
Mile

ARTHUR BANKS

beyond Haywards Heath, others of the Berkshire Downs between Didcot and Wantage or of Richmond Hill seen from across the Thames. Starting as a lofty cliff at the Alma's mouth they ran inland almost sheer for about a mile, and then for another mile or so their face was indented with a number of ravines. After approximately two miles, at the base of a high point known as Telegraph Hill from an unfinished telegraph station on its summit, the Heights curled into an amphitheatre about a mile across and half a mile in depth. On its further side stood another hill 450 feet in height, rising from the river by a series of undulations. This was the famous Kourgane, destined to become the key to the battle. On the near side of the Alma was to be seen a wide belt of vineyards, separated from the plain by stone walls and punctuated by three villages, the centre one of which was named Bourliouk and lay in the path of the 2nd Division. Finally, crossing the Alma to the left of Bourliouk and running through the middle of the amphitheatre, went the post road from Eupatoria to Sebastopol.

As anticipated, within a mile or more of the shore Menschikoff had stationed no troops on the Heights which the allied guns had begun to bombard since mid-morning. He trusted to their great natural strength to keep that part of his line inviolable. And so, with the minimum of care and intelligent engineering, it would have done. He knew, or he ought to have known, that a steep but climbable track ran up the cliff edge and that up the ravines went three country roads at least one of which was capable of carrying artillery. A few trenches dug across these roads, a handful of desperate men ensconced above each and he would have had little to fear. By an astonishing oversight Menschikoff took not one of these precautions, merely concentrating the greater part of his army of 39,000 men and 96 guns in a wide sweep from above and below Telegraph Hill round the amphitheatre to Kourgane and the knolls beyond. On the slopes of Kourgane and about halfway down was a ridge on which he constructed a battery of 12 powerful guns, usually named by British writers the Great Redoubt. It was protected by a low breastwork three feet in height and on either side ran a protective ditch or epaulement to accommodate infantry. Shallow

trenches between each gun had been dug for the use of sharpshooters. The Great Redoubt commanded all the ground
between itself and beyond the vineyards across the opposite
bank of the Alma. To its (proper) right about half a mile
away on the same ridge a lesser redoubt of nine guns had been
built. This, set back at an angle, overlooked a valley up which
any flanking attack would have to be made. On the other or
Western side of the Great Redoubt and at about the same
elevation a battery of 18 guns straddled the post road as it
climbed out of the amphitheatre. This third battery not only
dominated the road both north and south of the bridge over
the river but with the guns of the Great Redoubt could direct
a harassing cross- and plunging-fire on to the bridge itself.
Furthermore, along the top of Kourgane and at various well-
chosen points round the rim of the amphitheatre there were
field batteries capable of carpeting with shot and shell the
Great Redoubt if captured. Masses between and in the rear
of the redoubts and batteries, some in the folds of ground
making them invisible to the allies, were five regiments,
numbering in all 15,000 men. This force was in charge of
Gortschakoff with Kvetzinski his second-in-command.
Lastly, on the extreme right and rear of his line, Menschikoff
had placed his cavalry, 5,000 strong, in a large arc, ready to
deal with any flanking movement. Peninsular officers were
soon heard declaring that they had never seen anything so
intimidating as the Russian position. Menschikoff himself
was entirely of the same opinion. He believed he had created
another Lines of Torres Vedras against which the enemy must
fling themselves and be destroyed. So great was his confidence that he had that very morning invited a party of ladies
with their civilian escorts to watch on specially-constructed
stands on Telegraph Hill the annihilation of the French and
the 'island curs' who had dared to invade Holy Russia.

The advance had not proceeded far when the first Russian
batteries opened up and Frederick Berkeley, one of the only
two officers of the Scots Fusilier Guards to have seen active
service, drew out his watch with a magnificent flourish and
proclaimed: 'The battle begins at one o'clock.' (But his
watch was almost certainly half an hour slow.) At first, the
round shots fell short and there was a general disposition

to take them lightly. 'Great ponderous shot [wrote Tipping], they came bounding along the ground like cricket balls. As the men saw them approaching they opened their ranks and the balls went hissing past.' They even evoked merriment, as when a greyhound belonging to Captain Forman of the Rifle Brigade pursued them barking furiously. But when a man put his boot out to stop a cannon ball and his foot was carried away, the laughter ceased abruptly.

It was clearly time for the two armies to deploy into line from the right and while this was being carried out a sergeant of the Light Division was killed – the first death (it is believed) in the war.

Either through more poor staff work or sheer inexperience the British, who had started the day too remote from their allies, were now too close. When the order to deploy was given, the 2nd Division was jostled by Prince Napoleon's and it in turn crowded into the Light Division on its left, the 95th overlapping the front of Sir George Brown's right regiment, the 7th Fusiliers. Though Sir George at once ordered his men to take ground to the left in fours, this was difficult to execute under a fire which had now become heavy, and the congestion was never overcome. The British army had taken too little room and the error, which was to prove costly, was discovered too late.

Following their imperfect deployment the two leading divisions were commanded to lie down. In their rear but still out of effective range the 1st and 3rd Divisions were halted and stood at ease. To the sound of much cheering, some British nine-pound batteries raced forward, unlimbered and attempted, even using rockets, to reply to the Russian guns, but these were at too great an elevation and after a short time they gave up and withdrew.

Now began for the British soldier a period of irksome inactivity, the more exasperating inasmuch as while they could do nothing they were being shelled with impunity. 'I think [wrote Hugh Hibbert of the 7th] the worst part of the whole affair was the lying down in lines before we received the order to advance. ... The shells bursting over us and blowing men to pieces, arms, legs, and brains in all directions.' The fire, although not particularly severe and causing relatively few

casualties, was none the less for most men the first in their
lives and it affected everyone differently. Sergeant Gowing,
also of the 7th, 'felt horribly sick, a cold shivering running
through my veins'. Captain Montgomery of the 42nd was
'afraid for the first time in my life and flinched at every shot'.
On the other hand Colonel Warren of the 55th sat bolt upright
on his horse 'like a statue with a single glass to his eyes, never
moving when a shot or shell passed close to him'. As for
Pennefather, the notorious 'swearing' general in command of
Evans's left brigade, he repeatedly slapped his thigh and cried
out, 'Blood and 'ounds, boys, I like that!'

For nearly 90 minutes the men lay inert, watching little
black dots emerge from the layers of smoke enshrouding the
batteries, following their approach as they gradually enlarged,
wondering one moment whether they would bring death and
the next being covered with some comrade's blood. For untried
soldiers it was a scarifying ordeal, which none but British
soldiers (affirmed Hibbert proudly) could have borne. They
joked and they chaffed one another; they gave the Russian
guns female names with Rabelaisean additions; they never
complained. Of all men the most concerned was the kind-
hearted Raglan. In an endeavour to draw off the shelling he
ostentatiously rode about, to the alarm of his staff, conspicuous in his blue frock coat and cocked hat. After 40
years behind a Whitehall desk he was under fire once more
and he was enjoying every moment of it. It was said that on
him the whistle of a bullet or the whirr of a shot had the effect
of a glass of champagne – 'he used to clutch the stump of his
right arm with his left hand and chuckle.'

The reasons for this last and gruelling halt had been the
need to await the results of French operations on the right.
These had been begun by the impetuous Bosquet, who had
been fuming with impatience all morning. Zouaves of his
first brigade led by Bouat and followed by the Turkish
battalions could be seen swarming 'like bees' up the undefended cliff path and topping the plateau; but here, having
no artillery and it being contrary to French training and tradition to advance without its cover, the men halted and played
little further part in the battle. Meanwhile on either side of
the first road up the heights, which Bosquet's binoculars told

him could carry artillery, the skirmishers of his second brigade under Autemarre went scrambling up, firing in-
discriminately not at the enemy (for there were none) but
to indicate the course of their progress by the resultant puffs of
smoke. As soon as Autemarre accompanied by Bosquet had
got his men and (after some struggling) his artillery on to
the Heights, St Arnaud issued his next command. This was in
furtherance of the French aim – an attack on three echelons
by the right – and it was of singular simplicity. 'With men
such as you [he told Canrobert and Prince Napoleon] I have
no orders to give. I have but to point to the enemy.'

Despite this grandiloquent *envoi* things began at this point
to go awry. Canrobert went forward but found the road ahead
of him (the second from the sea) unfit for artillery, which he
accordingly sent off to his right to follow in the wake of Autemarre's. This created a delay which was nearly fatal. His
division reached the edge of the plateau less its guns and therefore like Bouat's brigade unable to proceed further. On the
other hand the Russians were by this time reacting sharply to
the threat to their centre. Guns were being rushed to the
northern slopes of Telegraph Hill and were soon sending shot
and shell into Canrobert's troops as well as directing plunging
fire on Napoleon's division spread out in the vineyards below.
A crisis, as perilous as it was unanticipated, had suddenly
developed. With Bosquet isolated on the Heights, Canrobert
clinging to the slopes and his artillery somewhere on its way
up, the Prince's division suffering casualties (which though
not numerous easily led to exaggerated estimates), the entire
French plan was cracking and their position at the hands of a
resolute enemy could have become critical. It was clearly
time for their allies to act. Just after three o'clock an urgent
message from French Headquarters reached Raglan stating
that the Prince's troops were being 'massacred' and that
Bosquet's were being 'compromised': begging in effect for
the British to enter the battle.

It had been Raglan's intention to attack as soon as the
French were on the Heights, but it had by now become
impossible for him to hesitate much longer, regardless of what
the French had or had not achieved. The sight of his men
suffering for so long under fire had become unendurable and

there is little doubt that the French request anticipated his orders by a very few moments. These orders now given deserve to be noted, for they were the only ones issued to his troops by the commander-in-chief during the whole of the coming battle. The line was to advance and not to stop till the Alma was crossed. If Raglan had any other plan in his head (which is doubtful), he kept it from his generals.

'I shall never forget that excited look of delight on every face when I repeated the order', said Major Lysons, acting temporarily as Evans's Assistant Adjutant-General. The men of the leading divisions sprang to their feet and notwithstanding continued fire from the Russian batteries were carefully dressed in line, two deep. Only when the officers were completely satisfied was the order given to advance. In this magnificent alignment, two miles in width, the British army went forth to battle for the first time on European soil since Waterloo. In front were the men of the Rifle Brigade, in skirmishing order, preceded on horseback by Colonel Lawrence and Major Norcott, and looking to the Russians on Kourgane as they cleared the vineyards of their own sharpshooters like 'green flies'. It was approximately at this moment that there occurred 'a notable incident of the battle', according to Hamley, whose *Operations of War* ten years later was to become a military classic and who was present as an Artillery captain. This was the setting fire to Bourliouk by the Russians in their retirement. In a few minutes its houses stuffed with coarse hay and straw presented a raging furnace, billowing forth thick, acrid, impenetrable smoke on a front of well over 300 yards. The stroke was clever and well-timed, taking the British by surprise. With less disciplined troops it could have had serious consequences, for the 2nd Division, confronted by this impassable obstruction, was brought to a standstill. The Light Division, by a seaward drifting of the smoke, was unaffected, and Codrington's Brigade immediately facing Kourgane pressed on, the 7th Royal Fusiliers on its right shouldering their way through the overlapping 95th, the leftmost regiment of Pennefather's halted brigade. Such humiliation was more than the Derbyshire men could stomach. Moved by some common impulse the left half of the regiment cut their brigade traces and rushed on in the wake of the 7th. By now the fire from the batteries had become a great deal heavier. Though the pace of the Light Division's advance had been too swift for the Russian gunners hitherto to aim with much accuracy or effect, once the men were across the wall and among the vineyards they began to fall on all sides. Here not only was their rate slowed down but the enemy had with remarkable foresight scattered at various points white posts topped with straw bundles, giving them exact ranges. In addition, their skirmishers having retired across the river were lining the southern bank and picking off their enemies as they struggled through the vineyards. Here the cause of deceleration was the peculiar Crimean viniculture which, because of the shortage of timber, consisted of digging hundreds of large holes three or four feet square up the north side of which the vines were trained. To men disciplined 'to march like a wall and wheel like a gate' these unanticipated obstacles were disrupting. Once the line was broken, so was what might be termed corporate discipline. Shakoes, tin kettles, even haversacks – anything that impeded movement was tossed away with that thriftlessness which characterized the British soldier on active service. Some paused to pluck and eat the grapes and went on into the fight with bunches dangling from their lips. Others, whom Alfred Tipping called 'the unwounded and uninjured except in the nervous system', found the protective shelter of a wall too tempting to resist. So great indeed was the confusion in crossing the vineyards that the errant 95th strayed so far to the left that it merged with the 23rd on the other side of Codrington's Brigade. By the time the Alma was reached all trace of alignment had been lost.

With orders not to pick their way most men dutifully leapt straight into the Alma, holding their rifles and ammunition pouches above their heads, and found the water in this stretch rarely more than waist high or up to their armpits. A few hesitated on the bank where it was deeper till it collapsed or until pressure from behind tumbled them in – provoking in either case much laughter, despite the firing from the other bank.

As they crossed some stumbled and fell, drenching themselves and, which mattered more, their powder, others who were hit slumped forward with a groan, never to rise. Some hurried across, others in whom the recent meal of salt pork had raised an unquenchable thirst paused unconcernedly to drink and fill their waterbottles.

The south bank of the Alma lay a little way back from the actual river (a cart track ran between the two) and rose to a height of about eight to 15 feet. It was to become a feature of the first importance in the fighting now developing. Without it there might have been no British victory or victory only at a hideous cost.

As the part to be played by General Buller's brigade on the left of the Light Division was small so far as the 77th and 88th were concerned, it can be disposed of briefly. Buller – 'Gentleman George' – was not a general of distinction. The weight of his responsibilities for the left flank of the army seems to have numbed his faculties. Having led his brigade across the Alma with less difficulty than Codrington because in his path there were fewer obstacles, he seems to have been content to have complied with the command not to stop till across the river. About his next step he was so much in the dark that he actually turned for enlightenment to his youthful ADC, Henry Clifford, who advised an advance similar to Codrington's on the right. While Buller was making up his mind to agree, Egerton in command of the 77th on the extreme left had spotted a large number of helmets over the crest of a hillock some hundreds of yards to his left front. Fearing an attack he wheeled his regiment round and formed line facing the Russians. When Buller's orders to pursue the advance reached him he decided to ignore them, to remain where he was and to explain his reason later. This, as it turned out, there was never any need to do. Egerton was one of the army's most proficient officers and it was clear after the battle that he had performed an invaluable if unspectacular service. A few moments later and Buller himself discovered another force which, from their helmets seen topping a ridge, he wrongly imagined to be Menschikoff's cavalry. He instantly stopped the forward march of the 88th (whom he was accompanying) and ordered it to form a square – an order most reluctantly and indifferently obeyed by the turbulent but dare-devil regiment. A similar order was passed on to the 19th on his right. Fearing that what he thought to be cavalry had every intention of attacking, Buller was justified in his precautions. But the 19th saw it in another light. They were some distance from any threat to the left, but they were very much nearer the battery on the Great Redoubt. Now a square was the approved method of dealing with a cavalry attack, but a square formed within range of the powerful 12-gun battery on the slopes was inviting disaster. The officers of the 19th declined to accept the order and with commendable indiscipline veered off to the right and attached themselves to the 95th and the 23rd Royal Welch Fusiliers.

Codrington's Brigade already swollen in numbers had been running into difficulties which the addition of the 19th only worsened. In the 23rd and 7th it contained two of the most highly trained regiments in the army, but in order to do themselves justice it was essential that they advance in line, the virtues of which (over column) had been taught since the Napoleonic Wars. Break that formation, send them forward in the matted state in which they had reached the south bank and all the benefits of their training would be sacrificed; the moral and physical effect upon the enemy of an unbroken, outflanking line, grandly advancing, would be lost. But for the bank's being lined by Russian marksmen, this would have provided cover in which to re-establish order, but the bullets whistling down from above made it impossible. The only commands the men would heed were 'fix bayonets' and 'come on!, come on!, anyhow!' Codrington very soon saw it was hopeless to attempt any reorganization and in his deep sonorous voice could be heard shouting, 'Get up the bank and advance to attack'. Thereupon, not as they had been trained to fight but in a great, ragged, bundling body, they went into the assault. As they crowned the bank the Russian marksmen could be seen in retreat, leaving between the river and the Great Redoubt above a bare obstructionless glacis of 500 to 600 yards in length. Over the edge of the low breastwork ahead pointed the muzzles of the 12 guns silent only till their own men were clear of their fire. Behind the epaulements and between the guns infantry were massed looking 'like the dense crowd you would see on Derby Day', but with faces described as being oddly white and expressionless. Codrington's men had not gone far when the breastwork above flashed into one continuous line of flame, as shot, shell, canister grape and bullets tore down the slope.

In the face of this searing fire men tended to close in rather than to scatter, thus aggravating and intensifying the initial disorder. 'They went forward as a horde', declared an eye-witness, and Sir Colin Campbell, watching from the 1st Division in the rear, cried out, 'My God! Those regiments are not moving like British soldiers!' At some points the men were 16 deep. Casualties in consequence were severe. Clifford saw 14 men killed by a single discharge of grape. John Pearson of the 33rd 'never expected to live another moment'; but as a private he had more chance than an officer. Conspicuous in his uniform with its epaulets and wealth of gold braid, well in the front of his men, waving his sword and trying to restore some kind of order, an officer was particularly vulnerable. To carry the colours was to risk almost certain death – the 95th lost every ensign in succession as well as five sergeants.

Though it seemed to all anxious spectators that the Light Division was losing that effective concentration of fire power which can come only from perfect alignment, the impression conveyed to the Russians was happily very different. They had been trained to resist dense columns similar to their own, but a long line, even though irregular and knotted, stretching out far beyond their flanks, was something not in their military vocabulary. 'We did not think it possible [wrote Captain Hodasevich] for men to be found with such firmness of morale to be able to attack in this apparently weak formation our massive columns.'

The consequences of this incredulity could never have been anticipated. After one last withering volley their firing ceased and, to the amazement of all, the Russians were seen through the smoke limbering up and withdrawing their guns, using cavalry horses for the purpose equipped with lasso harness. 'Stole away! Stole away!' hallooed a young subaltern. 'He's carrying off his guns.' Another, young and lithe, darted from the ranks of the 23rd holding in his hands the uncased colours of the regiment with its 75 holes. Henry Anstruther, barely 18, reached the breastwork in which he was just about to plant the colours when a bullet struck him in the heart. Close behind him rode Codrington, conspicuous on his grey Arab, and following him and cheering lustily as they covered the last few yards came the men of the Light Division. They reached the Redoubt just as the last two guns were being dragged away. Captain Bell of the 23rd flung himself at one, tore off its driver and with the point of his sword scribbled '23' on the barrel. Captain Heyland of the 95th, who had lost an arm on the way up, similarly took possession of the other. At the same time those who had paused to look around them saw higher up against the sky-line where the post road climbed over the col a flurry of ladies streaming away with their gentlemen friends in the direction of Sebastopol and shedding shawls and parasols in their flight.

To Hamley this 'discreditable withdrawal' was the turning point of the battle. Yet it should be said at once that this was no craven act. The Russians when adequately led were as courageous as any of their foes.* Their retreat derived from an uncompromising order of the Czar, who believed that Wellington had never lost a gun (he had in fact lost four, although they were Portuguese) and had determined that no Russian gun should ever be taken. So anxious, however, was the Russian commander to comply with that order that, as we have seen, he left it nearly too late.

One regiment of Codrington's Brigade had not partici-pated in the assault on the Redoubt. The line which the 7th Royal Fusiliers took brought them somewhat to the right of Kourgane. They too crossed under the same storm of lead and found Russian skirmishers established on a ten-foot bank. 'These [wrote Hibbert] began to shoot us like rats in a trap. For one moment I thought we were done for when Coney who was carrying the regimental colour sprang up the bank and planted it for the rest to rally round. Then in a

---

* There was never any question regarding the bravery of the Russian common soldier: it was their field officers who so often set them a deplorable example. For that bravery there was according to a Russian officer (in a conversation with Gadsby) a cynical explanation: 'No wonder our soldiers are brave! They have so little to lose that they lose nothing when they lose their life. The way to make a soldier good is to make him careless about his existence.'

moment we all rushed up and the time of retribution for the Russians began.'

In front of them instead of a redoubt 500 yards away there were two battalions of the left half of the Kazan Regiment descending upon them in tight formation. Although outnumbered by more than two to one, the 7th had in Colonel Lacy Yea one of the finest officers and strictest disciplinarians in the service. He was devoid of fear and was devoted to his profession and his regiment, from which in turn he demanded the utmost courage and devotion. For him there could be no turning back, whatever the odds. The Fusiliers must fight and die where they stood. Keeping up in his deep throaty voice a steady flow of oaths and imprecations, he rode up and down on his hunter, butting into and driving his men into something like a line capable of bringing to bear on the Russians' close column the maximum firepower.

At a distance which the inventions of a dozen or more years would make impossible the Royal Fusiliers and the Kazan regiment began pouring fire into each other's ranks. Sometimes the range increased, sometimes it diminished. Sometimes small groups of English and Russian soldiers would lose patience and rush together in bloody hand-to-hand conflict. It was in one of these that young William Monck ran his sword through two Russians before being shot dead at pointblank range. In another Hibbert saw 'Persse fire his revolver's five barrels at some men close to him, miss with all and throw the pistol itself at a fellow's head and call him a damned coward.'

The fight was not so unequal as the difference in numbers or so deadly as the closeness of the combatants might suggest. Only the two front ranks of the dense and narrow Russian column could fire and then only with an 1832 smooth-bore musket recently altered from flintlock to percussion and hardly lethal at 100 yards. The Fusiliers from their much extended line presented a less vulnerable target and their Minié rifles had infinitely greater range and penetrating power. This celebrated rifle, the invention of a Frenchman and manufactured by licence in England, had been issued to the troops only recently but not to all – it was to be several months before the 4th Division was equipped with anything better than the old Brown

Bess. While this slogging match was in progress, the rest of Codrington's Brigade with its adhesions were spreading themselves excitedly over the conquered redoubt higher up to the left and the more wary were looking over their shoulders with growing uneasiness.

Good timing and good psychology is only another way of saying good generalship. The lull which follows achievement is as critical a period as any in battle. When the Light Division reached the Great Redoubt after their exhausting and perilous attack it was inevitable that tension must relax. Survivors would be given time to reflect on their lucky escapes and while doing so would lose something of that reckless courage that only the heat and excitement of actual fighting can create and sustain. Nor, if it were necessary to renew the fight, would it be so easy to recapture that *élan* which had carried them up the Kourgane now that the regiments were intermixed. Herein lies the danger behind the counter-attack. The moment that his victorious troops were in the Great Redoubt, the controlling and directing hand of a great commander-in-chief should have been in evidence. Now should supports be arriving to reinforce the victors and fortify and inspire them against counter-measures. But as the wearied Light Division looked back they saw nothing on the long slope leading up from the Alma but the dead and wounded 'lying like grass on the ground'. As they glanced to their flanks the prospect was even more discouraging. To the right and left were massed columns of Russian soldiers from whose throats came 'a long, sorrowful, wailing sound', the ominous precursor to some desperate venture. Nor had they long to wait to learn its significance. First the field batteries on high Kourgane opened fire, next emerging from a hollow directly to the front where their existence had been concealed came a third body of Russians, two battalions it turned out, of the Vladimir Regiment bearing in their midst the image of the blessed St Sergius. No fire came from their lowered muskets because what they were engaged upon was a bayonet charge but of a style and tempo so different from our own that it remained unrecognized as such and led, as will be seen, to a grievous mistake.

Although Codrington's Brigade had been hit severely and many had exhausted their ammunition, its high percentage of toughened long-service soldiers guaranteed its capacity still to put up a fight. The fire from their Miniés into the dense Vladimir columns would have shaken them, perhaps even enabled our men to hold them back till reinforcements arrived. But it was a moment when nerves are easily lost, when perception is blunted and credulity ranges uninhibited. A frantic figure of a staff officer on horseback, perhaps misled – that at least is the most charitable explanation – by the Russian failure to fire, came galloping along the ranks shouting, 'Don't fire! Don't fire! – the column's French!'

Few stopped to ask themselves how the French could have moved to the British front from having been not half an hour earlier on their right flank, nor how they came to be dressed in long grey overcoats reaching to their ankles. Obediently one bugler after another from left to right sounded the 'Cease Fire' followed by 'Retreat'. To Colonel Chester of the 23rd this was insanity. 'No, no,' he shouted. 'It's a Russian column, fire! Fire!' They were his last words and they were unheeded. He was found by Russell after the battle lying 'dead with a scornful frown, his sword clutched in the death grasp'.

But for its tragic sequel the immediate consequences of this crazy command (the identity of its author was never discovered) were almost humorous. The Russians, astonished at not encountering any fire, seemed to have suspected some subtle trap and their ponderous advance ground to a halt. Without this pause what followed must have been doubly disastrous. With many of their officers and NCOs dead or disabled and the bugles insistently sounding the Retire, the Light Division started to fall back down the slope, 'a scattered crowd without regular formations', but dourly, sullenly and frequently stopping, despite the heavy fire under which they now came, to turn and make some reply. Codrington, who had foreseen the danger, had meanwhile dispatched an ADC to General Bentinck to hurry on his brigade of Guards who were no nearer than the crossing of the Alma.

Where was the commander-in-chief and why was he not in such control as to have made such an appeal unnecessary?

Lord Raglan had no sooner issued his first and last order than accompanied by a handful of his staff he had made his

way to the right of the burning village. Here he forded the
river and riding past some astonished French skirmishers
operating on the left of Prince Napoleon's division, he entered a lane, never once hurrying and paying no more attention to shot and shell than he would to whirling autumn leaves.
This lane, evidently detected that morning in the course of
his scrutiny through his glasses, led on to a knoll which was
really a lower spur of Telegraph Hill at the angle where it
turned into the amphitheatre. On this eminence, far in advance
of his army and quite isolated – indeed it was virtually within
the enemy lines – this astonishing man sat coolly on his horse
Shadrach watching the progress of the fighting. It was magnificent but it was not generalship.

From this advanced observation post Raglan (Kinglake
naïvely tells us) 'had to bear the anguish of finding that the
ground where he longed to see the supports marching up was
still left bare'. If Raglan had been where a commander-in-
chief ought to have been at this moment, that is somewhere
in the centre of his army, he would have seen in time, and
provided for, the needs of his first line by ordering up reinforcements on the heels of the Light Division instead of, as
we shall see, leaving this to others.

The 1st Division had remained deployed in line when the
Light Division had started its advance. Having received no
precise orders, the Duke of Cambridge appears to have been
at a loss when to act and how far to act. He advanced his
division after a time to behind the first wall of the vineyards
and then caused it to lie down. Like all members of his royal
house he was intensely brave, but on his young and inexperienced shoulders the responsibility for the fate of the brilliant
Brigade of Guards weighed heavily. The previous night when
most of the army slept he had been seen restlessly pacing in
and out of his tent till dawn broke. And now as he watched
with concern the Light Division disrupting themselves in the
vineyards and raggedly climbing the opposite slopes, he seems
to have doubted the wisdom of committing his precious division to a similar fate. While he hesitated Richard Airey, who
had not accompanied Raglan, saw how things were going and
hurried across to the Duke whom on his own authority he
ordered to advance. Some further time was lost while instruc-

tions were carried down to Sir Colin Campbell on the left. When at last on the command, 'The line will advance', this magnificent division went forward it was in time to bring victory but too late to prevent a temporary setback.

Ordered to break ranks when they came to the vineyards and 'get over as best you can', the Guards like Codrington's Brigade before them were rapidly disorganized by the physical obstacles and the fierce cannon fire. 'The grape and canister [wrote one officer] was falling around us like hail – the flash of each gun being instantly followed by a splash of grape among the tilled ground like a handful of gravel thrown into a pool.' But after all, commented another, 'what does one expect to find in a vineyard but *grape-shot*?' In any case, remarked a third, 'once we commenced advancing and firing one lost all feelings of nervousness.'

Being the centre and therefore the directing battalion of the Guards Brigade the Scots Fusilier Guards were the first across the river. They had just started to align themselves when Codrington's ADC reached General Bentinck pleading for instant support. Bentinck, a dull-witted man, who reminded Arthur Earle of a stud-groom, thereupon lost his head and without awaiting the arrival of the Grenadiers and Coldstream spurred his horse up and down shouting, 'Forward, forward, Fusiliers, what are you waiting for?' After that, wrote Captain Gipps, 'it was impossible to restrain the men and up the ascent we went in imperfect formation and not even our bayonets fixed'. The Scots Fusilier Guards, reputed to be the finest of all the line regiments, surged forward 'little better than a mob'. Francis Haygarth and other officers, after vainly haranguing their men, abandoned the attempt to get them into line and rushed on ahead through a fire described as so fierce that 'you could hardly conceive it possible for anything the size of a rabbit not to be killed'. But the enthusiasm and courage of all ranks of the Fusilier Guards were not enough to compensate for their increasing isolation as they forged up the hill with nothing to their left or right.

The Grenadiers and Coldstream had not, it seems, received Bentinck's urgent command, or if received their commanding officers had no intention of complying with it while their men were in confusion. Colonel Hood of the Grenadiers had been watching the progress of Codrington's Brigade and considered that their loss of power derived from the loss of order. He would have none of it. Sternly commanding the men to lie down under cover of the bank until all were across, he threw out markers and as coolly as if on parade set about aligning and dressing his regiment. Nothing would hurry him, not even a personal appeal from Yea who came galloping down from the right.

Further to the left the Coldstream, last across owing to a river bend in their path requiring a triple fording for some of them, were handled with the same care by Colonel Upton.* Meanwhile, as if to prove how little generalship played any part in the battle, the very worried Duke had somehow strayed to the left and reached the spot where Buller was standing near the 88th.

'What am I to do?' he asked. 'Why, your Royal Highness,' came the reply, 'I am in a little confusion here – you had better advance, I think.'

Before the Duke could give an order the Coldstream and the Grenadiers, their alignment completed, had surmounted the bank and with a wide gap between them where the Scots Fusilier Guards ought to have been, started to ascend the slopes of Kourgane. Here at this moment, although the picture is very confused, the layout seems to have been as follows. Codrington's men, obedient to their original command to retire, were still dropping back with frequent haltings to return the fierce Vladimir fire. On their right Lacy Yea's Fusiliers were at grips with the Kazan battalions. With their lead of about five minutes the Scots Fusilier Guards were halfway up the hill roughly in the centre, advancing in ragged formation with their Colours carried by Lindsay and Thistlethwayte well up amongst the leaders but somewhat to the right. On the left slopes of Kourgane beyond the Coldstream the Highlanders had crossed the Alma and were beginning to form up.

The Grenadiers and Coldstream had not gone far when the

* As an illustration of how uncertain can be the evidence even of one writing home on the evening of a battle an officer of the 19th describing his advance up the slopes declared that owing to its bends he had had to cross the Alma *twice*.

23rd, with hardly an officer left standing and their nerves shattered by the terrible ordeal they had undergone, suddenly gave way. They turned and cannoned into the Scots Fusilier Guards toiling up in their rear with such force that they carried back a large number with them in their retreat, hurling some to the ground and breaking at least one set of ribs. This would have been damaging to the morale of the finest troops without a baser addition. A shout was heard and was taken up and repeated on all sides: 'Fusiliers, retire!' The origin of this command and the direction from which it originally came have eluded discovery. There were within call three fusilier regiments for whom it could have been meant – the 23rd, the 7th, and the Scots Guards. The probability is that it was given (like the previous order) by some agitated, officious staff officer and was intended for Yea's regiment, becoming increasingly isolated on the right as the rest of the brigade retreated from the Great Redoubt.

Heard in the heat and confusion of battle it was not unreasonable that the Scots Fusilier Guards should take it as applying to themselves and, highly disciplined, should obey the command. All but a small rebel minority gathered round the Colours turned and in the words of Lindsay, who bore the Queen's colour, 'went rapidly downhill'.

Elated by the success of its counter-measures the Vladimir Regiment marched ponderously down from the Redoubt. With its lines of skirmishers protruding on either flank it looked like some monstrous beetle. As it came within their range the Russian artillery ceased, but instead of pressing on the regiment inexplicably halted as others in other battles ahead were to do in similar circumstances. The air which had resounded with the noise of battle became still, save for the groans of the wounded and dying. The halt and the lull lasted only a few moments. But when the Russians resumed their downward march they had lost their advantage. The Coldstream and the Grenadiers were so much the nearer, striding up the hill, each man armed with a deadly Minié.

They had passed in their ascent Sir George Brown, erect on his horse. His contribution to the battle had so far been nil, but he was reputed to have been the only man in the army to have shaved that morning. They had opened their ranks to

let through broken units of the Light Division and the
95th and then had placidly closed them as if it had been a
peacetime exercise. As they approached the vicinity of the
retreating Scots Fusilier Guards, they looked up in amazement and, ignorant of the cause, were heard to cry out in allu-
sion to Queen Victoria's alleged partiality: 'Shame! Shame!
What about the Queen's favourites now?' Pressing on they had
cleared the stragglers and had just opened fire on the Vladimir
Regiment heading for the gap when for the third time within
fifteen minutes that panic cry was heard: 'Retire! You're firing
on the French! Retire!' A frantic figure on horseback whose
cocked hat proclaimed him to be on the staff was seen, but whose
speed as he rode from right to left across the front of the
Guards made identification impossible. This time the order
was too ridiculous to be heeded. The Grenadiers on the right
halted only long enough to dress back to their left so as to
be able to pour flanking fire into the descending columns.
Tipping recounts the next few minutes:

Our gallant regiment stood in line as if in Hyde Park, the
enemy coming down within 80 or 100 yards and firing from
behind the hill as well. We delivered our fire and they dropped
by dozens, another and another volley and the cool determined
stand we made in that awful bottom cut them down in crowds, as
they came on.

At such short range the Miniés struck like a wall of lead.
With their inadequate muskets the Russians could make no
effective reply. As they withdrew, the Scots Fusilier Guards
having rapidly reorganized their broken ranks were once more
on the way up the slope to take their proper place between
the Grenadiers and the Coldstream. Then, as if they had been
under the eye of Her Majesty at a Birthday Review the
Brigade of Guards resumed their forward march in one unbroken line of scarlet topped with bearskin. It was a sight
which those who saw it never forgot. Their lofty headgear
gave the impression of an array of giants moving effortlessly
into battle. Even the Russians could not withhold admiration.
'C'était trop majestueux', exclaimed a captured general that
night.

Firing volley after volley as they went – the rear rank shooting as the front rank halted to reload – they had expended 16 rounds by the time they were within 40 yards of the Redoubt. At this point the order to charge was given and with ringing cheers, audible more than a mile in the rear, the Guards broke into a run and swept into the Redoubt. They had defeated but not routed the Russians. Notwithstanding the awe they had inspired and the fearful casualties they had inflicted their foes withdrew 'in very tolerably good order, firing at us and in no confusion or disorderly haste'. Indeed, but for a fresh threat on their flank, it is possible that the Russians, never more courageous than in defence, might have been allowed to put up a resistance long enough for reinforcements to arrive. The threat was to be seen in the bonnets of the 42nd Highlanders as they topped the ridge on the Russian right. Only a retreat could now save them from being taken in the flank.

In his last halt before his brigade had crossed the Alma Sir Colin Campbell, drawing on his own war experiences, had addressed his men. He had warned them to pay no attention to the wounded, to let them lie till picked up by bandsmen and stretcher parties. To be in no hurry to fire. In fact, to wait till ordered to do so and then to aim low. To be steady and to keep silent. 'The army will be watching you,' he concluded. 'Make me proud of the Highland Brigade.'

When the march had been resumed the Alma was reached at a point where it took a north-easterly bend, compelling – happily as it turned out – the three regiments to cross in echelon. Though Russell has confessed to have learnt after 40 years as war correspondent how impossible it is to synchronize the events of a battle with any certainty, it is probable that while the Scottish regiments were still reforming on the South bank the Scots Fusilier Guards were falling back, for the Duke, now more agitated than ever, rode up to Sir Colin as he stood with the 42nd on the right of the brigade and insisted that there must be a disaster unless the division was withdrawn. Campbell's reply was characteristic: disaster was certain *if* there was a withdrawal. A few moments later (though not in the presence of the Duke of Cambridge) he roared out, 'It were better that every man of Her Majesty's

Guards should lie dead upon the field of battle than that they should turn their backs upon the enemy.' With permission to carry on given only reluctantly by the Duke – Private McAusland heard him muttering, 'We shall be tried for this, Sir Colin' – it had not taken this tough old brigadier long to decide his tactics. While the Guards assaulted the Great Redoubt he would bring one regiment after another up the eastern shoulder of Kourgane, overrun the Lesser Redoubt and, bringing forward the left shoulder, take the Russians in the flank. Having dispatched orders to this effect by Anthony Sterling, his brigade-major, he put himself some way in advance of the Black Watch and uttered just two words, 'Forward, 42nd.'

Making, says Sterling, 'a deliberate parade ground movement of regiments in echelon, right in front' the Highlanders started up the incline at a smart pace. On the left they brushed by the 77th still in line facing east and on the right they went through the 88th (The Connaught Rangers) halted in their irregular and distasteful square, from which angry Irish voices were heard shouting sarcastically, 'Let the *Scotchmen* go on! – They'll do the work.' Striding in perfect silence they fired no shot and took no notice of those knocked over. Such few casualties as the brigade received were caused by some ill-directed fire from the Lesser Redoubt and this soon ceased as the threatened guns were towed away.

Well ahead of the 42nd went the skirmishers under Captain Montgomery. As he reached the first or outer ridge he could see the Guards on the right breaking into the Great Redoubt and the Russians streaming away to join the right half of the Kazan regiment which was driving on straight in the path of the approaching 42nd. Montgomery's skirmishers, to whom naturally Sir Colin's prohibition did not apply, were just about to open fire when there was heard the same cry from presumably the same agitated staff officer making his way from right to left across the British front – 'Don't fire! They're French!' But a Highlander next to Montgomery called out 'Na ... na ... there's na misstakin thone deevil' and sent a Minié bullet into the column. Half a minute later they were joined by the main body of the 42nd, moving with speed, up the hill. Too blown by their swift climb to charge

they were commanded to do what Sir Colin had trained them
to do in such circumstances, although unauthorized by regu-
lations. They marched on firing without halting and as they
marched they cheered. No body of soldiers in close formation
could withstand such execution. The Russians wheeled round
and retired.

Yet it was not to be quite as simple as all that for the
Highlanders. The troops which Buller had imagined to be
Menschikoff's cavalry were part of the uncommitted Sousdal
Regiment. These, moving from left to right behind a spur of
Kourgane, came straight on the flank of the advancing 42nd.
Now was the value of the fortuitous Highland echelon formation
to be proved. As the Russians approached over the outer ridge,
eager for battle, the 93rd appeared in line taking two battalions of the Sousdal in the flank as they intended to do to the
42nd. But, though subjected to murderous fire, the Russians
did not, in Sir Colin Campbell's words, 'yield easily', and
while they resisted they enabled the remaining two battalions,
accompanied by some cavalry, to hasten forward and threaten
the left flank of the 93rd. As they came on hopefully over the
ridge, still further to the left, the 79th were tearing up the
hill. Alternately cheering and firing the men of the Cameron
Highlanders made straight for the Russians, pouring volleys
into their exposed flank and driving them over the outer ridge
and down into a hollow on the far side. As all four battalions
drew away two horse batteries which had followed on the heels
of the Highlanders and had discovered a ford across the river
came galloping up and directed a deadly enfilading fire into
the retreating Russians who, to their credit, never increased
their pace beyond that of a quick step despite the punishment
they were receiving.

Here on the left it was a complete Highland victory, gained
at surprisingly little cost – 15 killed and 83 wounded. But it
could so easily have been, if not a defeat, a success purchased
dearly. Had the Highlanders moved more slowly or had the
Russians reacted more speedily they would have established
themselves on the outer ridge across the line of the brigade's
advance. In that event (wrote Anthony Sterling) 'God knows
what would have been the loss to the Highland Brigade even
if we had succeeded in pushing them back.'

The battle of the Alma was now over on the centre as well as the left. From the 79th on one side across to the Grenadiers on the other bonnets and bearskins were being raised on the points of bayonets. The cheers of the conquerors of Kourgane passed down through the 2nd and 3rd Divisions to the 4th well in the rear, till more than 20,000 throats were sending out paeans in celebration of the greatest British victory for 40 years.

'I shall never forget that cheer [wrote one who heard it] as long as I live.' When later in the afternoon Raglan sent for Sir Colin Campbell there were tears in his eyes and his countenance quivered. He could only shake him by the hand; he could not speak. In reply, Sir Colin's sole request was that he might have permission to wear henceforward a Highland bonnet instead of the general's cocked hat. It was granted, and the difficult task of building one combining the three hackles was secretly entrusted to Lieutenant Drysdale who, working most of the night, produced next morning the finished article for a delighted Sir Colin Campbell.

On the British right the results of the day were equally satisfactory though not so spectacular. For this some credit is attributable to Lord Raglan though not to the extent claimed by Kinglake. According to this writer the 'apparition' on the knoll within their own lines of a 'gay looking troop of horsemen whose habits and white plumes showed that they were staff officers' brought consternation to the Russian command and even more than the approach of the Light Division hastened the withdrawal of the guns from the Great Redoubt. It is Kinglake's hero-worshipping at its worst. There is no reliable evidence whatsoever that the appearance of such a group (even if noticed in the murk of battle) created either alarm or diversion. The general responsible, Kvetzinski, declared that he ordered the guns to be withdrawn because the regiment responsible for their defence had been defeated. Raglan's contribution to victory does not lie in his foolhardy and extraordinary appearance far in advance of his army but in the calling up of two guns, although even in this he merely expressed a wish for something to be done which was already being carried out. It had occurred to him that the Russian guns ranged across the post road might, from where he was

standing, be very nearly taken in reverse by artillery. Accordingly he had dispatched a staff officer to order Turner, whose
battery was attached to the 2nd Division, to send forward
a couple of guns. Turner, acting under De Lacy Evans's
orders, was already trying to do this when Raglan's message
reached him. He merely increased the pace of his advance
but in doing so reached the knoll with his guns so far ahead
of his men, that it was only with the aid of some of the
staff that he was able to lay the first gun. Now, according to
young Calthorpe, who was with his uncle Lord Raglan at
the time, the latter had just exclaimed, 'Look how well the
Guards and Highlanders advance!' when that first gun was
fired. In other words the battle was by then three-quarters
over.

The range from the knoll to the 18-gun battery was extreme for Turner's nine-pounders and the first shot fell short.
The second was on the target and killed two horses; the third
blew up an ammunition wagon. It was enough. Together with
what was happening at the Great Redoubt, which the Guards
were fast approaching, this shelling from a new angle filled
the gun-conscious officer in command with alarm and the battery was withdrawn to a spot higher up the post road and
out of Turner's range. This withdrawal at once brought much-
needed relief to the 2nd Division, whose exploits alone remain
to be described.

It is no disparagement of Evans's fine division, destined to
play a glorious part in the fighting to come, to say that at the
Alma their contribution was less than that of the Light or 1st
Division. It was not their fault. The burning of Bourliouk
across their line of march had made it impossible to proceed
abreast of the Light Division. Worse still, they were split into
two as they went left and right of the village. On the right
the 41st with most of the 49th forded the Alma well below
the post road bridge, but because of its depth in those reaches
with some delay and difficulty. There, on the other side, un-
accompanied by any officers senior to himself, they were discovered by their acting Adjutant-General, Lysons. Despite the
desultory fire from some daring Russian sharpshooters, who
had remained behind hidden in trees (where their bodies were
found next day) this most efficient officer had, by ordering out

markers, succeeded in getting the men of the two regiments into some formation when their brigadier, Adams, arrived and took over. At the same time a message was received from Raglan desiring the Brigade to advance on the knoll. This it reached just as the fight was ending with a total loss of no more than six men killed and 36 wounded.

In Pennefather's Brigade on the division's left those men of the 95th who had not disappeared on the tail of the 7th Fusiliers and most of the 55th had been unaffected by the burning village to their right. The 30th, the third regiment in the brigade, together with the 47th and part of the 49th from Adams' were immediately behind the blaze and to get round it to the left were compelled to move in fours. In this congested formation they became particularly exposed to the 18-gun battery directly ahead of them across the bridge. Attempts at reply by artillery brought forward were no more successful than before. 'Shot and shell of various calibres whistled and bounded incessantly along this spot that it seemed [declared one officer] a marvel that anyone escaped.' It was just about here that Sergeant Keeshan of the 55th had his arm severed and quietly picked it up and walked to the rear.

Owing to the delay thus caused, by the time the left portion of the 2nd Division had cleared the village and started to deploy prior to crossing the river, the Light Division were approaching the redoubt and there was some easing of the rain of shells falling on the former. On the other hand as the 2nd Division drew nearer to the river they came under heavy fire from skirmishers established along the Southern bank. Their bullets in addition to the shot, shell and grape which still came from the 18-gun battery straight ahead caused many casualties in the crossing. The right half of the 95th moving down the post road should have passed over by the bridge but the cry went out that it was mined. There was immediate confusion and some faltering during which every officer of one company was struck down, but Captain Champion shouting, 'Come on, 95th – show 'em the way', restored confidence and led his men over. The remainder of Pennefather's Brigade and its adhesions from Adams' Brigade crossed below the bridge suffering not only a number of casualties from Russian fire but (especially in the 30th) from drowning in unexpectedly deep pools. Under cover of the bank and some quarry excavations the men lay down and started firing at a range of 600 yards on the 18-gun battery ahead. As soon as Turner's two guns on the right front had compelled this to withdraw and the weight of gun fire had lessened, Evans gave the order to advance. In the very best traditions of the service the officers brought their men to the top of the bank and putting out markers dressed them in line. Only when this had been done to the satisfaction of Colonel Mauleverer of the 30th did he resume his place in the rear and was heard unconcernedly asking Major Patullo for a light for his cigar. After that 'in perfect parade ground order' the advance of the division went ahead along the line of the post road into the heart of the amphitheatre. What remained of the 95th had meanwhile drifted off towards where the Grenadiers were starting their climb, leaving the 55th the leftmost regiment of the division. To the latter's left front the Royal Fusiliers were dourly carrying on their private battle with the Kazan Regiment. The slaughter of the Russian officers, especially of one who seemed to have been the inspiration of its fight, had been steadily weakening morale. But having received a visit from Gortschakoff and orders for a supreme effort, the Kazan Regiment was starting to move down against the nearly exhausted Fusiliers when Colonel Warren, entirely on his own responsibility, hurried the 55th forward. Using the right flank of the 7th as a pivot, he wheeled his regiment through an angle of 90 degrees, thus positioning it on the flank of the advancing Russians. While his men poured a killing fire from their Miniés into the flanks, Turner's two guns on the right with depressed sights cut what Captain Hume called 'regular lanes' through the Russian ranks. No effective reply came from the Kazan regiment, nor was it possible. Only the front ranks could use their old smooth-bore muskets and they had small hope of inflicting injury; the remainder merely fired aimlessly into the air. It halted, stood for a short time, its surviving officers bravely exposing themselves, shouting, sword-waving, exhorting, even shaking recalcitrants by the throat. The ordeal was more than any soldiers hopelessly handicapped by their unwieldy formation could stand. They turned and retired, at first slowly. But now on the heels of the 2nd Division followed the artillery, galloping across the bridge. Fanning out right and left they poured accurate fire on all remaining Russian columns within sight. 'We opened from 18 guns [wrote an Artillery officer]; they stood it for some time ... at last they broke, flung away everything and ran like fun.' To another they scattered 'like sparrows'. To Captain Heath watching through a telescope from the maintop of *Niger* these last moments of Russian resistance on Kourange brought to mind a curious analogy. 'The Russians did not deploy but gave way whilst still in their solid formation and ran off, beginning at the rear of the mass ... with a few individuals, but the numbers increased every minute until the formation became exactly like a rocket, or a comet with a bushy tail.'

It had not been more than 35 minutes since the British attack had opened and already everywhere the Russians were in retreat. On the heels of the artillery came the fresh and almost scatheless 3rd Division. Crossing the Alma in column they quickly deployed into line and advanced in the track of the Guards who had pressed on beyond the redoubt. The French having at last got their guns on to the Heights were pounding the congested Russian columns as they closed in to get through the gorge through which the post road ran. It was at this moment that a general of genius might have thrown in his cavalry force, small though it was. It was the opinion of Sir George Cathcart that 'Those fellows have had such a dressing they will never meet us in the open again', and outside Headquarters it would have been greeted with loud acclamations. Raglan thought otherwise. He believed the Russians had not only the capacity but the mind to turn and make a stand. Once again as on the previous day he considered he ought not to risk his only mounted arm. His cavalry it was his confessed intention to 'keep in a bandbox'. He had issued no orders to them either before or during the battle. Furious and frustrated they had been forced to hang about on the extreme left flank while the Infantry and even the Horse Artillery were garnering glory. The very young cornet of horse who some weeks before at Varna was heard to ask 'whether the *inphuntry* would be employed at Sewastopol' was getting his answer and it was not to his taste.

Still without orders, Lucan, by this time nearly speechless with anger, led the Light Brigade across the Alma and up to where the victorious Highlanders had halted on Kourgane. In the distance the Russians could be seen streaming away towards Sebastopol, broken at last and disheartened. Now if ever was the opportunity for cavalry to take up instant pursuit, rounding up prisoners, capturing guns and converting a retreat into a rout. But instead there came from Raglan three successive orders, each more unpopular than the last. Lucan on the left and Cardigan on the right were to escort the artillery into a forward position but – and the injunction was sternly repeated – on no account were the cavalry to attack. But when their menial task had been performed they could not resist pressing on and sweeping in prisoners. Instantly came the second order: the cavalry were to return. This having been ignored, a third command was received: the cavalry were to desist forthwith and return. It was insupportable. Even the prisoners taken had to be let go. That night the dashing Captain Edward Nolan stormed into William Howard Russell's tent lambasting the High Command and shouting, 'There were a thousand British cavalry looking on a beaten army – retreating – guns, standards, colours and all – with a wretched horde of Cossacks and cowards who had never struck a blow, ready to turn tail at the first trumpet, within ten minutes' gallop.' Robert Portal of the 4th Light Dragoons complained furiously of being commanded 'by a pack of old women who would have been better in their drawing-rooms'. Charles Windham, whose division (the 4th) was never involved, writing a week later declared in connexion with a cavalry follow-up: 'The more I think of the battle the more convinced I am that it might have ended the campaign. I thought so at the time and I think so more strongly now.'

It may have been so. The question whether Raglan's caution was justified, whether he was right in his determination to keep the only allied cavalry 'in a bandbox', is never likely to be settled. The argument may best be disposed of with a quotation from Sir George Higginson. Writing 60 years after the event he confessed not to 'feel justified even now, being fully aware of all that happened subsequently, in passing any judgement'.

With the unimpeded dispersal of the last Russian troops the battle of the Alma ended. It was a victory, St Arnaud assured Sir John Burgoyne, worth 20,000 additional troops. The position which Menschikoff boasted to his Czar he could hold for three weeks he had failed to hold for three hours. His propaganda had denigrated the British as sailors conscripted into military uniform; but the infantry had dismayed his men by fighting like 'red devils', the Guards like 'hairy devils'. As for the Highlanders, no one had warned them about these terrible 'soldiers in petticoats'. All, Guards, Highlanders, infantry, had that extra mobility and that more extended fire-power derived from their line formation which enabled them to overcome men whose courage matched their own and whose numbers – on Kourgane – exceeded their own.

Nevertheless the price of victory was severe. The killed numbered 362, the wounded no fewer than 1,621, of whom many were to die that night under the surgeon's knife as they lay (for lack of trestle tables) on the bare ground or later in the so-called hospital ships or still later amid the pre-Nightingale horrors of Scutari. These losses appalled the country but only because they came after so long a spell of peace. The younger generations knew nothing of Albuera and Salamanca with the cost of which Alma compared not unfavourably. Far greater were the Russian casualties, estimated at 5,500, of which 1,800 were killed. French losses were given as 1,343 but these were either deliberately exaggerated or included cholera casualties; 500 would be a correcter estimate.

It was the density of the casualties even more than their number which wrung the hearts of the survivors. Between the Alma and the Redoubt the dead are described as lying in swathes. In the Redoubt 'they lay in ranks. One [Russian] company seemed to have fallen as it stood. There was no heaping of bodies one on another, but it would have been difficult to step between them.' 'I cannot liken the field of battle to anything better than an abattoir', wrote a surgeon. On the eastern slope of Kourgane, where the retreating Sousdal Regiment had been raked by the batteries in the rear of the Highlanders, Arthur Tremayne 'never saw a more ghastly sight than rows of Russians with their skulls blown off'.

When darkness fell only a fraction of the wounded had been tended, and though the work went on by lantern light countless numbers were left out all through a bitterly cold night in pain and tortured with thirst.

Not anything [wrote Hibbert] that one reads can come up to the realities of a field of battle after an action; the horrible sights of the mangled bodies and wounded men praying for the love of God for a drop of water and begging one not to let them bleed to death, are far worse than the actual fighting.

In the attention so inadequately rendered to the stricken it is pleasant to learn that no distinction was made between British or Russian. Indeed the solicitude shown by our men to their foes struck Clifford as 'quite beautiful'. There were on the other hand a few shocking instances of Russians shooting the men who had just given them a drink, but most showed almost pathetic gratitude, kissing the hand that held the flask.

That night there was little elation among the troops as they prepared to bivouac. Too many had lost dear friends or comrades; the men of the Light Division spoke bitterly of having been sacrificed. When once they had ceased to speculate on the question (heard on all sides) 'What will they say at home?' they settled down to write or to sleep, using in many instances a Russian corpse for a desk or a pillow, according to their need. Among the officers, once mutual congratulations on survival had been exchanged, conversation centred on two topics: the lack of generalship and the failure to follow up victory.

'The only orders that were given at all were received by the 1st Division who were ordered when under a galling fire to lie down – a moment after, an ADC ordered them to advance.' This may not be an entirely accurate statement, but it is not wide of the mark. 'We (the actors in this horrid business for I can call it nothing else though a victory) think [wrote Captain Patullo of the 30th] that there was a great want of generalship and much loss of life in consequence.' 'There was little or no generalship before the action began [wrote Hugh Clifford] and none after we had got into it. We advanced on the position and nothing but the bravery of the officers and men going slap at it as *Englishmen can do*, took it.' In Russell's opinion no higher qualities were shown than

'a bulldog rush at the throat'. Hamley was even more outspoken: 'All that we have to be proud of was the dash and
valour of the regiments engaged.' 'Though each of the divisional generals acted as he thought best, there was [contended
Sir Evelyn Wood] no concerted action.' Lord Raglan played no
greater part in bringing about victory than a chairman's wife
who breaks a bottle of champagne on its bow does in the launch-
ing of a ship. 'The only orders I ever received from him [one
aggrieved officer told Russell] from the time I left Bulganak till
I arrived at the crest of the Alma were "March" and "Halt".'

Alma was a soldiers' and a field officers' battle. It was won
by men like Hood and Yea, Sanders of the 19th, Chester of
the 23rd, Warren of the 55th, officers who without orders
(because there were none) used their own surpassing initiative, yet none was mentioned in Raglan's dispatch.

More serious because of its repercussions on the campaign
was the complaint that the victory had not been immediately
followed up and was therefore a victory *manqué*. Levelled
against Raglan such criticism is not wholly sound. There is no
doubt that he wanted to press on (using as his spearhead the
fresh 3rd and 4th Divisions) as in like circumstances his
master, Wellington, would have done; but unlike Wellington
Raglan was not a free agent. St Arnaud declined to play on
the ground that his infantry could no more proceed without
their knapsacks than without their artillery, and that the first
had been left behind at the foot of the Heights and the second
had fired away all its ammunition.* It may well be doubted if
the impetuous Bosquet, had he been in command, would have
proffered such excuses, but Bosquet was not, like St Arnaud,
a sick, indeed a dying man.

To St Arnaud's objections Raglan had either to defer or
else risk taking independent action, trusting that the French
army would never, knapsacks or not, remain passive spectators. With the need to preserve the Anglo-French alliance
lying like an incubus on his chest it was difficult for him to

---

* A cynical French ADC put forward to J. H. Skene another –
perhaps the true – reason: 'Nous ne voulons pas que les Russes
cèdent trop vite – nous voulons beaucoup de tapage. Nous aurions le
tambour, nous aurions la gloire – nous aurions ce qui est creux – tout
ce qui fait du bruit – nous autres de la Gr.r.rande Nation!'

take any other course than that adopted. But if the criticism against Raglan's inaction is confined to the two days following the Alma, it is very much more difficult to rebut. On the morning after the battle the French were ready to move on, but it was now Raglan who demurred. It was necessary, he insisted, to bury the dead and embark the wounded (which included 500 Russians) – an excuse which would prevent any victory from ever being followed up. Nor is it consistent with Raglan's professed anxiety to press on the evening before. One explanation may be that St Arnaud's excuses had wakened Raglan's only lightly dormant Francophobia and having once started to attend to the wounded he was glad to have excuses himself for paying back St Arnaud in kind. Lord George Paget, dining the day after Alma with Raglan, reported Headquarters to be eloquent with hate against the French and the commander-in-chief very much dissatisfied with his allies. 'Once during dinner, when he heard in the distance their endless trumpet sounds, he said quite petulantly, "Ah, there they go with their infernal too-too-tooing; that's the only thing they ever did." '

And so, while the whole army was engaged in burying the dead and with the cheerful help of the sailors carrying the wounded on improvised stretchers to the seashore three miles away and to the hell that awaited them on board ship, the Russian army with its guns and most of its wounded were reaching Sebastopol and recovering their morale. There, there was no talk of capitulation. Menschikoff ordered a line of ships to be sunk, blocking the entrance to the harbour. Admiral Vorniloff who bitterly opposed the idea, preferring to put gallantly to sea and give battle, nevertheless caught the general enthusiasm to resist to the end. He told the army: 'If I myself give the order to retreat, kill me with your bayonets.'

When at last on September 23rd, and then not till two precious hours after sunrise, the allied army turned their faces towards Sebastopol it had missed its chance of taking the city by a *coup de main* on the heels of its dispirited defenders. Exactly how dispirited the Russian army had become as it covered the weary miles back to its base was to be seen in the litter of abandoned equipment. Even had they the will to resist, they would have had no assistance from nature. Robert

Lindsay, visiting the battlefield 30 years later, could not find a scrap of cover 'good, bad or indifferent for eight miles of the Alma behind which half a company of men could find shelter either from guns or cavalry pursuing. Only fine qualities of horsemanship and sportsmanship were needed to break up the flying column after the battle.' Whatever their other faults, these two qualities were not lacking in the Light Brigade. Within 24 hours it was generally reckoned the French and British armies could have been lining the northern shore of the harbour in a position to demand its surrender.

The Crimean expedition, made so late in the year and with a knowledge of its uncertain equinoctial weather, was a gamble and it could only succeed if risks continued to be taken. A hundred years before Wolfe in his wisdom wrote: 'In war something must be allowed to chance and fortune.' This allowance neither Raglan nor St Arnaud was prepared to make. Whatever their reasons, something in the ensuing pages will be learnt of their cost in human lives.

3

Balaclava

'No matter what mistakes a General might commit the pluck of the British army would set it all right.'

– *Sir Harry Smith*

WHETHER THERE SHOULD have been an attempt to take Sebastopol from the north or whether this should come from the south, where the allies would have good harbours in their rear instead of a much exposed coastline, is the concern of a general history of the Crimean War. It is enough to say that the second plan was adopted (largely on Sir John Burgoyne's advice) and that this necessitated the famous Flank March to the south, unquestionably one of the more fantastic operations of the war. With few maps and working mostly by compass a combined army of more than 50,000 led by the British moved through a tangle of scrub and forest so dense that 'you could not see the man just ahead of you' and the twigs of the undergrowth beat out strange primitive tattoos on regimental drums. No less dense, however, seems to have been the intelligence service on either side, for when the British van was approaching the farm of an early Scottish settler named Mackenzie high above the head of Sebastopol harbour it blundered into and captured the baggage train of the army which Menschikoff in ignorance of the allies' intentions was marching out of Sebastopol in order that it might be free to operate in the field. In addition a few prisoners were taken, including an artillery captain too fuddled with drink to escape. Now, it might have been amusing to loot and auction in carefree manner a variety of articles (which included ladies' underwear and improper French novels), but had the encounter taken place three hours earlier it could have proved disastrous for the scattered and disorganized British army.

From the neighbourhood of Mackenzie's farm, where the troops bivouacked, the road taken next morning dropped into the valley of the Tchernaya, across which behind some hills lay Sebastopol. More to the left a narrow defile led into the valley of Balaclava from which through a gorge there was access to the port of that name.

The only justification for this hazardous Flank March was, in the opinion of many, an immediate assault upon the town. Sir George Cathcart pleaded with Raglan for instant action. 'We could run into it even in open day, risking only a few shots from the redoubts. We see the people walking about the streets in great consternation.' And well might they be concerned. The chance discovery five days later in the house of an Englishman named Upton whose father had built the Sebastopol dockyards of a plan of the fortifications revealed little more than could be seen – a martello tower known later as the Malakoff and what Cathcart called 'a low park wall not in good repair'. As there could never be an investment proper while the enemy occupied the northern shore of the harbour the longer the assault was deferred (it was argued) the more desperate it must become. But here again the reasons which led Raglan and Canrobert, who had taken over from the dying St Arnaud, to postpone the attack are irrelevant. It is enough to suggest that, when a year later the allies entered Sebastopol, the few thousand survivors of the magnificent British army which had descended into the Tchernaya valley may have wistfully recalled the objections of Burgoyne and others who opposed immediate attack. They had reckoned its cost to be too heavy: and this cost they had put at 500 dead.

Instead of making plans for instant assault the allies pressed on to Balaclava and the Chersonese upland to the south of Sebastopol. After a brief bombardment and a token resistance Balaclava surrendered next day. Than the sequel to this easy prize there is nothing more ironic in the whole campaign. The French claim always to occupy the right would have meant their taking over Balaclava and the British moving on to the port of Kamiesh some miles to the west. Canrobert, however, courteously left the choice to Raglan, merely stipulating that whoever got Balaclava must take the right flank in the siege operations. With the knowledge that he had or

ought to have had of the army's deplorable lack of transport
and of the extent of the ground to be occupied Raglan should
not have hesitated. To choose Balaclava would not only be to
extend the line of defences far beyond the capacity of his
army but would separate it from its base by over six miles of
travel, which included a steep climb to the Chersonese Upland. Without experience of command and (it is thought) too
proud to yield to his sometime enemies what his army alone
had captured, Raglan decided to retain Balaclava. Any doubts
he may have had were removed by the impetuous Admiral
Lyons, a man whose knowledge of logistics was even frailer
than his own. But for that decision, the responsibility for
which Raglan cannot escape, the battles which lay ahead might
never have been fought and the sufferings of the troops have
been greatly reduced. The choice so lightly made by Raglan
proved to be the choice of calamity.

While the French passed through to take over the port of
Kamiesh and to open *en règle* siege works facing the town
of Sebastopol, the British set about preparing for the defence
of Balaclava with such troops and ordnance as they could spare
from their siegeworks, which began in front of the Karabelnaya suburb across the Dockyard Creek and continued eastwards as far as the Inkerman Heights. To appreciate the
magnitude of this task and its bearing upon the battles of
Balaclava and Inkerman, it is necessary to describe the topog-
raphy in some detail.

The Chersonese Peninsula is shaped like a Norman shield
lying on its side with its point to the west. Its base is a steep
escarpment which stretches from near the head of the inner
harbour in a more or less southerly direction till some two
miles north-west of Balaclava it merges with a coastal strip
of high ground running east and west. This escarpment is of
an average height of about 600 feet and is uniformly steep and
in some places unscalable. Named the Sapounè Ridge, it
was traversed by three roads only, one to the north being the
post road from the interior to Sebastopol, the second four
miles to its south, known as the Woronzoff road, which by-
passed Balaclava and connected Sebastopol with the extensive
estates of Count Woronzoff and other Russian noblemen to
the south-east; the third, near the end of the escarpment,

which linked the harbour with Sebastopol by way of the Col de Balaclava.

In the disposition of the allies' armies the Sapounè Ridge from the Col de Balaclava to two miles beyond the Woronzoff road was occupied by two French divisions forming the 'Army of Observation' under Bosquet. North of him lay the camp of the British 1st Division and beyond this Sir De Lacy Evans's 2nd Division guarding the extreme right of the allied line with the Inkerman Heights to its front and the Tchernaya valley to its right. The port of Balaclava lay outside what might be termed the main allied perimeter. It had to be provided with a defensive system of its own. How far this task was beyond Raglan's capacity the battle of Balaclava was to prove.

A land-locked harbour carved out of the cliffs connected to the north by only a gorge, Balaclava had powerful natural defences. On the other hand once through this gorge there was little ahead except a valley roughly three miles in length and width. This, though closed to the west by the Sapounè Heights, was open to the east and throughout its extent was freely manoeuvrable by all arms. To the north the valley was bounded by a bow-shaped cluster of hills called the Fedioukines over which ran a road from the interior. Midway between the Fedioukines and the gorge a number of hillocks, strung out in an east–west line, formed a low ridge which divided the main valley into two. Along this ridge went the Woronzoff road once it had descended from the Sapounè ridge. These Causeway Heights, as they were called, were sufficiently lofty to conceal all that was happening in the north valley from anyone placed in the south. An enemy could thus sweep into the north valley either from due east or over the Fedioukines and breast the Causeway Heights within two miles of the port before being seen. To meet such a threat, and not as Raglan's biographer suggests, to protect this road, five redoubts had been built roughly half a mile from each other along the causeway and a sixth on what was called Canrobert's Hill slightly to the south and on the extreme right of the British defences. This protective outer line had been hastily constructed – one redoubt had been thrown up in a day – and the defences were so shallow that a man on a donkey, it was said, could pass them with ease. Into them nevertheless were placed nine 12-pound naval guns from HMS *Diamond*, three on Canrobert's Hill and two in the next three redoubts running west, the remainder being unarmed. For garrisons, Raglan distastefully and unwillingly had to resort to the Turks: one battalion in the Canrobert redoubt and a half in the other three. The Tunisians so selected were admittedly not the flower of the Turkish army but, led by experienced European officers, they might have acquitted themselves as well as their comrades at Silistria. They were given instead one British Artillery NCO to each garrison.

The inner line of defence was supplied by the 93rd Highlanders and a field battery (Barker's) stationed at the village of Kadikol near the northern entrance to the gorge, and by Marine artillery distributed along the heights above the port. To round off the defensive system, Lord Lucan's cavalry division completed by the recent arrival of Scarlett with the Heavy Brigade, occupied the western extremity of the valley under the muzzles of Bosquet's men and guns. They were admirably placed to take any attack on Balaclava in the flank.

The best hope of getting the utmost effect out of such diverse and inadequate material was to create a single command. When after some days the Russians began probing in the direction of Balaclava and it was decided to send down Sir Colin Campbell to take charge of the 93rd, Raglan had his chance. Sir Colin had commanded a division at Chillianwallah and had seen more active service than anyone in the army. Given overall command of the valley it is certain that he would have made the best disposition of all available troops. Unfortunately Raglan's sensitivity for the feelings of others would not allow him to offend Lucan and so the evils of divided command, so crampingly felt on the Heights, was fatally reproduced in the valley below. Lucan and Campbell were to meet any Russian attack with independent authority.

It was not that Lucan was merely a stupid man, unbalanced in his judgements, unpredictable in his reactions, irritable in his manner. Supported by two good-natured, single-minded brigadiers, he would have cooperated willingly with Campbell, with whom he was on the best of terms. What unfitted him in the circumstances for independent command was his feud with Cardigan, a man even more unbalanced, violent and brainless than himself. It was impossible that two such men could work in harmony. What Maude had entered in his diary two days after the Alma he never had need to revise: 'The more I see of Lord Lucan and Lord Cardigan the more thoroughly I despise them. Such crass ignorance and such overbearing temper.' Raglan by his own weakness aggravated the relationship. Having approved Lucan's appointment the least he could have done was to support him loyally; but the soft-hearted commander-in-chief could never bring himself to put the jealous, petulant Cardigan in his place. Raglan was to be unfairly blamed for many of the failures and follies of the war, but nothing can excuse his complaisance towards Cardigan, in particular his allowing him to bring his private yacht *Dryad* into Balaclava where for weeks it occupied valuable space in a congested port and his consenting to his sleeping on board every night while his brigade and his divisional commander were enduring the hardships of life on rations under canvas. If anything more than such condonation betrayed Raglan's unfitness for command, it was his inability to foresee trouble in an emergency from two such bitter antagonists not subjected to the overriding authority of a third person. With Sir Colin Campbell in supreme command it is unlikely that the Light Brigade would have been sent to its destruction.

While preparations were making on the plateau for the preliminary bombardment to blast those defences which, undisturbed by a single shot day or night, the Russians – men, women and children – were feverishly building under the inspired direction of Colonel Todleben;* while siege guns were being dragged up by singing, cheery sailors, while the men were digging trenches in the difficult, rocky soil of the British sector, ominous signs of Russian intentions were in evidence. Once recovered from their surprise and the defeat of Alma

* Earle tells of a celebrated French engineer who a month or two later inspected our lines and asked about the Russian works facing them. When he learnt that they had been constructed since our arrival without molestation from us, he just murmured, '*Mon Dieu*', and went back to France. 'Accounts differ as to whether he fainted on the spot or not.'

having been explained away, the Russian army which Menschikoff had withdrawn from Sebastopol had reappeared on the
eastern flank. As it probed and discovered the weakness of
the defences it became bolder and more aggressive. Foraging
parties down to and across the Tchernaya, once light-hearted
affairs, were becoming dangerous. Vedettes were constantly
wheeling against the skyline indicating the approach of
Russian troops. There were frequent calls to 'Turn out
immediately' and the sounding of 'Boots and saddle'. In fact
a war of nerves extremely successful from the Russian point
of view was being waged. Their most valuable victim was
Lucan, whose nervous agitation produced the endless alerts
which in turn threatened the health of his division. 'The way
they keep turning us out', complained George Wombwell, 'is
too ridiculous. If a heavy dragoon or any other thick-headed
individual sees a Cossack he comes galloping into camp and
instantly magnifies the Cossack into five hundred. So of course
out we go and by the time we get there not a soul is to be
seen.' Once an aged cow paid with its life for being mistaken
for a Russian. Sometimes the cause for alarm was not so insignificant and then troops in reply to Lucan's urgent request
might be sent down from the Plateau and the Light Brigade
kept standing to horses all night long without even being
allowed to put on their coats.

In all these operations the cavalry's role had been sternly
defensive. To the indignation of Cardigan and of the whole
Light Brigade, burning to wipe out the frustrations of the
Alma, nothing aggressive was permitted. They were still not
to be let out of their bandbox. As they withdrew under orders
from one minor engagement after another, they had the morti-
fication of hearing the Russians jeer; they heard their divisional general called 'Lord Look-On' throughout the service
and their pusillanimity subjected to ribald jests and jibes. It
was unfair alike to them and to Lucan, because, as Lenox
Prendergast learnt when once sent to Headquarters with a
plea to be allowed to attack, there was on no account to be a
major offensive down at Balaclava. Even the worried Lucan's
request for an additional troop of artillery and a few more
infantry was rejected. Everything must give place to the siege.

For all that, the bombardment from the 73 British and 53

French guns which was to precede the assault did not open till dawn on October 17th, 21 days after the arrival of the Allies before the town. 'All artillery officers – French, English, and naval – [Clifford had written 11 days previously] say if once we get our guns up in position after a fire of 48 hours, little will be seen of Sebastopol but a heap of ruins.' The speculation proved academic. There was no 48-hour bombardment. Within three hours the Russian guns, served with admirable courage and accuracy, had exploded a large French magazine and dealt a damaging blow to French morale. For two days their batteries fell silent. The check was fatal to the success of the operations. Working indefatigably, as usual throughout the siege, the Russians succeeded in repairing every night the damage inflicted on them by day by the British guns, which continued to fire till they ran out of ammunition. The bombardment from the fleet having failed to make any impression and the French in their present mood showing no disposition to assault, it became evident before a week was passed that the first attempt against Sebastopol had totally miscarried. The distance at which Sir John Burgoyne insisted that the batteries should be built Clarke Jervoise of the 23rd considered too great and the line too extended to produce any marked effect in so short a time. 'I should have thought', wrote Arthur Godfrey of the Rifle Brigade, 'that a concentration of fire would have been more effective.' But what value was the opinion of two infantry officers?

Canrobert's insistence upon the siege's taking precedence over all other operations was warranted only on the assumption that the Russians concentrated equally upon resisting all efforts to assault the town. That they might decline to oblige and might think to use their field army for mounting a counter-offensive well away from Sebastopol, say against Balaclava, was one of those unpalatable contingencies which Headquarters chose from time to time to ignore. Thus when on October 24th the Turkish commander Rustem Pasha heard from a spy that the enemy proposed to hurl on the morrow an attack against Balaclava with 25,000 men under the newly-arrived General Liprandi, and had the message passed by way of Campbell and Lucan to Headquarters, all that Raglan, remembering the false alarms, replied was, 'Very well.' With a conventional request to be kept informed of events he returned the messenger to the valley. But this time there was no false alarm.

Early on the following morning, the anniversary of Agincourt, one hour before sunrise a great Russian host consisting of 22,000 infantry, 3,400 cavalry and 78 guns began converging on the eastern approaches to the Balaclava plain. In accordance with his practice Lucan at that hour was making a tour of the outposts, accompanied by his staff and trailing one or two cavalry officers, including Lord George Paget. As they approached Canrobert's Hill two flags were seen flying against the first streak of dawn. While their particular significance was being debated all doubts were scattered by the opening of a cannonade so powerful as to preclude any likelihood of a feint attack or a casual foray. Instantly the alarm was conveyed to the rear where the cavalry division had for some time (as was usual at that hour) been 'standing to horses' and the order just given to 'file to your lines'. As Cardigan was still asleep in his yacht, Lord George Paget, his second-in-command, went back at speed, mounted the Light Brigade and brought it forward in echelon with the Heavies to his right. Both brigades were halted just outside the range of Russian fire. Meanwhile Maude's battery of two howitzers and four six-pounders had raced up and unlimbered near the Causeway between the second and third redoubt. 'It was so dark at first [he noted in his diary] that nothing could be distinctly seen but the flashes of the Russian guns on which accordingly our guns were laid.' Galloping up on Maude's rear and taking up position to his left on the north side of the Causeway came Barker's battery dispatched by Campbell. Farther along the Woronzoff road vedettes could be dimly distinguished circling right and left, indicating an enemy advance by all three arms.

Contrary to uninformed opinion the Turks on Canrobert's Hill resisted stubbornly. Hopelessly outnumbered, seeing no sign of troops coming to their assistance, only able to reply with three guns to the Russians' 30, they had lost a quarter of their number when at last they fell back abandoning the redoubt. Even then they repeatedly halted to fire into the Russian

infantry now swarming towards the second redoubt. Here
the Turks had been bravely fighting without any sign of support, but the sight of their compatriots retreating and the
arrival of shells in their midst from the advancing artillery
broke their spirit and they, too, retreated, pursued by Cossacks
who cut them down without mercy. With the loss of the second
of the six redoubts Sir Colin Campbell, who had never liked
their construction and would have preferred a less extended
defence, began to be seriously alarmed for the safety of the
port and ordered Barker to withdraw towards Kadekoi. This
uncovered the northern flank of the third redoubt, strategic-
ally the most important of all. At the same time to its south
Maude's battery was deprived of its able commanding officer,
who was carried to the rear gravely wounded, and, its
ammunition running low, it too was ordered to retire by
Lucan. Seeing themselves thus forsaken the garrison of the key
third redoubt fled and they were followed by the Turks in
the fourth redoubt. Some ran looting through the Light Brigade camp, others made for Balaclava screaming, 'Ship! . . .
ship! . . . dok [too many] Rus!' The solitary British NCOs
could do nothing but spike the guns in the 2nd, 3rd and 4th
redoubts.

Condemned by all who watched from afar and unfairly
likened to curs and cowards, to flocks of sheep in panic, the
Turks had gained for their allies invaluable breathing space,
calculated at about one hour. When at length the Russians
pushed on from the captured redoubts the element of surprise
had been lost. In that hour Raglan had been informed and his
aides-de-camp were racing across the plateau whipping up
reinforcements. Until these arrived in the valley it would have
been contrary to military maxims for the cavalry to attack.
Consequently there came down from Raglan what is generally
known as Order Number One. It required Lucan (to his rage
and humiliation) to withdraw his division entirely, to bring it
into comparative safety to the south of the sixth redoubt under
the guns of the escarpment. 'It was [wrote Paget of the re-
treat] one of the most painful ordeals it was possible to conceive – seeing all the defences in our front successively
abandoned as they were and straining our eyes in vain all
round the hills in the rear for indications of support.'

The sun was now well up and this absence of support was as visible to the Russians as to Paget. They had only to press on with speed and enterprise to overwhelm the insignificant forces – not one-tenth of their number – between them and Balaclava. Whether they suspected a trap, whether they believed, despite the evidence of their own eyes or what their spies had reported, that no army could leave its base so ill-defended, they halted, and one of those curious but not uncommon lulls spread over the battlefield.

The troops which Raglan had ordered down were the Duke of Cambridge's 1st and Sir George Cathcart's 4th Division. The former got away promptly on their officers' having received a characteristically flippant message from the Duke's irrespressibly cheerful ADC, Jem Macdonald: 'There's a row going on down in the Balaclava plain and you fellows are wanted.' The 4th moved off only after a scene between Raglan's staff officer and Cathcart which might have been lifted out of a Shavian comedy. Cathcart held a 'dormant commission' giving him supreme command in event of Raglan's death; but he knew that Raglan preferred Sir George Brown's company and advice and he was increasingly grieved that his idea of an immediate assault had not been adopted. Altogether he was not in a cooperative mood when Raglan's messenger reached him as he was sitting down to breakfast in his tent. Asked to march his division immediately, he had replied that it was impossible. When the officer explained that the Russians were marching on Balaclava, Cathcart coolly retorted:

I can't help that, sir. It's impossible for my division to move, as the greater portion of the men have only just come from the trenches. The best thing you can do is to sit down and have some breakfast with me.

The staff officer having politely demurred, he went on:

Well, sir, if you will not sit down in my tent, you may as well go back to Lord Raglan and tell him I cannot move my division.

Of course in the end he did so. But the delay, which brought his division down full 40 minutes after the Duke's, had serious consequences.

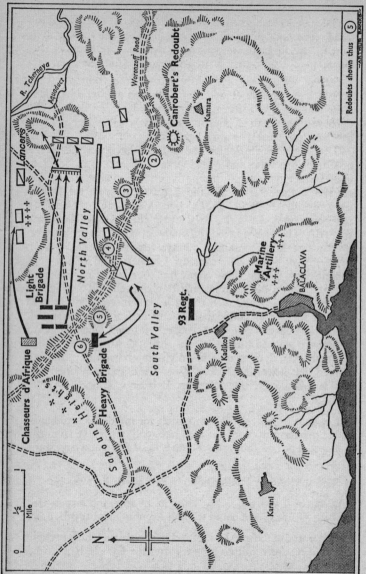

The Battle of Balaclava

The speediest approach to the plain was by the Woronzoff road. Had both divisions followed this they must either have forced the Russians to retreat across the Tchernaya, thus abandoning their gains, or to give battle. To make some such challenge may at first have been in Raglan's mind, but Canrobert who had speedily joined him on the escarpment still discouraged any major affair' outside siege operations. Raglan thereupon sent a further message strictly inhibiting the use of the road and requiring the divisions to march along the crest and to descend into the valley by the Col de Balaclava. It was while the 1st Division were taking this roundabout route that they were treated to a spectacle (as they looked over their left shoulders) surpassing in its action and excitement anything they had ever seen. There had been a Russian audience at the Alma, but it had soon fled. Here on the Sapounè Heights the spectators in perfect security were about to witness a scene, every detail of which they would remember all their lives. It has been commonplace to liken the battles of Balaclava as watched from the heights to theatrical displays, now exhilarating, now horrifying its audience. The simile is inadequate. What was seen was not merely the events performed before the footlights but the mechanics, as it were, of the play behind the scenes and in the wings.

At the foot of the escarpment the cavalry division had taken up their reluctant new position, the Light Brigade on the left at the head of the north valley, the Heavy Brigade on their right but on lower ground. All were dismounted and eating their frugal breakfast, washing it down with rum and smoking. A mile away to their right front the 93rd were halted in two lines on the crest of a low hill immediately north of Kadekoi. With them were 40 convalescent Guardsmen hurried up from Balaclava under the command of two Grenadier Guards subalterns, Verschoyle and Hamilton, and 60 invalids from various regiments under Colonel Daveney. On either flank were some Turks who had rallied after their retreat from the redoubts. Near at hand was Barker's battery. Making its way from the Col towards the Highlanders might have been seen a battery of Horse Artillery, which its commander Brandling had been keeping in a state of constant readiness for just such an occasion and was now the first of all reinforcements to reach the plain. In all these deployments there was nothing dramatic – even the exchange of occasional artillery fire hardly distinguished the scene from peace-time manoeuvres. It was only when the audience cast their eyes to the left that the picture assumed dramatic proportions. Moving up the North valley but unseen to all British forces below was an immense body of Russian cavalry in close formation accompanied by artillery and followed by infantry.

To *The Times*' correspondent, Raglan by the side of Canrobert no longer showed any trace 'of the divine calm attributed to him by his admirers as characteristic in moments of trial'. It was a worried and ill-at-ease Raglan who now dispatched a Second Order to Lucan. The sight of its bearer swiftly descending from the plateau indicated to the observant that something was afoot. Imagining the Russian objective to be Balaclava, Raglan instructed Lucan to advance eight of the ten Heavy Brigade squadrons to the support of Campbell, whose men under more intense bombardment had just been withdrawn to the foot of the hillock and ordered to lie down. While Lucan was giving his orders, four squadrons of the Russian cavalry detached themselves from the main body, wheeled to their left and traversed the causeway in front of Kadekoi. Campbell instantly ordered his force back to the crest. At the awesome sight of the Russian cavalry cantering down the slope towards them the last shred of Ottoman morale vanished. The Turks fired one wild volley and fled yelling, 'Ship! ... Ship!' This time there were no Cossacks to hunt them down, but one very irate wife of a Scottish soldier did her best with a heavy cudgel to express the general indignation felt for such cowardly behaviour. For those who stayed firm, the 93rd and the invalids, it was almost needless for Campbell to ride up and down and to tell them (and 'look as if he meant it') that there must be no retreat, that they must die where they stood.

Once more there was a hush in which those on the escarpment heard only the jingling of bits from the cavalry below. Then from 'that thin red line topped with steel' a volley rang out. The range was too long. No one was hit and the Russian advance continued. The second volley was delivered at about

350 yards and was supplemented by fire from the guns of Barker's battery and those on Marine Heights. This caused the Russians to swerve to their left, which Campbell took as an attempt to turn his right. He sternly checked an inclination to charge with the bayonet, exclaiming, 'Ninety-third, damn all that eagerness', and instead threw forward his right grenadier company under Captain Ross. This delivered a third and last volley which visibly shook the Russians. They wheeled almost in a half-circle and retired across the causeway.

According to the most reliable witnesses the Russians left no dead on the ground; yet it is hard to believe that three rounds, not to mention fire from the batteries, should have been without visible effect. What is the truth about the casualties? Is Lieutenant Stotherd of the 93rd right when he told his parents:

We gave them three British cheers and peppered them so much that they turned and swerved away and finally beat a retreat at a hard gallop, leaving many a corpse behind.

Or was Robert Portal in the not far distant Light Brigade more correct when he put the number at 50 killed, or Munro the 93rd's surgeon when he estimated the dead at 'not more than 12', or George Higginson watching from the Sapounè Heights who 'could not observe any casualties'? The solution is perhaps to be found in a conversation which Munro had some years later with a Russian officer, who took part in the charge. Considerable casualties were caused by the second and third volleys, he declared, but (he went on) a severely or even mortally wounded man will usually retain his seat long enough to ride out of danger before collapsing.

Whether the physical damage inflicted was great or small was of little consequence compared with the moral damage. The Russian objective had not been Balaclava, as Raglan thought, but the destruction of Barker's battery and this very limited purpose they had failed to achieve. The refusal of a few hundred men to be intimidated by the flourish and thunder of a thousand heavy horsemen was something on which they had not reckoned and it was altogether disconcerting. A worse humiliation was to come.

The main body, commanded by General Rykoff, had been

steadily advancing up the valley, still unseen by the Light
and Heavy Brigades. When level with the fourth captured
but empty redoubt they came under fire from one French
and two Turkish heavy guns on the escarpment. Several
saddles were emptied – one witness put the number at 20 –
and the Russians quickly wheeled to their left. This brought
them over the causeway ridge where 800 yards ahead the
eight squadrons of the Heavy Brigade had just started on their
way to Kadekoi. Whether surprised or not the Russian cavalry
came on at a slow canter.

The story that tells of the short-sighted Scarlett's glancing
to the left and asking what were 'those funny pointed things'
and getting the reply 'Thistles, sir', is probably apocryphal.
What is certain is that the Russians caught him unprepared
and at a disadvantage. First, his Brigade was strung out in
two lines. He had with him only two squadrons of the Scots
Greys and one (the second) of the Inniskillings – in all about
300. To his right but further along the path to Kadekoi
was the first Inniskilling squadron. Also to his right but
towards his rear were the 5th Dragoons and behind them the
Royals, halted because they had not been ordered to Kadekoi.
Further still to the rear but impeded by a vineyard on their left
rode the 4th Dragoons. Secondly, the force immediately with
Scarlett was not only very much smaller than the Russians but
it was at a tactical disadvantage by being on lower ground
and having also on its left a vineyard. Beyond this also on
the left lay the Light Brigade camp. This had been hurriedly
struck early that morning, then ravaged by the flying Turks
and was now cluttered with tent-poles and disordered picket
ropes.

With his red face and ample white moustache the Hon.
James Scarlett looked more than 55. He had seen no active
service. Nor was there anything remarkable about him except
his courage and his modesty. He had chosen for his ADC
Alexander Elliot, late of the 8th Bengal Cavalry, one of the
only five officers of his Brigade who had had any experience
of fighting. In circumstances where anything but resolute
counter-measures would have brought disaster, Scarlett,
counselled by Elliot, was just the man to lead the Heavy Brigade.

His first concern was to clear the vineyard and he coolly gave orders for the three squadrons to form line and show a front well to their right, thus leaving room for the 5th to come up on their left. While these deployments were taking place Lucan, who had seen the Russian change of direction, came galloping down and gave the order to make the charge, which Scarlett was already preparing to do. But to attempt this with troops not in perfect alignment was contrary to every precept he and his officers had learnt in Phoenix Park or on Hounslow Heath. To achieve the necessary conditions his troop officers were putting out markers and unhurriedly and without concern turning their backs to the enemy till the dressing had been completed to their satisfaction. Not even the divisional trumpeter's sounding the charge, by order of a fuming Lucan, was noticed or if noticed permitted to interrupt the ritual.

In the face of these singular parade-ground evolutions what were the Russians, between 2,000 and 3,000 strong, doing? In any war but the Crimean the answer would be incredible. They had halted. At 350 yards or more from the Heavy Brigade they had pulled up with such suddenness that in the still morning air the rattle of their accoutrements was heard on the Sapounè ridge. They stared to their front as if fascinated by what they saw. Perhaps they were intimidated by the imperturbability of the dressing, the absence of hurry, the air of complete confidence: they are known to have been puzzled by the appearance of the Scots Greys with their busbies and red tunics and to have thought that the terrible bearskins of the Alma had suddenly taken to horses.*

The consequence of their abrupt halt had been the pulling up of the flanks a little later than the centre. This had given to the tight phalanx a slightly crescent-shaped formation which was maintained when after a brief pause the advance was resumed, but at a slower and more hesitant pace.

As soon as the British alignment had been effected Scarlett put himself well in advance of his men. He was accompanied by his orderly, a trumpeter, a giant named appropriately Shegog, and Alexander Elliot. When satisfied that all was in order he turned to Shegog and said curtly: 'Sound the charge.' On the ears of the audience high above on

* The French hailed them as *grenadiers à cheval*.

the Sapounè ridge 'the shrill sound of the trumpet broke the awful silence', as it echoed from hill to hill.

Slowly at first because of the broken ground and never at more than eight miles an hour Scarlett and his three squadrons (the two Scots Greys on the left, the Inniskillings on the right) moved forward with the utmost deliberation upon the centre of the massive Russian column, as broad as it was deep and so closely packed that no intervals could be discerned between its files. On seeing this act of hardihood the enemy, who had been coming down the incline at a jog trot, slowed down to nearly a halt. Some discharged a few wild shots from their carbines, all, slightly bewildered and amazed, waited for an order that was never given. On the Sapounè Heights everyone had dismounted. None spoke a word. Only a low murmur likened to a great sigh passed across the crowd. The next instant Scarlett had broken into the enveloping mass, his sword swinging high above his head. Elliot by his side was seen to swerve and with expertise to cut down a Russian officer well in front of his men. Behind him and his three companions came thundering up the hill the Scots Greys and the Inniskillings, the first uttering their famous moan, the others a cheer.

It was a heavy Dragoon's dream of a lifetime come true. For this he had drilled and wheeled and charged in mock attacks. And now it was the real thing. No wonder he went into battle sublimated, forgetting in the white heat of his excitement self and danger, nor, if struck, noticing his wound. All that mattered was to charge and to kill.

Oh, God! I cannot describe it [wrote a dragoon]. They were so superior in numbers, they outflanked us, and we were in the middle of them. I certainly never felt less fear in my life than I did at that time; and I hope God will forgive me, for I felt more like a devil than a man. We fought our way out of them as only Englishmen can fight.

Another account was more dramatic.

Oh, such a charge. Never think of the gallop and trot you have often witnessed at Phoenix Park, when you desire to form a notion of a genuine bloodhot all mad charge such as I have just come out of. ... From the moment we dashed at the enemy I knew nothing but that I was impelled by some irresistible force onward, and by some invisible and imperceptible influence to crush every obstacle which stumbled before my good sword and brave old charger. I never in my life experienced such a sublime sensation as in the moment of the charge. Some fellows speak of it as being demoniac. I know this, that it was such as made me a match for any two ordinary men and gave me such an amount of glorious indifference as to life as I thought it impossible to be master of. Forward – dash – bang – clank – and there we were in the midst of such smoke, cheer and clatter as never before stunned a mortal ear. It was glorious, I could not pause. It was all push, wheel, frenzy, strike and down down they went.

Although Scarlett was soon deeply embedded in the Russian column, his sword rising and falling as he slashed about him, and his three companions were close in the rear, the squadrons behind in their cutting and hacking extended not much further than the fifth Russian rank. At this point all formation was lost. It became a mêlée in which sense of direction was lost; some fanned out right and some left, others had even turned about and were facing the way they had come. To the watchers on the hill the tension became almost unendurable. As the two Russian wings started to close in on the three buried squadrons it seemed impossible that any could emerge alive. All round could be heards sobs and cries of, 'God help them – they're lost!' Only Raglan (as he afterwards confessed) never had any doubts as to the outcome.

Lost they would certainly have been without the coming of supports. Happily the remaining seven squadrons either on Lucan's or Scarlett's orders, or in the case of the Royals without any orders, were already in motion. On the right the 1st Inniskilling squadron keeping a beautiful alignment and sitting well down their saddles came galloping up the incline over unencumbered ground to their front and tore into the Russian left, taking them obliquely on the bridle hand. Further to the left the 5th Dragoons stabbed into the side of the right wing as it was folding round the rear of the Scots Greys and at the moment when many of the Russians actually had their backs to the Dragoons. Beyond them the 4th Dragoons, having at last cleared the vineyard, were racing up parallel to the main line of attack until when they were well past the enemy's front ranks they wheeled to the right and to the cries of *Faugh a ballagh* hurled themselves in one unbroken line into the Russian flank. The force of their impact upon the enemy cavalry, now bewildered and confused by attacks on three sides, was such that they were able to hack their way through from one flank to another with the loss of only one man. The fourth and final blow came from the Royals. They had started to advance on a line which would bring them between the 4th and 5th Dragoons when a voice rang out, 'By God, the Greys are cut off! . . . Gallop! Gallop!' At this they put on such a spurt that all order was lost and never retrieved. In consequence their attack, which fell on the south-western angle of the Russian troops, lacked the driving force which regular alignment alone could give and before they had embedded themselves ineffectually in ones and twos in the enemy ranks Colonel Hodge caused them to be checked and recalled. As it happened further penetration was not necessary. Too late the Russians realized the fatal mistake of receiving the Heavy Brigade's charge standing instead of meeting it with a counter-shock. Already the great phalanx was heaving like some giant creature in agony. Slowly the files loosened, resistance relaxed and crumbled, there was a break-up on the left rear and a retrograde movement in the direction of the sheltering guns along the Causeway. Henry Clifford watching from the French lines on Sapounè thus describes the scene:

Like a shot from a cannon ball our brave fellows went at the astounded enemy like one man, and horses and men were seen struggling on the ground in every direction. The Russians fled in the greatest disorder, our splendid cavalry not leaving them till they had got under the protection of their artillery.

Pursuit in the circumstances was too hazardous to be allowed; on the other hand with no fear of hitting their own men Barker's and Maude's batteries, so far silent, were able to pummel the retreating Russians till they had disappeared over the Causeway skyline. Within a few minutes not a Russian was to be seen and the Heavy Brigade was looking as quiet and formidable as if it had never been engaged.

Casualties in this swift, fierce battle which lasted no more than eight minutes had, though involving at least 3,000 men, been surprisingly few for the British and relatively few for the Russians. The figures for the former were under 80, of which most were wounded; for the latter approximately 200, of whom again the great majority were wounded. For this there were two reasons: first the congestion which made it diffi- cult to use the sword with any freedom and secondly the bluntness of the sword when used. On neither side were the sabres sharp and on the thick overcoats worn by the Russians (wrote Fisher-Rowe) ours 'jumped off like india-rubber'. Only a mighty downward slash on a shako was really effective and more than one Russian dead was found with his head nearly cloven in two. If it be asked why the point was not used, the answer is that to do this with the pattern then issued was hardly possible.

'The most glorious thing I ever saw', a French general was heard to exclaim. Raglan, always undemonstrative, com- pressed his feelings into two monosyllables – 'Well done!' Sir Colin Campbell, pulling off his bonnet, cried, 'Greys, gallant Greys. I am 61 years old and if I were young again I should be proud to be in your ranks.' No doubt it was inevitable that the Greys, always conspicuous by the colour of their horses, had by participating in the first attack carried off the greatest credit; but Cornet Fisher-Rowe of the 4th Dragoons expressed a widely-held feeling among the rest of the Heavy Brigade when he wrote:

The only credit they had was that they happened to make the first charge in which they failed to rout the Russians who out- flanked and would have surrounded them had not the 4th and 5th come to their assistance; and so great was their confusion that they broke our line as they came full speed in the other direction.

No competitive assessment of the part played by the various regiments can affect the claim of the Heavy Brigade to have won a neat, clear-cut and important victory. It was no fault of theirs that this victory was not expanded into one of the greatest cavalry exploits in history. To grasp how incom- plete was Scarlett's triumph it is only necessary to ask one question: what was the Light Brigade doing when the Russian cavalry wheeled out of the north valley and, passing right across its front, went down to engage the Heavies? Not 500 yards separated Cardigan's men from Rykoff's. Every moment the 'gallery' expected this incomparable chance of a flank attack to be seized. To the dullest of brains there seemed no other possible course for this brilliant, dashing, eager brigade to take. But to the amazement of the spectators and the fury of the Brigade nothing of the kind was attempted.

While there is no excuse for this incredible inaction there is, for what it is worth, an explanation. The story has conflicting versions, but the most trustworthy is that which tells how Lucan just as he was riding off to join Scarlett and was still smarting under Raglan's Number One Order said to Cardigan, 'I'm going to leave you. Well, you'll remember you are placed here by Lord Raglan for the defence of the position. My instructions to you are to attack anything and everything that shall come within reach of you, but be careful of columns or squares of infantry.'

Had the two brigades changed places there is not the slightest doubt that Scarlett on his own initiative or on Elliot's advice would have led an immediate attack against so compelling a target. Cardigan, consumed with hatred and jealousy of Lucan, would not give his detested brother-in-law the slightest handle for making a complaint should the attack fail. He would 'work to rule'. For any errors arising therefrom Lucan, as his superior officer, not he the subordinate, would take the blame. Lucan had told him to defend the position and defend the position he would, even (there is no doubt) at the cost of his life. Although it irked him as much as anyone to see Scarlett's charge unsupported and though he was heard to mutter, 'Damn those Heavies – they've the laugh of us today', he declined to move. Not his was that moral courage which enables the good commander to seize the opportunity however great the risks involved or doubtful his orders. When Captain Morris in command of the 17th Lancers, an officer of much experience acquired in the Sikh wars, pleaded first for a general attack by the Brigade and then in desperation for one by his own two squadrons, Cardigan was adamant. Once possessed of an idea no argument would affect him. To all Morris's reiterated appeals the response came in parrot fashion, 'No, no, sir, we must not stir from here.' At length in his fury Morris wheeled round his horse and rode back to his regiment slapping his leg with his drawn sword and exclaiming, 'My God, my God, what a chance we are losing!'

No words were truer. The magnificent Light Brigade, after five frustrating weeks, was poised for attack. There were no vineyards or broken camps between them and the troubled Russians. In two minutes they could have been rioting in the enemy's flank and rear, driving them off the Causeway, past the redoubts and over the Tchernaya. There would never have been another charge that day and as one historian has written, 'Balaclava might have taken its place as a classic in military literature and the host of the Russian horse have suffered a discomfiture with few parallels in the history of war.'

It is unnecessary to consider the subsequent recriminations between Lucan and Cardigan or their mutual accusations. The case against Cardigan, cheekily summarized by Robert Portal of the 4th Light Dragoons: 'Cardigan has as much brains as my boot', becomes in Kinglake's prosy language 'an imperfect acquaintance with the business of war.'

For all this missed opportunity the battle of Balaclava was virtually over when the shaken Russian cavalry retreated to the bottom of the valley. Whatever their ambitions that morning, whether the destruction of Barker's battery, the routing of the 93rd or a mad dash at the harbour, they had not been realized. From having been aggressors they had become defenders and the dispositions which Liprandi was now making (including the bringing forward of infantry and artillery through the Fedioukine Hills) were designed to cover a retirement not to resume an offensive. Nor had their discomfiture been only military. The sight of their cavalry so ignominiously handled by a third of their number had had an unsettling effect on the morale of the infantry. Those occupying the three captured redoubts on the Causeway, pointing like a finger towards the British lines, were in no mood to remain in so isolated a position. Unless Raglan was prepared (as we know he was not) to have a full-scale engagement in the valley all he need have done was to hold his hand or at most keep up a little pressure. There was every sign that by morning the Causeway redoubts would be evacuated. Admittedly the guns might have to be written off but (as Canrobert is said to have impressed upon him) it was far more important to hurry on with the siege while the fine weather lasted than to indulge in diversionary engagements. But Canrobert could not be expected to feel the same compunction as Raglan. To the disciple of Wellington the loss of nine British guns was insupportable. Without being indebted to the French he believed both redoubts and guns could be retaken by the two divisions he had summoned, provided no time was lost. A mere demonstration by infantry and cavalry might be enough. The 1st Division had already reached the foot of the Col and in pursuance of Raglan's plan had been directed to a station south of the Woronzoff road. Of the laggard 4th Division there was no sign. As the minutes passed Raglan's impatience increased. His face no longer showed its habitual serenity. At length he summoned an aide-de-camp and to him dictated his Third Order to Lucan:

Cavalry to advance and take advantage of any opportunity to recover the heights. They will be supported by the infantry which have been ordered to advance on two fronts.

Whether there was (according to one version) a full stop after 'ordered', whether there should be no 'to' and 'advance' spelt with a capital A, the message is no clearer. What cavalry was to advance – the Heavy Brigade who in the south valley were nearer the redoubts or the Light Brigade farther off, or both? Where were the infantry who were to advance on two fronts? And what exactly were these fronts? The first division was clear enough to Lucan as he puzzled over the message but there was no sign of another. Nor from where he was standing could he see anything that was happening either in the north valley or on the Causeway Heights. In the circumstances he may well be forgiven for taking this obscure message as an interim or alerting order, pending the arrival of sufficient infantry to advance on the 'two fronts'. He therefore made preparations for future action by mounting his men and moving the Light Brigade left to the rising ground at the end of the Heights. Unfortunately he did not accompany them and so see what was to become visible to them in their new station.

While these deployments were being carried out Cathcart at length arrived. He had been told by orders received as he was moving down the Col to assault the important third redoubt held by Odessa regiment, the Guards to act as supports. But he had not recovered from his splenetic attack of the morning. Having drawn level with the fourth redoubt he ordered his division, half of whom had been up all night in the trenches and all of whom had just marched six miles, to lie down. It was the Guards and the Highlanders who ought (he considered) to do any immediate assaulting and the 4th to do the supporting. He showed no inclination to move.

As he viewed this inaction, Raglan could not conceal his exasperation. With the valley and its redoubts and bodies of cavalry and infantry spread out below him in high relief it looked so obvious. Time was precious and time was being wasted. The stump of his arm was seen to oscillate violently. He was nearing that state of mind in which the best commander can commit an indiscretion, when a voice was heard exclaiming, 'By jove! They're taking away the guns!' The Russians (it is believed) were doing no such thing, but the effect of the words on Raglan was dynamic. For him it must be the end of inaction. He called over to Airey and dictated to him the most celebrated order in British history. Had they been on manoeuvres what Airey wrote down on a flimsy piece of paper, using his sabretache as a desk, might have led to some choleric discussions that night in the mess. What he did write on the Sapounè Ridge with the whole valley spread out beneath him was to have the most fearful consequences.

Lord Raglan wishes the cavalry to advance rapidly to the front and try to prevent the enemy carrying away the guns. Troop of horse artillery may accompany. French cavalry is on your left. Immediate.

To be fair to Raglan and Airey, they might reasonably have thought it unnecessary, time being the all-important factor, to weigh words nicely: obscurities could be explained by the staff officer who carried the order down. This should have been Lieutenant Calthorpe, Raglan's nephew, who was next on the rota for duty. Unfortunately its urgency required the message to be taken straight down the escarpment, a feat calling for the highest qualities of horsemanship. For this there was one obvious choice – Captain Edward Nolan of the 15th Hussars, serving as Airey's ADC. There was no finer or more intrepid horseman in the army, but in selecting him Raglan was using a man devoured by such notorious and nervous excitement that, taking everything into account, his unsuitability should have been recognized. Nolan's excitement sprang from the master-passion of his life – light cavalry. Properly handled he believed it could in war go anywhere, do anything. Although only 35, this son of an Irish father and Italian mother had served in the Austrian army before transferring to the 15th Hussars in India and, having written two books on the subject, was an acknowledged authority on cavalry tactics. From the moment he had landed in the Crimea he burned to see his ideas put into practice. His enthusiasm was ingenuous. Only the day before, on running against an old friend, he had shouted, 'Isn't this fun? I think it's the most glorious life a man can lead.' Yet ever since his landing he had seen all fighting laurels appropriated by the infantry, while the cavalry had played the part of a molly-coddled invalid. For this he blamed Lucan. Outspoken, arrogant, intemperate, he had never bothered to conceal his contempt for Lord 'Look-On'. A couple of weeks earlier during a minor Russian attack when Maude reported Lucan as being 'all hesitation and for doing nothing but watch' and declining even to allow the battery to be used, there had been words between him and Nolan. Later Nolan had been heard to say to a friend, 'Wait till I get a chance and you'll see what we can do.' But when on the morning of October 25th a chance in a thousand had come and gone, when he saw the Light Brigade standing idle when they might have flung themselves upon the Russian flank, his rage became such that George Higginson feared he had lost all self-control.

And now at last he was the gloating bearer of an order which must force that stupid old woman to act. At last was come the hour for the use of the right, the only really decisive, military arm. If there was to be any quibbling about the order, he carried up his sleeve the ace of trumps. For just as he was riding off Raglan had called out, 'Tell Lord Lucan the cavalry is to attack immediately.'

As he reached the valley and flashed past the 17th Lancers on his way to Lucan, his friend Captain Morris, a pocket Hercules and almost as brilliant a rider as Nolan, called out, 'What's going to happen?' and received the excited answer, 'You'll see . . . you'll see.' When at length he drew rein where Lucan was seated in front of the Heavy Brigade he had worked himself into such a state that he was incapable of entering into any patient explanation as Calthorpe or any member of Raglan's staff might have done.

There could be nothing genial or accommodating in the meeting of Lucan and Nolan. Dislike was mutual. Lucan not only felt the common antipathy of divisional commanders towards Headquarters staff, but he could not have forgotten Nolan's recent behaviour nor have been ignorant of the bitter language he had been using in Staff circles about him and the scorn he had expressed for his management of the cavalry. No one could have been more insufferable to him than this self-assured young officer sitting astride a magnificent tiger-skin saddle cover and, in the conspicuous and brilliant uniform of the 15th Hussars, looking as if he had just stepped out of his military tailor's.

Lucan took and read the order (as he later admitted) 'with much consideration . . . perhaps consternation would have been the better word'. It was no more precise than its predecessor. To him standing in the South Valley it was even incomprehensible. Gone was all reference to infantry. Instead there was an artless mention of horse artillery. The cavalry (contrary to all military maxims it seemed) were, unsupported, to attack guns unspecified and in any case invisible to Lucan. And what was meant by front? Which front? There could be three. And where exactly was the enemy? From where he was Lucan could see none. Perhaps the most futile phrase was that concerning French cavalry. If Raglan meant to convey that the Chasseurs d'Afrique, just sent down by Canrobert to be of general assistance, were under particular orders to advance in step with Lucan's division, he was conveying information which was not true. If he intended Lucan to concert with d'Allonville, their commander, in a scheme of attack – a procedure which would obviously take time – how could this be reconciled with the word 'immediate'? Raglan, indeed, had worded his fatal Fourth Order as no French or Prussian commander-in-chief would ever have done. It was, as a French authority has put it, '*d'une forme peu militaire*'.

Had only a moderate degree of affability existed between Lucan and Raglan's messenger it is possible, though by no means certain, that from a question or two put and answered, Lucan might have learnt or rather deduced that front meant Causeway Heights and guns those taken from the *Diamond*. But ever since dawn Lucan had been fuming at his treatment by Raglan and now confronted by this smirking popinjay he lashed out against the absurdity of the order and the senselessness of cavalry attacking guns in battery. It was the trailing of his coat and Nolan stamped on it gleefully. He cut short Lucan's diatribe abruptly and imperiously with the words 'Lord Raglan's orders were that the cavalry should attack immediately.'

The word attack, not mentioned in the written order, was at least unequivocal and Lucan rapped out angrily, 'Attack, sir, attack what guns?' In a sentence that sent six score men to their death Nolan flung back his head, threw out his arm in the direction of the (hidden) North Valley and 'in the most disrespectful but significant manner', putting as much contempt as he could into his voice, cried, 'There, my lord, is your enemy. There are your guns!'

One of the several unsolvable problems of the Crimean War is what exactly Nolan intended to convey by that sweep of his hand towards the east and by those declamatory words. Did he really mean those Russian guns which the failure of the Light Brigade to support the Heavies had allowed the enemy to withdraw to the end of the valley? Or did he mean what Raglan meant, the British naval guns which it was believed the Russians were about to carry off? Why should he not have meant the Russian guns? He was not in Raglan's confidence; he had not been party to Raglan's conversation with Airey. When handed the Fourth Order in which there was nothing to gainsay such a construction, there is no record of his having been given any briefing beyond the parting injunction regarding immediate attack. The telling phrase may have been rehearsed by Nolan on the way down in anticipation of Lucan's proving hesitant and difficult; or, because he was quick-witted it may have come to him in a flash. In either case it was something too good to be lost against the one man whom he held responsible for the cavalry's deplorable inactivity. And so it came out, insolently, scornfully, provocatively but quite deliberately and unequivocally 'There, my lord, is your enemy. There are your guns!'

Lucan might have put Nolan under arrest for such intemperate language and behaviour. Instead, perhaps considering silence the best expression of contempt, he turned and dictated a message to Cardigan, while Nolan rode over to Morris and asked permission to accompany him in the charge.

Self-centred, without a heart, utterly inconsiderate for the feelings and convenience of others, Cardigan was nevertheless a brave man, prepared to die if need be at the head of his Brigade. But the sanity of this order, so contrary to every rule of war, he could not accept without a remonstration, notwithstanding his resolution of avoiding any argument with his hated brother-in-law. Accordingly he dispatched Fitz Maxse, his ADC, to tell Lucan that what he was being asked to do was to charge a heavy battery a mile or so ahead with more batteries on either side and the flanking hills lined as well with infantry.

Only a personal interview could settle the matter and Lucan rode over to Cardigan. It was for him the passing from one disagreeable tête-à-tête to another. The encounter that ensued was brief, formal and chilly, less akin to that of two generals discussing details of an attack than two seconds making arrangements for a duel. Had it been otherwise, now that Lucan for the first time that morning had a true picture of the state of the North Valley, Raglan's Fourth Order might have been restudied in association with the third and his true intention divined. Instead all that Lucan elected to reply to Cardigan's objection was a bleak and unaccommodating. 'Yes, I know it. But Lord Raglan will have it. We have no choice but to obey.'

There was nothing more to be said. Cardigan lowered his sword in salute and muttering (it is alleged) 'Here goes the last of the Brudenells', trotted over to give his orders to Lord George Paget, in command of the 4th Light Dragoons.

At this moment the Light Brigade was in two lines. The first (going from proper right to left) consisted of the 13th Light Dragoons, the 17th Lancers and the 11th Hussars. The second made up of the 8th Hussars and the 4th Light Dragoons was behind a knoll a little way to the rear, facing north-east and ready to deal with any attack coming round the Fedioukines. With half a squadron of the 8th acting as Raglan's escort the Brigade had that morning paraded 673 strong.

Looking down the valley (which if he had done earlier on might have helped him to understand the true meaning of Raglan's fourth order) Lucan realized that in such a wide deployment the Brigade was far too exposed for the coming attack and on his own authority, but to the jealous Cardigan's fury, ordered Colonel Douglas to move his 11th Hussars to the rear of the 17th Lancers. This caused them to become the second line with the 8th and 4th acting as the third. Maude's battery now commanded by Shakespear could not as Raglan envisaged 'accompany' them because much of the valley being ploughed land it would be death for it to advance.

Meanwhile Cardigan, having given Paget his orders, repeated several times and always with emphasis. 'I expect your best support, *mind, your best support*.' 'Of course you shall have my best support,' returned Paget, attributing these reiterated injunctions to an excitement which Cardigan sought to conceal under a mask of nonchalance. Nevertheless he felt nettled by them and no doubt to soothe his own nerves he lit up 'a remarkably good cigar'.

The trumpet having sounded in succession 'Stand to your horses' and 'Mount', Cardigan with drawn sword took his station in front of the right squadron of the 17th Lancers. Two or three horses' lengths behind him were ranged Wombwell, his orderly officer, his ADCs, Maxse and Lockwood, the last so incensed by Cardigan's failure to follow up the Heavies that he intended (so he told Maxse) to resign that very day. Also out in front but on the extreme right of the line sat one of two Sardinian officers who it appears had obtained permission to join in the charge.* Five lengths further

* The presence of these Sardinian officers (whose country had not yet entered the war) has never, I think, been recorded. They are

to the rear the troop officers were getting their men into perfect alignment in two ranks as though for a review. Magnificent in the uniform of his old regiment, the 11th Hussars (which he had paid £40,000 to command), with his long thighs encased in the famous cherry-coloured overalls, a crimson sabretache at his side, a fur cap on his head with its crimson bag and distinctive white and crimson feather, Cardigan looked every inch the cavalry leader of romance as he sat straight-backed astride his superb chestnut charger, Ronald. Only one detail would have betrayed to the acute observer that something more serious than a review was in contemplation: his heavily gold-braided pelisse instead of being slung over his tunic was being worn, giving his small (and almost certainly corseted) waist an almost boyish appearance.

When the last commands of the troop officers had died away there descended over the battlefield another hush. Neither cannon nor musket spoke from either side. There was a momentary interruption when in his 'strong and hoarse' voice Lord Cardigan was heard giving the command, 'The Brigade will advance. First squadron of the 17th Lancers will direct.' Then in a silence unbroken even by a trumpet,* the first line moved off, first at a walk, then at a trot. And now at last a sound reached up to those tense watchers on the Heights, but it was only that of the jingling of harness bits.

The artist has been much to blame for the popular misconception of the Charge of the Light Brigade which to begin with was not a charge so much as a controlled movement at trotting pace. In order to achieve the utmost dramatic effect not only is the breadth of the valley reduced from a mile to a few hundred yards but the Brigade is depicted as moving at breakneck speed, with its lines so close together that it is advancing almost in close formation. The facts are very

mentioned in two letters from Maxse. After stating that the Sardinian on his right 'fell horse and man some halfway down and was taken prisoner', he adds, 'there were two of them.' Thanks to searches made by the Italian authorities at my request their names have been discovered. They were Maggiore Govone (d. 1872) and Luogotenente Landriani (d. 1858). It was the last who was wounded and captured.

* The once much debated question whether any bugle was sounded has for answer 'Yes' and 'No'. It was sounded for the second and third line but not for the first.

different. The first line occupied only about one-fifth of the width of the valley. Between it and the second line there were roughly 400 yards, rather less between the second and the third; but between the two regiments in the rear there was such a drifting apart that they became invisible one to another. The whole operation was in effect less one charge than an aggregate of charges.

There was at first nothing to indicate to the spectators above that Cardigan was not going to conform to Raglan's intentions. It was only after he had covered some 200 yards and, instead of inclining to the right towards the redoubts and the captured British guns, continued straight down the valley (keeping it is said his eyes riveted upon one gun in the Russian battery) that the enormity of the error became apparent. It was then according to Kinglake and others who have followed him that Nolan, realizing the consequences of his rash words and gestures, spurted ahead diagonally across the path of Cardigan, waving his sword in the direction of the Causeway and shouting out words inaudible above the thunder of hooves. As against this account (based it would seem on the evidence of one nameless officer only) must be set the fact that no such conduct on Nolan's part is (so far as is known) recorded by any who rode in or in front of the first line (whose evidence alone would be of value). Neither Wombwell nor Maxse mention it in their letters. Ten years later after reading Kinglake's version the latter vehemently declared that he had 'no recollection of Nolan having attempted to create a divergence either by deed or gesture'. He remained convinced that 'Captain Nolan (though I cannot think he realized their position) intended to charge the guns we did charge and no other'. Nolan certainly went ahead, ignoring a restraining shout from Morris, and there is no doubt that he outrode Cardigan, to Cardigan's fury, waving his sword and shouting; but there is no evidence that these actions were inspired by anything more than exhilaration at being at last in a Light Cavalry charge and being impatient at the slowness of the pace set.

It is idle to speculate further on the question. The harm had already been done in that brief exchange of words with Lucan. Poor Nolan's motives as he raced ahead will never be known, for by a stroke of retributive justice he was the first to pay the price of his unruly words. The first Russian shell fired by a battery on the Fedioukines, bursting between him and Cardigan, sent a splinter into his chest, piercing the heart. From his throat came such a ghastly shriek that Private Wightman of the 17th could never think of it without a shudder. His sword dropped from his hand, his body crumpled up but the right arm remained erect over his head. While the horse wheeled round in terror the rider's knees, the knees of an incomparable horseman, kept the body in the saddle till it had been carried through the ranks of the oncoming 13th Light Dragoons.

As the advance continued straight down the valley into the eye of the Russian battery at the end there burst from the watchers on Sapounè cries of 'Stop! . . . Stop! . . . It's madness!' Men sobbed and tears ran down their cheeks as they beheld those five magnificent regiments riding to their doom. '*Mon Dieu!*' gasped an old French general into Henry Clifford's ear. '*Mon Dieu! Que vont-ils faire? Je suis vieux, j'ai vu des batailles, mais ceci est trop.*'

Soon the fire was coming from both sides of the valley, from massed infantry armed now with Miniés as well as from the batteries; and before long, as they came within range, from the 12 guns which were the Brigade's objective. It had been the first time that the men had been under serious fire.

'I felt at that moment my blood thicken and crawl [wrote one of them], as if my heart grew still and quiet like a lump of stone within me.' Their natural instinct was to quicken their pace into a charge, but Cardigan was too accomplished a cavalry leader not to know that for this to happen before they were on their target would be insanity. Above the turmoil, above the oaths, the shouting and the cheering his deep voice could be heard calling out repeatedly 'Steady. . . . Steady the 17th Lancers . . . steady, Captain Morris.' Once when Captain White of the first squadron came edging up on Cardigan's left he found a sword laid across his chest and heard Cardigan without removing his eyes from the battery ahead very properly telling him not to ride level with his commanding officer.

After leaving Cardigan, Lucan had returned to the Heavy

Brigade which he ordered out in support. The Greys and the Royals moved off preceded at some distance by Lucan himself and his staff. Riding over the ploughed land more slowly than the Light Brigade they began to suffer severely when they came under fire. Lucan was hit in the leg, two of his staff were wounded and a third was killed. 'The shot and shell and bullets came down on us like hail and every second I expected to get one.' Captain Stocks of the Royals was to be lucky, but a dozen of the regiment had been wounded by the time it was level with the third redoubt. It was then that Lucan made a decision that proved that he was no more deficient in moral than in physical courage. Turning to Lord William Paulet, riding at his side, he exclaimed, 'They have sacrificed the Light Brigade; they shall not have the Heavy, if I can help it.' The halt was sounded and the Heavy Brigade pulled back till it was out of range but still sufficiently far forward to shorten considerably the agonizing journey to safety which the remnants of the Light Brigade were soon to be making up the valley.

For the Light Brigade it was less a test of courage than discipline. Courage can stem from an instinctive resolve to live or can be inspired by rage, rage in this case at seeing comrades struck down, at being bespattered with their brains and blood while being powerless to retaliate. Discipline on the other hand is never instinctive, it can be acquired only the hard way. And it was discipline which kept the Light Brigade, as they rode through that inferno of fire, from breaking their ranks and riding on anyhow, the quicker to get amongst the guns and sabre the gunners.

With Cardigan out in front the influences which kept him riding 'in capital style', 'as steady as a church' were more complex. First there was a cocoon of egotism. His thoughts were exclusively occupied with himself and his own concerns. Maxse, who bore him no ill-will, believed that he rode down the valley 'in a state of phantasmagoria of self and never saw or thought of anybody but himself doing his duty as a leader well'. Compared with that nothing else is likely to have counted. He saw Nolan forging ahead and he heard his shriek but the action clearly failed (as will be seen) to pierce his armour of unconcern. He would certainly have deplored what

was happening to the men who rode behind had he con-
descended to look round, but to do so he would almost as
certainly have regarded as showing plebeian curiosity, an
almost womanish weakness, instead of the proud indifference
of an aristocrat to everything not intimately related to himself. And what could be more intimately related to him than
his old feud with Lucan fired to a new pitch of intensity by
the latter's interference with his authority in his Brigade by
removing the 11th Hussars – *his* regiment – to the second
line. Then there was Nolan who, it seemed quite clear to him,
was attempting to usurp *his* – Cardigan's – authority. To
anyone as shallow-brained as himself anything impinging upon
his personal rights and dignity became of paramount consequence, taking precedence of all else. Two such affronts within
ten minutes were enough to keep his temper at boiling point
and render him immune from physical fear.

But there was a limit even to the incomparable discipline
of the Light Brigade. After a time it was impossible to keep
down the pace. George Wombwell could do nothing to hold
back the troopers in his rear. 'We broke into a gallop every
man feeling convinced that the quicker we rode through the
awful showers of grapeshot, musketry, and shells which
they poured into our flanks as we passed the better chance he
would have of escaping unhurt.' A blood lust, too, as one of
them confessed, was whipping the men to a fury. 'My heart
now began to warm, to become hot, to dance again and I had
neither fear nor pity. I longed to be at the guns. Every man
was seized with a cannibal hunger and could have eaten
a squadron without salt.' Moreover, once the pace increased
yet another factor spurred on the men – a devil-may-care
rivalry between the 17th and the 13th to be first in the battery.
The last words Arthur Tremayne of the 13th heard before
his horse fell dead beneath him were, 'Don't let those b——s of
the 17th get in front, come on, come on.'

With this pressure from the rear Cardigan was soon unable
to cope and to escape being engulfed he was progressively
compelled to increase his own pace until, when some 100 yards
from the battery, he was heading what might at last be termed
a charge, although he himself would never agree to a speed
of more than 17 miles an hour.

At this moment the Russians fired their final salvo. The flashes from 12 guns lit up as though by lightning the clouds of smoke behind which they were by this time hidden. Horses reared up, men died with a cheer or an oath in their throats, the erudite Trooper Melrose with a Shakespearean quotation on his lips – 'Wish not a man from England. God's peace, I would not lose so great an honour.' For those who survived and charged the guns, sitting firmly in the saddle and with heads well down, the worst was temporarily over. But for two reasons these would have numbered only a handful. First there were by then so many gaps in the line that some of the shot passed harmlessly through. Secondly there had been a tendency by the Lancers to veer to their left and one half of Morris's squadron passed altogether clear of the guns.

On reaching the battery the adventures of four out of the five regiments had certain features more or less in common. First there was the settling of accounts with the Russian gunners. On them 'hand over hand the thirsty sabres with a hissing sweep came down. ... It was something more than kill *or* be killed. It was *kill* whether or no and in any way, don't mind it and [confessed an Hussar] I didn't.' Next to this ragged fighting around the guns there followed a number of separate disjointed attacks upon isolated groups of startled Russian cavalry, all of them at first successful and all of them succeeded by a desperate withdrawal through forces massing in the rear.

To take first the exploits of the 13th Light Dragoons on the extreme right. In the rear of the guns in this part of the field the Russian cavalry were massed at a halt, apparently bewildered by what they had seen, evincing no tendency to counter-attack and inviting the charge which they duly received. 'Our wretched remnant [relates Captain Jenyns] dashed on with such a good right cheer', that they set the enemy scattering left and right 'like sheep'. Having carried their pursuit a quarter of a mile beyond the battery, the 13th halted, rallied and looked back. There were the guns cleared of Russians but no one to carry them off. As they deliberated on their next move, this was determined for them by the appearance from the direction of the Causeway Heights of a very strong regiment of Lancers. With blown horses the 13th wheeled round and cut their way through, but with such losses that at one time it was feared the regiment had only nine survivors.

On the left, when Morris and about a score of survivors of his squadron had passed clear of the battery, they too found themselves confronted by startled Russians at least two squadrons strong with others visible in the background. But they also were halted and Morris's experienced eye was quick to appreciate his advantage. 'Remember what I've told you, men, keep well together,' he shouted and innocently believing that he had the bulk of his regiment behind him dashed on furiously. Singling out, like Elliot, a senior Russian officer in front of his men he made straight for him, flung his guard with dexterity and drove his own sword so far into the other man's body that despite his great strength he was unable to withdraw. As he struggled to do so, he himself was struck down and fell insensible to the ground. His squadron, however, profiting by their shock tactics, pressed on and actually drove the Russians back as far as an aqueduct which crossed the end of the valley. Here they realized the hopelessness of further pursuit and seeing Cossacks forming up across their rear decided they had 'done enough for honour'. Rallying to the great booming voice of Nottingham-born Corporal Morley, shouting 'Coom 'ere, coom 'ere, fall in, lads, fall in', the 20 Lancers, who had suffered no casualties during their pursuing, turned and went back through the enemy 'as if they had been made of tinsel paper'. Riding obliquely across the valley they, like the survivors of the 13th, reached safety.

The right squadron of the 17th having rushed the guns were finding their lances not very effective against the artillerymen when they were rallied by George Mayow, the brigade major, to deal with a body of Russian cavalry who, though halted, he believed were about to attack. Unlike Morris he realized how absurdly small – fewer than 20 – was this little remnant of Lancers, but having witnessed the success of the Heavy Brigade he concluded that cavalry at the halt might be assaulted with impunity by a very much smaller body of resolute men. His deductions proved correct. Before the vicious onrush of the Lancers – crazy by parade-ground standards – the astonished enemy gave way. They too were pursued half a mile beyond the battery until the neighbourhood of the Tchernaya was reached. Here Mayow very properly halted his men, while he looked back in confident expectation of seeing supports coming up. None being visible, he began the return journey.

Support for the 17th Lancers should have come as Lucan intended from the 11th Hussars. These, however, had never got truly in the rear but rather to the left of the Lancers. Advancing down the valley nearer than any other regiment to the Fedioukine Hills they had in consequence suffered losses (over and above those from the artillery) from infantry formed up in a square. 'The very air hissed as their shower of bullets passed through us.' On the other hand when level with the battery their left squadron passed altogether clear while their right just 'brushed' its flank and was delayed no longer than was needed to dispose of the few gunners who had escaped the lances of the 17th and to receive the surrender of a much-decorated officer. A hundred yards farther on Colonel Douglas called a halt. It was while debating within himself as to the next move that he was joined by Lord George Paget.

All the way down the valley as Paget rode at the head of his 4th Light Dragoons, his cigar still between his teeth, there had been running through his head those parting mandatory words of Cardigan, 'Your best support, mind, your best support.' This had been rendered difficult to give because of Lucan's last-minute switch of the 11th Hussars to the second line which had caused Paget to be further from the first line than Cardigan had imagined it would be when he issued that injunction. Nor was that Paget's only worry. The 8th Hussars instead of keeping at a squadron's length started to incline towards the right. As Sherwell would not tolerate the slightest increase in pace, his regiment began to fall out of alignment with the 4th Light Dragoons and to become in effect a fourth line, leaving Paget's men exposed to fire on both flanks. After vainly shouting orders to close up, he abandoned the attempt and concentrated on catching up on the right of the 11th and so providing that 'best support'. His men had just about drawn level with the Hussars' rear rank when a subaltern burst into a 'View Halloa' and the battery showed up in the smoke. The next instant they were cutting and thrusting at the surviving gunners in the centre. With one remarkable exception their onslaught was not very successful. In their eagerness they tended to use the edge, not the point, of the swords which for the most part fell like those of the Heavies harmlessly on thick overcoats. The exception was Major Low, who for a few moments was carried away by a lust to kill and striking right and left with his sword accounted for no fewer than 11 Russians and afterwards when reaction had set in burst into tears. With such work Paget, who had not even drawn his sword till the guns had been reached, decided to take no part. It was, he considered, his duty rather to observe and direct than to occupy himself with the 'immediate destruction of the foe'. Thus on looking round he had caught sight of Douglas ahead and rode over to where he was standing. With Cardigan's words forever in his ears he was even more troubled than Douglas about the next move. But it was Douglas who got in the question first. 'What are we to do now, Lord Paget?' What indeed? – there was only one man competent to supply the answer and of him there was no sign. 'Where's Lord Cardigan?' Paget's reply was obviously rhetorical, for without awaiting an answer he turned back to rally his men, who after their losses on the way down looked to him more like a party of skirmishers than a regiment.

Left to himself and having no orders to retire, Douglas on seeing a large number of Russians forming to his front (a detachment of those who had been earlier routed by the Heavy Brigade) decided that audacity was the only answer. 'On the impulse of the moment' and confident that reinforcements of cavalry, artillery, and even infantry must be on their way, he decided to drive the enemy into the gorge which constricted the valley as it approached the river. 'Give them another charge, men,' he shouted. The result, something of an anticlimax, has been well told by Sergeant-Major Loy Smith.

Waving our swords over our heads on we galloped expecting the next minute to be amongst them, but to our surprise when not more than 20 yards off they wheeled about and galloped away in front of us, we shouting and feeling rather amused, for they were 20 to one, there not being at this time more than about 80 of us of the Eleventh left.

Picking up a straggler or two from the first line the Hussars carried on in pursuit of the Russians till they like the Lancers were near the aqueduct. Then occurred a scene which might be regarded as fiction coming from a less reliable source:

Near the bridge was a moderately steep hill which formed the end of the valley up which they rode a short distance, their rear being to the foot close to us. They now halted but remained for a few moments with their backs to us looking over their shoulders. Seeing there were so few of us and without supports they turned about and we sat face to face, our horses' heads close to theirs. As we looked up at them they had all the appearance of a vast assemblage in the gallery of a theatre. The stillness and suspense during these moments was terrible; at last it was broken by their officers calling out to their men to follow them and break through us which they attempted to do by driving their horses at our front rank, but the men failed to display the same courage as their leaders and our men showed a firm front, keeping close together and bringing their swords down to their right front guard, keeping them at bay. Many of them now took out their pistols and fired into us and the Cossacks began to double round our flanks and get in our rear; many of the flank men now became engaged and several were killed.

The only explanation of such astonishing behaviour is that the Russian morale had been severely shaken by the charge of the Heavy Brigade and none of them was prepared to stand up to the onslaught of a British mounted man. It is equally clear that with adequate supports the 11th Hussars might even at this stage have converted the battle into an indisputable victory. Indeed on looking round Colonel Douglas fancied he saw just those supports in a body of Lancers coming down the valley. Raising his voice, he shouted to them: 'Rally, men of the 17th Lancers.' But Cornet Roger Palmer with keener sight detected a difference in the pennons and replied, 'I beg your pardon, Colonel, that's not the 17th Lancers, that's the enemy.' 'Then fight for your lives!' cried Douglas.

The Russians were part of Jeropkine's Lancers who had come over the Fedioukines and had debouched into the plain. It was a well-conceived plan which should have annihilated the 11th whose horses were now nearly blown and they themselves isolated. It failed because at a decisive moment the Russians neglected to show here as so often in like circumstances active as opposed to passive courage, that élan which as a rule only armies of free men can produce.

The form which the 11th unintentionally adopted for their retreat was that of an oval, caused by some horses being less fagged, setting a faster pace. Behind them as they turned for home the Russians they had been pursuing came on shouting, 'Bussu ... bussu ... English.' The Hussars had not gone far when they were joined on their left by the remnants of the 4th under Paget who was still seeking how and where to support an invisible first line and an invisible Cardigan. But his men had had enough. Like the Lancers they had done sufficient for honour. On meeting the 11th without a word of command from Paget they went about and joined in their retreat.

The pursuing Russians were meantime steadily gaining on the tired British. Only by some venturesome stroke could the peril be averted. Raising his voice Paget shouted, 'Halt, front! If you don't front, my boys, we're done.' Rather to his surprise the men of both regiments obeyed 'as coolly as if they had been on parade'. The trick worked. Before this resolute line now facing them the Russians once more stopped and when the British continued their retirement they made no further effort to follow, being content to hand over to their Lancer comrades now strung out across the Hussars' line of retreat.

For the British it was an occasion which had already occurred and was repeatedly to recur in the campaign. Salvation came by a combination of British daring and Russian inertia. First it was necessary to form the men up in as tight a body as possible. Crying 'Rally ... rally' and holding aloft their swords, the surviving officers brought them into some sort of order. Then 'helter-skelter we went at those Lancers as fast as our poor tired horses could carry us'.

For all this intrepidity Paget was filled with misgivings. While his men were little more than a rabble numbering barely 70 the Russians ahead were two squadrons strong at least. Moreover, as the British approached they wheeled very neatly to the right in such a way as to enable them to take their enemy obliquely upon the right flank. They had in fact begun to close in at a trot when, instead of going on, they halted irresolute and began feebly and ineffectually with their lances to prod the British as they 'shuffled' by at merely a horse's length. Incredibly not a man of the 4th or 11th was lost. 'How, I know not,' said Paget. 'It is a mystery to me. Had that force been composed of English *ladies* I don't think one of us could have escaped.' Once past the Russian lancers Robert Portal who was one of his subalterns told his family 'we retired in perfect order to the position we had come from'. He adds that the fire was 'more severe than before', but as that from the Fedioukine Hills had been very much reduced since the outward journey, this may be doubted.

For this partial abatement of Russian firepower the Light Brigade owed a debt of inestimable gratitude to d'Allonville and his Chasseurs d'Afrique. On seeing the British plight he had hurriedly ordered two squadrons of 150 men, nearly all veterans with at least a dozen years' service, to attack and silence the battery on the Fedioukines. In their loose Algerian formation and conspicuous on their white horses they dashed skilfully over the ground not unlike that of their native Africa. Although in the end compelled to withdraw before the advance of two fresh battalions of the Vladimir regiment they succeeded at some cost in bringing about the withdrawal of the guns. The result was that though the survivors of the Light Brigade while making their way back were subjected to a new menace from roving bands of Cossacks they were at least spared shot and shell from the Fedioukines.

The last regiment to reach the now-silent battery were the 8th Hussars on the right. In Colonel Sherwell they had a commander who like many Crimean officers combined bravery with a rigid piety. No cavalry regiment was more highly disciplined. The standard of behaviour upon which he insisted had been well illustrated not half an hour previously. Sherwell had gone sick, but hearing that a fight was in prospect he had thrown off his blanket and had come galloping up from Balaclava. Perhaps as a result of 'the Old Woman's' absence men had relaxed somewhat as they stood to horses. The order to draw swords having been given some were even smoking when the colonel arrived. 'What's this?' he exploded. 'One, two, three, four, seven men smoking *and* swords drawn. I never heard of such a thing. No regiment except an Irish regiment would be guilty of it. I'll have this breach of discipline punished.' Calling up a sergeant he ordered him to take the names of the defaulters. Some died in the charge, but at least one of those who returned was in fact punished on the following day.

Once started on their slightly oblique course down the valley the 8th not only fell behind into what was virtually the fourth line and so lost all touch with the 4th Light Dragoons on their left, but approached the guns and infantry on the Causeway nearer than any other regiment. For this, as Edward Phillips tells us, they paid a cruel price:

We advanced at a steady trot, soon to a faster pace; we had not advanced 200 yards before the guns on the flanks (our left and right) opened fire with shell and round shot; two regiments of Infantry drawn up on the right under the guns began firing volleys of Minié balls and almost at the same time the guns at the bottom of the valley opened with grape. In spite of this awful fire we galloped over the ground strewed with the men of the first line, and our own dropping at every yard; every sound was there, the bursting of shells, the deep dash of the round shot as they struck the ground, and the whistling of the storm of Minié balls and grape shot. We passed the Infantry, the guns on our left and right, and approached the guns at the bottom of the valley, which the first line charged in the midst of a fire that swept down the men by dozens and carried off almost all the officers.

The rôle of the 8th at Balaclava was the least spectacular of the five regiments, but perhaps the most self-sacrificing. Having arrived at the battery in tolerably good order, Sherwell, still keeping his men under firm control, continued some way towards the rear, when seeing no Russians but those who in scattered groups were retreating towards the river, he felt he had gone far enough and halted. While in this position he was joined by Mayow and his small band of Lancers making their way back obliquely across the valley. Between Mayow and Sherwell as between Paget and Douglas the same question was debated: where was Cardigan? While they considered the next step they, too, saw Lancers forming across their rear – in their case having descended from the Causeway Heights. Only for an instant did Sherwell, like Douglas, mistake them for the 17th. With the cry, 'By God, they're Russians – keep together men – death or glory – we'll ride them down', he wheeled his regiment about and (continues Phillips)

. . . we charged bang through them, thus opening a way for the remnant of the first line now quite broken by their losses. As soon as we had charged through the Lancers opposed to us, another lot was sent at an angle to cut us off and thus from the awful fire in advancing, and now charging we had suffered immense loss; there were not sufficient left to charge them and of course everyone made his way back through the same awful fire as before; however any one of us escaped the storm of shot and shell and bullets is miraculous. On our return out of the fire and rallying, only 44 men turned up out of 104.

The transit of the Russian lancers was described by another Hussar as like 'cutting through a thick-set hedge with a bill-hook'. The losses incurred in these two engagements were heavy, but they cleared the southern portion of the valley and enabled men in other broken regiments to get back more easily than would otherwise have been possible.

But what of Lord Cardigan, of whose whereabouts four of his five regimental commanding officers (Oldham of the 13th having been killed) had been asking? Up till the moment when he disappeared into the smoke of battle Cardigan had fulfilled the highest traditions of a cavalry leader. He had, as Morris, no partisan, had conceded, 'led like a gentleman'. It was only later that he showed his unfitness for the command. Passing through the guns, on one of which he nearly crushed his leg, he like Paget thought it beneath his dignity to concern himself with the dispatching of Russian gunners and continued coolly on his way. His ADCs having fallen wounded and Britten dead, he was alone with his thoughts and (from the sequel) there is little doubt that these were still concentrated on Lucan and Nolan. He had gone perhaps 300 yards when, like Morris and Mayow, he came face to face with a large body of halted cavalry. What must have been the impact on the superstitious and ignorant Muscovites, accustomed from infancy to pay the most abject respect to rank, when they saw emerging out of the smoke this magnificently caparisoned officer, with his sweeping moustache and sword carelessly carried at the slope, can only be deduced from what followed.

They stared in wonderment, none venturing to move. Cardigan, reining in Ronald, stared back impassively and coldly. The spell was broken only when an officer named Radzivill recognized the apparition as the Lord Cardigan he had met in London society and offered a tempting reward to his men to capture him alive. Thus inspired some Cossacks edged forward with circumspection and one actually drew close enough to prod him with his lance but so gently as merely to tear a rent in the cherry-coloured overalls. At this affront to his person Cardigan merely turned round and in Kinglake's turgid phrase consented to 'disengage himself from the reach of his assailants by a sufficing movement of retreat'.

If not when the battery had been reached, certainly when some minutes had passed, a good cavalry leader would have felt some responsibility for his brigade; he would have endeavoured to make some contact with his regimental commanders; he would have shown concern for the fate of his men. Not so Cardigan, of whom it was said that 'he played the part of a hero but not of a general'. Having led his first line up to the guns he seems to have felt that he had done all that was required of him; to have considered that his duty extended only to the first line and that this having vanished there was nothing left for him to do (as he told Kinglake) but 'to retreat gradually and slowly in the rear of the broken parties of the first line up the hill, rather than turn and ride through the Russian cavalry in search of my supports'. With the same indifference for anyone and everything not intimately related to himself he accordingly retraced his steps, neither hurrying his pace nor paying any more attention to Russian bullets and shells than if they were raindrops and he had been riding wearily home from a meet. The 8th Hussars having not yet arrived on the scene there is no record of anyone having sighted him until he overtook Sergeant Mitchell of the 13th toiling back on foot. He passed him without a word but (was it the first stirring of a conscience?) turned back to ask rather unnecessarily, 'Where's your horse?' 'Killed, my lord.' 'Then you'd better make your way back as fast as you can or you'll be taken prisoner.' With this unhelpful advice Cardigan proceeded once more up the valley. His next encounter was with Captain Shakespear and provides a supreme example of British sangfroid. There was no mention on either side of a charge or the fate of the Brigade. Cardigan merely pointed to the tear made by the Cossack lance and said (as if he might have been referring to a rent in his hunting breeches) 'Damn nice thing this, Shakespear, and nothing to keep the cold out.' 'Pardon me, my lord,' replied the equally imperturbable Shakespear, 'the artillery are always prepared for an emergency.' With that he beckoned to his trumpeter who carried his flask and handed it to Cardigan.

Having drunk, Cardigan continued at a walking pace till he met Sir George Cathcart to whom he addressed five words: 'I have lost my Brigade.' Seeing no sign of it ahead he once more wheeled about and rode down the valley till he met the 8th Hussars with whom he returned. This time he did not stop till he saw Scarlett at the head of the Heavy Brigade. To him, an officer of his own rank, he released the dammed-up fury against Nolan. 'Imagine the fellow, screaming like a woman when he was hit.' 'Say no more, my lord,' was Scarlett's dignified reply. 'I have just ridden over Captain Nolan's dead body.'

Not half an hour had passed since Cardigan had set forth at the head of 673 officers and men, finely mounted and wearing uniforms which, if become shabby and threadbare, were amongst the most decorative in Europe. Now 195 jaded figures, many helmetless, all dishevelled, covered in mud and blood, were riding back in scattered, dispersed groups. A fifth of the Brigade lay dead or dying in the valley, a number which would certainly have been greater had Russian flanking fire been more accurate. A hundred and thirty-four wounded and double that number who had been unhorsed were straggling back over the heavy ground, some running, some limping, some crawling, all harassed and threatened by roving bands of Russian Lancers and Cossacks, or where these were not active by continued fire from the flank. Men who might have escaped death so far met it here from the savage prod of a lance as they lay wounded or were hunted down and transfixed as if they had been wild pigs.

As the immensity of the losses became apparent to Cardigan a kindlier side of his nature was revealed. He sought out d'Allonville and proffering his hand thanked him for his help.

The callous, haughty demeanour which had marked his behaviour and which he was soon to resume had vanished. When
Earle met him later in the day he declared he had 'never seen
a man so grieved'. Nor is there any truth in the story of his
going straight back to his yacht, a bath, a bottle of champagne and a good dinner. He may have done so much later
that night, but it is known that he made his way to where
his ADC Maxse was nursing a wounded foot beside a camp
fire. Here after a time reaction set in. He wrapped himself
in his cloak, lay down on the ground and under the stars fell
asleep, a man physically, emotionally and nervously exhausted.

Of the many facts of outstanding physical endurance that
day those associated with the names of Sir William Gordon
and Captain Morris are without parallel. The first who was
that night described medically as the only patient 'with his
head off', though blinded by blood and without stirrups can-
tered boldly through intervening squadrons of Russians to survive for many years to come. The second, having recovered
consciousness, found himself set upon by Cossacks whom he
managed to keep at bay by ceaselessly twirling his sword
around his head in windmill fashion till, a Russian
officer guaranteeing his life, he surrendered the weapon. This
left him completely defenceless when the officer was called
away and the Cossacks once more closed in. With blood pouring from his wounds he nevertheless succeeded in breaking
away, and mounting a stray horse; but this was brought down,
pinning Morris beneath him. With three wounds by now, a
fractured arm and several broken ribs he fainted for the second
time. Soon recovering consciousness he staggered and stumbled up the long valley till within the security of our lines he
collapsed for a third time, by a macabre coincidence along-
side the body of his friend Nolan.

Many, too, were the acts of bravery, as men stopped and
risked their lives to help the wounded or to surrender a horse
to those incapable of walking. It was here that the only
Victoria Cross awarded to a cavalry officer in the campaign
was won by Alex Dunn of the 11th Hussars, a man of immense
wealth, who went to the assistance of a stricken sergeant-major
and wielding a sword many inches longer than the regulation
article, hewed down his assailants and saved his life.

Typical no doubt of the survivors was the adventure of Edward Phillips.

I had not gone far when I found my mare begin to flag and presently I think she must have been hit in the leg by a round shot, as she suddenly dropped behind and fell over on her side. I extricated myself as quickly as possible and ran for my life, the firing being as hard as ever. After some distance I found myself cut off by some Lancers who had got in my front. . . I made sure my time was come; I drew my revolver but seeing they kept their distance, until an officer coming up ordered them back, as they were too far in advance, so I escaped this danger. Some little distance on I reached one of our poor fellows lying on the ground, dead or dying, his horse standing beside him; the saddle had turned round and what with excitement and running for one's life I was so done that I had not the strength to right it, therefore undid the girths and by standing on the saddle managed to climb on his bare back. Never was I so happy as when I felt a horse under me again.

There were things seen that day at Balaclava which men never forgot. The terribly wounded without hope of return, horses writhing, disembowelled, trying to walk on three legs; Sergeant Riley of the 8th riding with 'eyes fixed and staring, his face as rigid and white as a flagstone', dead in his saddle; Sergeant Talbot of the 17th careering on, his lance gripped tightly under his arm and he headless.

But there were episodes which could be recollected with pleasure. There was Jeremy, the little rough-haired terrier of the 8th, who followed his master throughout the charge, was wounded in the neck but survived to return to England. There was the memory of John Veigh, regimental butcher of the 17th, who at the last moment dashed up wearing his occupational smock covered with blood and bellowing, 'I'll be damned if I'll be left behind and lose all the fun'; who then lit up a short black pipe, selected a sword (with which he cut down six men in the battery) and came back scatheless, his pipe still alight. There was Lieutenant Chamberlayne of the 13th who, while mourning the loss of his horse, was advised that it would be more difficult to get a new saddle than another horse; and then putting it on his head made his perilous way up the valley past Cossacks who mistook him for a Russian pillager and rode by. There was Captain Percy Smith of the same regiment who from a previous accident could not use his sword without an iron contraption which he had left behind and had so gone into action unarmed. When faced by Cossacks on his retreat he drove his hunter straight at the first Russian, leaped over him and reached safety, the only officer of his regiment not to lose his horse.

With the Light Brigade reduced to what Captain Seager described as 'stage soldiers fit for nothing', it was at once apparent to Raglan (without being reminded of the fact by Canrobert whose attentions were consistently riveted upon Sebastopol) that even if the lost redoubts were recaptured – as easily they might be – by the two infantry divisions present they could hardly be held with the cavalry force now at his command. The operations were therefore suspended and the Russians left in control of the first three redoubts. The 1st and 4th Divisions returned to the plateau, the former without its two remaining Highland regiments which Raglan ordered to remain in the valley under Campbell's command.

In British military history Balaclava must ever remain a victory *manqué*. October 25th might have been a brilliant little success had nothing more succeeded the charge of the Heavy Brigade and the Russians given time to withdraw from their isolated position on the Causeway. It could have been a triumph had the Light Brigade been allowed to cooperate or had the infantry been employed with better skill. As it was the day remains a testimony to British valour, and, because to the unexcitable Anglo-Saxon mind glorious failure has a greater sentimental appeal than meritorious success, it is probable that of a hundred who can quote a complete stanza from Tennyson's 'Charge of the Light Brigade' scarcely one can repeat a line from his 'Heavy Brigade' who

> *Rode like Victors and Lords*
> *Through a forest of lances and swords*
> *In the heart of the Russian hordes.*

To have ridden behind Cardigan moreover brought in after years greater fame than to have ridden behind Scarlett into battle.

> *He who outlives this day, and comes safe home*
> *Will stand on tip-toe when this day is named.*

Twenty years later when it was decided to celebrate Balaclava day by a Balaclava dinner for the survivors of the Light
Brigade, no fewer than 750 attended claiming to have taken
part in the charge!

If to have captured and retained three redoubts and to have
carried away amid jubilation seven out of nine enemy guns is a
criterion of victory then Balaclava was a Russian victory. We
had neither spiked (because no spikes were issued) nor removed
the guns overrun and our cavalry had withdrawn with crippling losses, leaving the valley under Russian domination. But
Balaclava was not simply an affair of the Light Brigade. Russian accounts are understandably reticent about Scarlett's
action. In their encounter with the Heavy Brigade the Russian cavalry had put up a wretched performance, the effect of
which on their morale had been visible within an hour at the
bottom of the North Valley. Nowhere had they shown thrust,
skill or enterprise. 'If they had any pluck at all [wrote Portal]
not one of us, if we had been ten times as strong, could ever
have come back again.' Only in hunting down stragglers and
prodding disabled troopers to death did their men show any
aggressive spirit. The chivalrous Liprandi when interviewing
prisoners that night might insist the whole Brigade must have
been drunk, and a Russian general during a truce might refer
to 'une charge d'insensés', but from the day of Balaclava till
the last shot in the campaign the Russians were altogether
demoralized at the prospect of meeting British cavalry. If
according to Napoleon the ratio of moral to physical courage
is 3 to 1 the losses incurred by the Light Brigade were not
suffered in vain. Nor were these at 157 dead heavy when
considered in perspective. Before very long a surgeon was
writing, 'We bury three times the number of men every week
and think nothing of it.'

'History,' declared Camille Rousset, 'has sometimes witnessed the generous sacrifice of a cavalry which has immolated
itself to save an army, or even the noble despair of men who
did not wish to survive defeat. But here there was nothing of
the kind; neither defeat nor peril threatened the British army.'
'If we had been French [wrote Tremayne] nous sommes
trahis! would have been the cry; as it was men seemed to be
glad that they had not let the Heavies have the day all to them-

selves.' Nevertheless it was clear from the moment of return that a terrible mistake had been made. Who was the guilty party? Cardigan was at once acquitted. When Raglan came down and loudly declared that 'the cavalry have been wantonly sacrificed', there was no traversing Cardigan's reply: 'I received the order to attack from my superior officer in front of the troops.' That superior officer, Lucan, believed and with justice that, Divisional General though he might be, he had, despite what Raglan asserted to the contrary, no discretionary power in the face of so imperative a command. This leaves Raglan who conceived the order, Airey who wrote it down and Nolan who carried it down. The first two cannot be absolved on the grounds that they did not intend the Russian guns to be charged. The point is, had they made their meaning clear? If the Fourth Order is taken by itself, the answer cannot be in doubt – the meaning was not clear, it was equivocal. Nolan was responsible for interpreting it as he did, but any blame for this depends upon how far he knew the true intentions of his chiefs and to what extent he deliberately flouted them. There is no evidence that he knew these intentions or that he had received any verbal instructions beyond Lord Raglan's parting injunction. The whole tragedy of Balaclava derived from an order *capable* of being misinterpreted and for this order Raglan and Airey must share the blame with Nolan, but not in equal portions. Although a man of some ability Airey was noted for his tearing energy. It is evident that he dashed off the message without putting, as a responsible staff-officer should have done, his commander-in-chief's hasty, almost ejaculatory, orders into clear and unmistakeable language or at least giving the bearer exact instructions. Conveniently for all concerned Nolan perished and on his gallant shoulders was eagerly with almost indecent haste heaped the responsibility for converting what could have been a day of rejoicing into one of mourning. 'Never was such a mad order given, Nolan is the man to blame.' 'We think it was a judgement on him for getting us in such a mess.' So wrote two survivors of the Charge, Jenyns and Portal, but then, as Lieutenant Richards of the artillery told his family cynically, 'A dead man can carry a heavy weight.'

4

Inkerman

'None know with what majesty the British soldier fights.'
– *Napier*

IN THE BATTLE SCROLL of the British army Inkerman is without comparison. To none other can be applied more fittingly Wellington's aphorism that the history of a battle is like the history of a ball. Inkerman is the grand total of as many encounters as there were bodies of soldiers ready to follow a leader, be he officer, non-commissioned officer or fellow private. 'Colonels of regiments led on small parties and fought like subalterns, captains like privates. Once engaged every man was his own general.' And, Hamley might have added, he did so for most of the time in a fog. It is therefore scarcely surprising that those who took part in Inkerman, those who like Russell watched it from the wings and those who wrote later of it, agree in one particular – Inkerman eludes description. Inkerman must be treated, if it is to be appreciated as one of the noblest battles ever fought by a British army, for what it was: a series of isolated, largely distinct conflicts, loosely threaded together by one common purpose, which was to repulse the Russians everywhere. The sequence of events cannot be accurately determined and chronology must be ignored for the reason that combatants, who in any case knew nothing of what was happening away from their own narrow front, had no time to check movements by a watch.

Nor is any treatment of Inkerman comprehensible which does not begin with geography. Happily, unlike the battle itself, the ground over which it was fought is easily describable. At Inkerman, in contrast with Alma, it was the Russians who from the plain attacked the allies on the Heights. A massive spur of land, likened to the stock of a rifle and of an

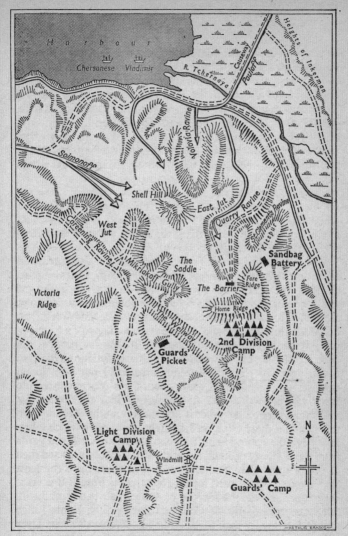

The Battle of Inkerman

(*As the battle lasted nearly eight hours it would be misleading to show troop dispositions at any one time. By using the map in conjunction with the text it is hoped that the reader will be able to follow the movement of troops throughout the battle.*)

average height of about 400 feet, thrust itself forward at the
North-East end of the plateau beyond the Sapounè ridge. Its
butt-end lay parallel with the harbour and along its base and
connecting the town with the interior ran a military road. On
either side of the stock the land fell away sharply into the
Tchernaya valley on the East and into the Careening Ravine
(which divided it from the Victoria ridge) on the West. Out
of the latter went two re-entries to the Inkerman Heights by
means of gullies, the first (if coming from Sebastopol) being
the Mikriakoff, the second the Wellway. From the Tchernaya
valley on the other side there were three similar approaches
by way of the Volovia, Quarry, and St Clements Ravines.
Of these the most important and (for the British) the most
dangerous was the Quarry Ravine inasmuch as it alone of all
five approaches carried a road, the important post road from
the interior to Sebastopol.

The butt at its base was two miles wide, but as it narrowed
towards the south it threw up a ridge with a pronounced
hump in the centre and two shoulders running out right and
left. The hump, for reasons soon to be obvious, became known
as Shell Hill and the two shoulders as East and West Jut.
South of this, the ground fell away, tapering to an isthmus,
scarcely more than 450 yards wide between the head of the
Mikriakoff gully on the west and the Quarry Ravine on the east.
South again of this, the isthmus broadened out and sloped
upwards to a shoulder in width about three-quarters of a mile
from where on one side it fell steeply into the Tchernaya
valley to where on the other it descended into the Wellway. On
this shoulder there was a further slight elevation to which Kinglake gave the name Home Ridge. This began some 500 yards
from the Wellway descent, ran eastwards for 400 yards and then
at rather more than a quarter of a mile from the Tchernaya
slopes took a sharp turn to the North. This Fore Ridge, as it
was named, carried on for 500 or 600 yards when it gradually
fell away towards the St Clements Ravine. The Home Ridge
was 30 feet higher than Shell Hill and 1,200 yards away. Over
the isthmus or saddleback between the two the greater part of
the battle was fought. It was thickly covered, as were the sides
of the ravines, by scrub, chiefly stunted oak about three or
four feet high, interspersed with rocks and boulders.

The defence of this difficult territory, approachable from
so many directions, had been committed to Sir De Lacy Evans
and his 2nd Division whose camp lay a short distance to the
south of the Home Ridge. Since the remainder of the Highland Brigade had been moved down to Balaclava, the Inkerman Heights had become the weakest joint in the allied line.
With a total force of 3,000 and 18 field guns Evans's nearest
supports were the Guards encamped more than a mile to the
south. The Light, 4th and 3rd Divisions were ranged to the
left fronting Sebastopol at approximately one and a half, two
and three miles respectively. The closest French troops were
Bosquet's Army of Observation strung along the Sapounè
Ridge overlooking the Balaclava plain from the Col to within
a mile and a quarter of the Guards' camp. Nowhere else could
the Russians attack knowing that they would be immune from
the guns of the fleet and that allied reinforcements, if
properly confused by diversionary movements, would take so
long a time to arrive, if at all. Any doubts as to their preoccupation with the Inkerman position should have been
removed on the day following Balaclava.

Among the several remarkable features of Inkerman was its
being given a dress-rehearsal. At half past one on the afternoon of October 26th, the Russians in the hopes no doubt that
the British were depressed and unsettled by the events of the
previous day down at Balaclava sent out 5,000 men,
preceded by skirmishers and carrying entrenching tools,
together with four light guns. Leaving Sebastopol by the
Karabelnaya suburb, they crossed the Careening Ravine and
swinging right surmounted Shell Hill. A picket from the 49th
and 95th, greatly outnumbered, but equipped with Miniés,
fell back on the Barrier, a low, stone-built redoubt which had
been constructed astride the post road as it climbed out of the
Quarry Ravine. Its purpose was rather to provide casual protection for pickets than a strong defensive post. Nevertheless
the men halted here and encouraged by the voice of the
pious Major Champion crying 'Slate 'em, boys, slate 'em',
defied all attempts at capture by the Russians. De Lacy Evans
with his experience of similar fighting in Spanish wars resisted
the temptation to give battle on ground of the enemy's
choosing. Beyond sending out a couple of companies to

reinforce one hard-pressed picket, he refused to unleash his division. Wherever and whenever the Russians came within range of the Miniés or guns they were to be attacked. If, notwithstanding, they succeeded in pressing back the pickets then he was ready for them behind the Home Ridge with everything at his command. It never came to such a fight. Before the fire of the pickets and the batteries the Russian columns melted away and their four guns were knocked out. Within three hours of the time of their appearance they had been thrown back with a loss of 250 killed and 80 prisoners.

After the gloom of the previous day this was a tonic indeed. 'Sebastopol will soon be ours now, these are their last efforts,' wrote Fisher-Rowe complacently. It was, thought a civilian spectator or 'Travelling Gentleman', one of the prettiest actions of the whole campaign, the only one on which any generalship was shown, the exact reverse of Balaclava, in that we inflicted heavy losses on the enemy at infinitesimal cost to ourselves. Nevertheless, from the Russian point of view it was not, as we were soon to discover, an entirely profitless affair. They had learnt something of the British defences on Inkerman, and, above all, the precise range of the British lines for any guns mounted on Shell Hill.

In the ten days which followed the battle of Little Inkerman, there is no evidence that Raglan ever visited this danger point, that he ever rode to the head of Quarry Ravine and examined the post road as it climbed up from the Tchernaya valley. It is true that he did feel, and express, some anxiety about the weakness of his right flank, although according to one officer of the Engineers, when advised to strengthen the Inkerman position, he is said to have replied, 'Nonsense! They will never dare come again.' It is known that he did ask help from Canrobert, who replied that he too was short of men. In such circumstances there was all the more reason for making this exposed flank as defensible as possible, even if it entailed withdrawing some men employed on contructing trenches near the French lines. What had been done? Seven hundred yards to the east of the Barrier and at the base of the Kitspur, a tongue of land which ran out between the Tchernaya valley on the right and the St Clements Ravine on the left, a small two-gun battery, usually referred to as the

FIELD MARSHAL, FITZROY JAMES HENRY SOMERSET,
1st BARON RAGLAN, 1788-1855.
From a portrait by WILLIAM SALTER, in the
National Portrait Gallery, London.
reproduction by kind permission of the Trustees

Lord Raglan

Sir George De Lacy Evans

Prince Gortschakoff

Marshal St Arnaud

General Todleben

Lord Raglan's Room

Battle of the Alma, showing Kourgane on the left and Telegraph Hill on the right

The Charge of the Light Brigade at Balaclava. A good example of the War artist's licence. The Regiments are far too close to each other and the Brigade appears to take up the entire valley instead of about one-fifth of it

The Night of Balaclava. Captain H. F. B. Maxse has identified the three figures: asleep, Lord Cardigan; standing, Lieutenant F. A. Maxse, RN, ADC; sitting, Captain Maxse himself

The second charge of the Guards at Inkerman

'A Hot Day in the Batteries' (facing the Redan). In the foreground the famous 13-inch mortars are in action

An artist's impression of the fall of Sebastopol, September 8th, 1855

Sand Bag Battery, had been made, not as part of any scheme of defence but solely to deal with a solitary Russian gun which had been harassing our men from across the valley. This having been silenced, the two guns were withdrawn. What was left was something useless for defence – a rampart nine feet high pierced by two embrasures but without any banquette on which men could stand and fire. Unless strengthened (not a difficult operation) or integrated with the defences of the Home Ridge, 800 yards in the rear, it should have been dismantled and abandoned. Instead it was left to acquire a spurious value as a symbol of victory. Of no tactical value to the British, French or Russian, its possession seemed to promise a guarantee of victory.

It might have been thought that at least steps would be taken to strengthen the Home Ridge in front of the second division camp. Instead, nothing of any kind would have been done but for the insistence of Colonel Herbert, Evans's Assistant Quartermaster-General, that some sort of rampart be built, if only to protect the guns in battery on either side of the road. The rampart, described as 'more like ordinary drains than fieldworks' – it was only two feet high and 100 yards long – was duly built, but only in the teeth of Headquarters' opposition in which Sir John Burgoyne was prominent, and until the day of the battle, but not afterwards, was christened Herbert's Folly. Even more reprehensible was the failure to clear the ground for several hundred yards in front of the ridge. Yet here were hundreds of stunted oak trees capable of affording cover to any attacking force and impeding any counter-measures, but also capable of yielding much desperately needed firewood. If it was objected that there was insufficient labour in view of all the trench and picket work to be done, the rejoinder was that in the rear of Balaclava there were 11,000 Turkish troops and behind them across the waters of the Black Sea and in Asia Minor there was available an inexhaustible labour force. Unfortunately in Raglan's eyes the Turks who had abandoned the redoubts had written off their fellow-countrymen alike as soldiers and as labourers as altogether contemptible. That was not the view of Eber, the great Hungarian patriot sent by *The Times* to join Russell. 'Vat dam nonsense you make because dree battalyons did not beat sevendy battalyons. You have not enough men, I tell you and I know de war and you shall want de Turks.' He was right. The very day after the battle all necessary works on the Inkerman Heights were put in hand – by Turkish labour.

The battle of Inkerman could never have taken place had any ordinary care and intelligence been shown by those who selected the positions for our outposts. ... In all the history of modern warfare I do not know of another instance of such culpable neglect on the part of divisional commanders of all the well known and long established precautions that should be taken by troops in the field against surprise.

This celebrated indictment by Lord Wolseley is not wholly fair – with the best of wills there were tasks beyond the capacity of the army and its Headquarters' staff, and responsibility for failure to perform them rests rather upon the Government of Lord Aberdeen and every government which since Waterloo had wielded the economy axe. Nevertheless it is hard to find an excuse for one failure that was to cost many lives – the neglect to bring up to the Inkerman Heights sufficient ammunition for any emergency from the ample stores in Balaclava.

The truth seems to be that at Raglan's Headquarters, where one officer was heard to complain that his bedroom faced north, there was a deliberate intention of applying the soft pedal on all that concerned the Inkerman flank. Plans were being prepared for an allied assault upon the town before winter closed in and ended all active operations, and care was being taken then as always that the commander-in-chief should not be disturbed by unpleasant or alarmist reports. These included advices transmitted from Berlin of a terrible retribution about to descend on the allies, of warning from spies and deserters of an impending attack, of a large influx of Russian troops, notably the 4th Army Corps from Odessa, of the morale-boosting arrival of the 'two cubs,' the Czar's sons Nicholas and Michael; but all, it is safe to say, reached Raglan in a reassuringly edited fashion. From this complacent frame of mind it was but a step to the last enormity of any Headquarters staff – the underestimating of the enemy. Writing only a few days after the battle Calthorpe, who, from his position on the staff was a reliable witness, makes with reference to Inkerman this at once honest and damaging confession: 'It is only a new proof of how much we have all along underrated the strength and resources of the enemy.' He might at the same time have added 'and their intelligence service'. Unlike the gentlemanly Raglan, the Russian commander-in-chief Menschikoff had no scruples about employing spies. From their reports it must have been clear that if Russia was to strike it would have to be before, not after the allied assault which the appearance of scaling ladders about the camp showed to be at hand. It was a deduction which Raglan and his staff seemed unwilling to make.

It had rained throughout Saturday, November 4th, and when the temperature rose at nightfall there spread over the plateau a heavy, clinging fog. For this reason the night pickets on Shell Hill were withdrawn from their usual forward and isolated position to others well South of its crest. No alternative precautions were taken. But for the curiosity which impelled Sergeant-Major Williams to creep forward, the sound of many wheels turning and the vague noises of movement might never have been heard muffling up from below. He reported what he had heard to his officer, who took the view that it was merely the usual nightly procession of country carts carrying provisions into the city. When towards the morning carillons rang out from the church towers of Sebastopol the same officer no doubt remembered that it was Sunday morning. He was not to know that the wheels were not those of carts but of gun-carriages and that the bells were not merely summoning the faithful to prayer but inspiring the devout conscript to fight for Holy Russia. Shortly before dawn the night picket was relieved and began to withdraw.

As originally devised Menschikoff's plan was for an army of 19,000 men and 38 guns under General Soimonoff to leave Sebastopol, cross the Careening Ravine and march up the road which would lead them to the western shoulder or jut of Shell Hill. There he was to establish his artillery and under its cover advance against the British in echelon from the right. At the same time General Pauloff with 16,000 men and 96 guns was to descend from the neighbourhood of Mackenzie's Farm, cross the Tchernaya by the bridge and then split his forces into two. The first part was to take the military road leading to the Eastern Jut, the other to bear south and follow the post road up the Quarry Ravine. Once having gained the Heights, both Pauloff's and Soimonoff's armies were to pass under the direction of General Dannenberg. To prevent any succour being rushed to the doomed 2nd Division, Prince Gortschakoff with 22,000 men and 88 guns was to demonstrate opposite the Sapounè Ridge and pin Bosquet down. At the other end of the allied line Timovieff was to make a real not a feint attack on the French left and the Sebastopol garrison facing the British were to seize every occasion to create diversions, real or feigned.

In this plan, formidable on paper, there were two weaknesses, one general, one particular. In general it depended upon too many contingencies; it required very exact timing upon a difficult and extensive terrain ironically less familiar to the newly-arrived Russian forces than to the British. In particular the ground chosen for attack was too narrow in its waist or saddle and its sides too steep for the deployment of two such vast armies as Soimonoff's and Pauloff's. Dannenberg seems to have been the first to appreciate the dangers of this bottleneck and at five o'clock on Saturday afternoon he prepared a plan which should have been the British army's death warrant. Shell Hill was to be left altogether to Pauloff while Soimonoff advanced along the half-mile-broad Victoria Ridge with his left on the Careening Ravine. In other words he was to attack the very vulnerable right centre where there, to oppose him, was only Sir George Brown's much-reduced Light Division numbering 1,200 and a few guns. Once this was pushed aside there was nothing to prevent Soimonoff from splitting the British army in two, cutting off the 3rd and 4th Divisions to the west and taking the Guards in the flank and Bosquet's men in the rear.

If everything had gone according to Dannenberg's plan nothing could have failed to fulfil the boast Menschikoff was making that: 'Future times will preserve the remembrance of the exemplary chastisement inflicted upon the presumption of the allies.' The plan went awry for two entirely disconnected reasons – the mist which developed during the night and Soimonoff's last-minute refusal to adopt Dannenberg's amendment. So far from requiring a fog the Dannenberg scheme postulated a dawn of good visibility in order that his troops could find their way about the unfamiliar Inkerman Heights and take all the advantage given to an attacker by their deceptive indentations and contours. Secondly, for reasons which died with him an hour later, Soimonoff decided to adhere to the original plan and marched his men across the Careening Ravine and up the west shoulder of Shell Hill.

Soimonoff's men scored an immediate and soundless victory when an isolated picket of an officer and 13 men, thinking they were British, approached and were taken prisoner. But a few moments later Captain Goodlake and a picked body of roving Coldstream Guardsmen were not deceived, and their opening fire raised the curtain on the battle of Inkerman.

It is to be doubted if any battle has ever been fought for so many hours by so many men over so narrow a field. This prolonged congestion together with the fog and the roughness of the ground combined to create what as the story is told will become a recognizable Inkerman pattern.

When the first grey figures emerged from the fog no longer wearing helmets but flat muffin-type caps, the night picket had already been relieved and were on their way home. The day picket, 500 in number and armed with Miniés and knowing the ground well, might have been depended upon, if the example of Little Inkerman counted for anything, to have delayed the Russian advance till supports arrived. Unfortunately the Ordnance Department had anticipated nothing but fair-weather fighting. The British soldier, unlike the Russian, had been issued with no means of keeping the rain from running down barrels when arms were piled while the men slept. Until treated – a process which took time – the weapons were unusable. From a letter of Captain Elton to his father some idea of the preliminary picket fighting and its handicaps is obtained.

About an hour after we had been on picket duty we heard firing from our advanced pickets and soon after the word was passed to 'stand to our arms for the enemy were coming in force'. I was sent to support the advance and on trying the muskets to my horror I found that only about 15 out of the company would go off and out of these 15 only about six men would follow me to the front. However there was nothing to be done but push to the front and I soon joined the advance picket which I found in much the same state with regard to the arms as my own. We retired gradually before them as they were coming on in masses of columns supported by very powerful artillery and soon had most desperate work, almost hand to hand in the thick brushwood with the guns playing on us in a most fearful way, and ours answering them over our heads, while we were firing musketry into each other at between 15 and 30 paces distance, now and then charging and driving them back and then being driven back by superior numbers again.

Despite the heavy odds against them, losses were surprisingly light owing as much to poor Russian shooting as the skilful use of cover provided by brushwood and fog. Nonetheless the Russians had gained their first objective. Cleverly and with remarkable expedition they had got their 24- and 32-pounder guns in battery on the crest of Shell Hill whence having obtained on October 26th the range of the 2nd Division camp they were soon straddling it with shot and knocking out all guns on the right of the road. As Russell hurried to the front the sky over Inkerman reminded him of the 'play of lightning amid the thunder clouds as the evening closes on a sultry day'.

To the cries of 'Stand to arms' and the sounding of Assembly, as the first shots fell, the British army had sprung to life.

Few of those who were roused from their sleep [wrote Hamley], will cease to retain throughout life a vivid impression of the scene which followed. The alarm passed through the camps; there was mounting in hot haste of men scarce yet half awake, whose late dreams mixed with the stern reality of the summons to battle, many of whom hastening to the front, were killed before they knew well why they had been so hastily aroused. Breathless servants opened the tents to call their masters, scared grooms held the stirrup and staff officers galloping by called out that the Russians were attacking in force.

No time was lost in dressing because of a recent order that

all should sleep in their clothes. Within a few minutes the men of the 2nd Division had fallen in and were marching into the fog, heading for the firing and leaving the divisional camp empty save for stricken tents and disembowelled bat-horses.

Had De Lacy Evans not been thrown from his horse a few days earlier and been sent down to a ship at Balaclava to recover from the shaking, it is certain that he would have adopted the tactics so successfully employed at Little Inkerman; the pickets would have been gradually withdrawn and the second division with its artillery have awaited its enemies from behind the Home Ridge. Whether they would have succeeded when the Russians mounted not four field pieces but 100 powerful guns and attacked with not 5,000 but nearer 40,000 is doubtful. To have extended his division behind the Ridge and yet within range of the Russian artillery would have been to incur staggering losses. Pennefather, who had taken over command, had other ideas. The adoption of any Fabian-like measures was unpalatable to an Irishman whose maxim in war is said to have been, 'Whenever you see a head, hit it.' Wherever the Russians showed themselves, there, at the first possible moment, they must be fought. The pickets must be fed, not retired. The ground must be held and the enemy resisted with bullets while these lasted and when these failed with that 'queen of weapons', the bayonet. The Russians must be met as they came struggling breathless up the steep slopes, or down towards the saddle, in any case they had time to deploy their immense forces in the open.

There is no doubt that Pennefather's tactics were right in the circumstances. When about seven o'clock Raglan arrived he made no attempt to interfere with his audacious defence; and whatever his failings as a commander-in-chief he was no indifferent tactician. Yet how much easier would have been Pennefather's task had the two-gun battery been converted into a great strong point and some attempt made to close the Gap – the name given to those 700 yards between the Barrier and the Sand Bag Battery – with a line of fortified posts.

While Pennefather's surviving artillery began a hopeless

duel with the far heavier guns on Shell Hill, the infantry, in conformity with his plan, went over the Home Ridge and down into the swirling mists beyond. Only 500 men from the 95th and a hundred from the 55th were held back as reserves. As a corollary the division went forward not in regiments but strung out in groups of 300 or 400 men. With nothing to guide them save Russian yells, British cheers, the sound of musketry or an occasional flash seen through the gloom, they quickly lost touch with each other and some with all sense of direction. As a result within its first half-hour Inkerman developed those features which have made it singular among battles.

It was like this [said John Campbell of the 36th but lent to the 95th], you might find yourself with a party belonging to several regiments pursuing the Russians with joyous shouts, 'They're on the run, keep them going.' Presently you ran up against a stronger party, perhaps a formed-up body; it was now your turn to fall back, the Russians did not pursue very far, or hotly, being afraid of being trapped in the mist, but our party diminished, some found their own regiments, some dispersed to collect ammunition from the pouches of the killed and wounded, some wandered, a few might go to the rear, not many, for men were full of resolution. Presently you might come across another fellow with a party, or groups of men under non-commissioned officers, then you would all join up and have another go at the Russians and so it went on.

To Major Patullo of the 30th* it was simply a case of

Where the enemy was thickest there each soldier forced his way without regard to regiment and there he fought or fell, drove the enemy before him or was repulsed as fate and fortune ordained.

Henry Clifford's opinion is even more succinct: 'No order could be given owing to the fog. All we could do was to charge them when they came in sight.'

Alone or in little bunches men wandered or stumbled across the broken ground, moving like shadows amongst the

---

* Throughout the battle when any regiment is mentioned it is not meant to imply that the whole of it was engaged. Such was the confusion and the broken state of the ground that no regiment remained homogeneous for long.

stunted trees. On that 'raw, ugly, drizzling peep o' day to cool
our courage and damp our powder' a stout pair of lungs was
worth more than a sword to an officer or a rifle to a
sergeant.

To the left front went detachments from the 47th and 49th,
others from the 49th together with units from the 30th
advanced straight ahead, to the right Brigadier Adams led
the whole available strength of the 41st, numbering 500, with
orders to reinforce the picket in the Sand Bag battery and to
hold it. Although here was to take place the bloodiest fighting of the whole battle, it was for the moment quiet. The real
threat was coming on the British left.

While Soimonoff in accordance with the original plan was
awaiting Pauloff's arrival on Shell Hill he had sent out three
bodies to act like exploratory fingers, searching out the ground
to his right. The first either by accident or design wandered
down into and then up the Careening Ravine. Here after
its capture of the small British picket it pressed onwards and
finally turned South-east into the Wellway. Had it persevered
it would have emerged on to the Heights between the 2nd
Division and the Guards Brigade, creating a most dangerous
diversion. That it failed to do so was due to the Guards'
practice of stationing a small independent picket, remote from
their camp, on a spur of land between the Careening Ravine
and the Wellway. It was in charge that morning of Prince
Edward of Saxe-Weimar, who catching a glimpse of the
Russians coming up the gully lined his men along the edge and
began a smart enfilading fire. This surprised and sent the
Russians into retreat and for the rest of the day this dangerous
sector was free of incident.

Across the Wellway the other columns were faring not
much better and for this the fog was partly to blame. While
this enabled the Russians to mount their first attack and bring
up their artillery, once their surprise was spent the effects
were wholly injurious. The mist not only concealed from
them the scantiness of the British forces but imbued them with
an understandable misconception. More than half Soimonoff's
regiment had not yet met the British in battle and now seeing
a line of soldiers materializing through the fog and extending
right and left far beyond their own close-knit columns they

had no reason to suppose that this was not the front rank of a phalanx similar to their own only deeper because wider. Assuredly no other explanation can satisfactorily explain the astonishing events about to happen wherein (again to quote Hamley) 'the extravagant achievements of chivalry were almost outdone by the reality'.

The 47th had not gone far when through the gloom it came face to face with the centre of Soimonoff's three advance columns coming over the Southern edge of the Mikriakoff gully. They were uttering their 'regulation howls', having been excited by a generous issue of *raki* that morning. They outnumbered the 47th by at least three to one but the Loyal Regiment was strung out in line and its men effectively armed with Miniés. At 80 yards range their commander, Major Fordyce, ordered them to fire. The effect from such an extended line on a dense column was startling. The Russians stopped in their tracks and for a few moments made a brave show of replying with their antiquated muskets, but the rain of bullets with the penetrating power of the Minié was more than they could resist. Imagining that from its breadth a large force was ahead of them they turned and made off rapidly, pursued by the 47th to the edge of the gully. Here Fordyce prudently ordered his men to halt and lie down.

A short distance only to the right the 41st were having a similar encounter with the third column except that here the fog was so thick that Major Grant had only time to shout, 'Give 'em a volley and charge!' Again the Russian reaction was consistent with a belief that they were confronted by an overwhelmingly larger force. They too wheeled about and were followed by Grant's men alternately cheering and firing. Here, no gully intervening, the pursuit was maintained till the 41st were on the forward slope of Shell Hill within sound though not sight of Soimonoff's main body awaiting the command to advance.

Nettled, it is thought, by these minor reverses, Soimonoff hesitated no longer to launch his offensive without awaiting Pauloff's arrival, keeping back 9,000 in reserve. Even so the attacking force outnumbered by nearly two to one all that Raglan could spare for the defence of the Inkerman Heights. This, under increased artillery cover (more guns having been brought up), he now threw forward, moving in echelon from its right in order to allow Pauloff elbow room when he arrived on the left.

Before such an avalanche Grant and his men fell back, fighting stubbornly, though unaware of the fact that they had gained invaluable time. Already reinforcements were arriving. The first on the scene were four companies of the 88th. These, Pennefather (whose oaths could be heard streaming out into the foggy air above the crackle of musketry) at once ordered to the left where the fighting and cheering indicated exciting developments. As the 88th advanced they ran into what were probably some of Grant's men falling back. 'What's going on?' shouted Captain Browne. 'You'll soon find out. There are 6,000 on the brow of the hill.' The reply was an understatement, but the real figure of 9,000 would have made no difference to the men of the 88th, still smarting under their frustrating experiences on the Alma. Indeed to show how much they meant business they had already discarded their great-coats and shakoes. Having spread out in line they were descending in order to cross the Mikriakoff gully when from the other side emerged a great grey mass of Russians, their white, pudding-like faces looking ghostly in the half-light. Their onslaught split the Connaught Rangers in two. The right half fell back about 150 yards, beyond which the enemy perhaps suspecting a trap ceased to pursue them. The left on the other hand at once counter-attacked and charging and cheering drove the Russians not only down the gully but up a spur of the West Jut at right angles to its mouth. Near the top ran a five-foot stone wall and behind it to recover their wind the men halted and took cover. On the other side could be seen a large number of columns, which formed in fact part of Soimonoff's reserves. Though any advance in such circumstances would be suicidal 18 excited Rangers scrambled over the wall and rushed further up the slope where next day their bodies were found perforated with bayonet wounds. Others might have followed their example had not a bugle from the rear sounded retreat. The survivors fell back followed by the Russians and on regaining the plateau found themselves in front of three guns of Townshend's battery which had come up from the 4th Division. There were no horses and no limbers and when the Russians came over the edge with the Rangers in front firing became impossible. In the circumstances the guns were abandoned but not without a struggle which, in a battle memorable for individual exploits, is outstanding. Lieutenant Miller, ordering his men to draw their swords and those without them to use their rammers, sponge staves or even bare fists, flung himself on the Russians. He and his men failed to stop their advance but the fury and grandeur of their fight seems to have either cowed or so staggered the enemy that they pressed on without attempting to resist and Miller lived to receive the Victoria Cross.

At such moments of achievement, whether it was the taking of a gun, a trench or a height, resolution and initiative seemed fatally to drain away from the Russians. Having captured the guns with loud cries of joy they came to a standstill. Whether they feared to advance farther into the fog, whether they felt the need for reinforcement, is not clear, but their hesitation saved the 88th. A short distance behind the abandoned guns the left was joined by the right, and, their ammunition being exhausted, they lay down. When Major Maxwell their commander had hurried back to Pennefather pleading for reinforcements or at least ammunition, the latter replied that he knew not where to put his hand for a man or a cartridge. The 88th 'must stand their ground, giving the Russians the bayonet or be driven into the sea'. Returning from this discouraging interview he ran into Canrobert, who was hastening up from the French Headquarters, and to him he repeated his tale of woe. It is clear from his reply that the Frenchman must have previously studied the terrain. '*N'importe,*' he said, '*retournez, deployez en ligne . . . fixez les bayonettes . . . faites une apparence.*' Accompanying Maxwell to where the 88th were lying he added knowingly, '*C'est une position très importante . . . Il faut faire une apparence.*' It would be enough simply to raise their bayonets above the brushwood to show the Russians that this dangerous approach to the British rear was guarded. The 88th acted on his advice and the ruse worked.

The 77th, the next regiment of the Light Division to arrive, had been directed by Pennefather to the extreme left of the Heights directly abutting the Wellway. It consisted of 259 men under Colonel Egerton, the tallest officer in the army, and was accompanied by their Brigade commander, Buller, and his ADC Henry Clifford. In addition it had gathered up a number of fragments from various regiments lost in the fog and eager to get into the fighting line. All were moving in the direction of the firing when out of the fog, especially dense at the moment, the Russians showed up suddenly in great force only 15 yards away. Clifford, who was riding next to Buller, thus describes the events of the next few minutes which were to win him the Victoria Cross:

It was a moment or two before I could make General Buller believe they were Russians. 'In God's name,' I said, 'fix bayonets and charge.' He gave the order and in another moment we were hand to hand with them. Our line was not long enough to prevent the Russians outflanking our left which was unperceived by the 77th who rushed on with the exception of about a dozen who, struck by the force on our left and who saw me taking out my revolver, halted with me. 'Come on,' I said, 'my lads', and the brave fellows dashed in amongst the astonished Russians bayoneting them in every direction.

Of his little band only he and two others were not killed or wounded.

With friend and foe striking out blindly in the fog, lurching through the brushwood, stumbling over the boulders, with pickets falling back here, advancing there, with men of different regiments merging together, fighting under the command of any officer whom they could see or hear, the confusion of the next half-hour of this part of the battleground makes it impossible to give any kind of coherent account. Even those who fought, and theirs is necessarily the sole first-hand testimony, have knowledge only of what occurred on a very narrow frontage, which because of the fog was sometimes no more than ten yards in width and depth.

According to the regimental records the main body of the 77th got Egerton's order to 'Give them a volley on the knee and load' when the Russians were hardly five yards away. At this distance the Minié bullets aimed with great coolness and precision tore into the right column, passed through several bodies and created a great wall of dead and wounded in the path of the Russians. Having paused to reload, as if on parade, the men followed up with a charge. Though badly shaken the Russians resisted courageously, even daring to cross bayonets, but before the fury of the 77th – one of the most highly trained in the army – resistance crumbled.

The mass began to waver and reel; their muskets went up in the air and they fairly turned and fled, impeded in their flight by the rear divisions of their own columns. Then a terrible scene of slaughter took place, our men plied them fiercely with fire and steel and driving them through the oak copses in our front sent the broken remains headlong down a small ravine [probably the Mikriakoff] about 450 yards from where the fight commenced.

Like Grant's men before, the 77th still pressed on, picking up small parcels of men from the 30th and other regiments till they too reached the skirts of Shell Hill. Here Egerton coolly halted his men and dressed them by the centre, brushed off a feeble Russian attack and remained in this advanced position till the close of the battle.

The Russians who had given ground before Egerton's men infected those to their left facing the 88th. They too retreated, even giving up possession of the three captured guns. The 88th, whose Quartermaster, a veteran of the Afghan War, had opportunely arrived leading bat-ponies loaded with ammunition, were able to follow them up, overrun the guns in front of which they halted, lay down, set their sights at 800 yards and for the rest of the battle continued to fire away whenever they saw a puff of smoke.

The crisis on the British left was over – the bold conduct of scarcely more than 1,200 had halted and thrown back at least three times their number at remarkably little cost. There the Russians had achieved nothing – their only success, the capture of three guns, being short-lived. But in the centre and on the right the battle had only just begun and many hours of desperate fighting lay in front.

Soimonoff's main body spreading like lava across the saddle were approaching the Home Ridge with its pitifully inadequate garrison and with half its guns silenced. Yet this great host might have been arrested far down the slope – for the nature of the ground favoured defence – but for the inexcusable failure of ammunition without which the finest rifle becomes a mere cudgel. Seven miles away in Balaclava there was all the ammunition the army could have wanted, but no one had made it his business to see that it had been brought up where likely to be needed. To attempt 'to feed the pickets' without feeding their pouches was useless. Furious and sullen, Patullo's detachment of the 30th and others fell back, despite Pennefather's insistence that no ground should be yielded. Luckily behind them on the Home Ridge three guns of Turner's battery had just arrived and having taken up a position to the west of the road were well placed to deal with the advancing Russians. Two rounds of canister went through their tightly-packed mass like the sweep of a great broom. Rank after rank collapsed; the remainder after brief hesitation turned and melted into the mist of the saddleback. With a great cheer the British rallied, leapt to their feet and joined by those behind the ridge went in pursuit, not pausing till they had driven back to Shell Hill a number reckoned to be ten times their own. Once again excellent timing, initiative, resolution, and perhaps a touch of deception had led to the rout of greatly superior forces. Yet the deception was not all one-sided. As these same Russians fell back they skirted the right flank of the 77th established as we have seen near the base of Shell Hill, but in their grey coats they were mistaken for British and were permitted to slip by without interference.

No sooner had this attack been repulsed than another developed farther along the Ridge at the angle where it turned north. It was here, directly in the line of fire from Russian artillery, that the British guns had been knocked out and the only possibility of resistance came from a small force of 183 men of the 49th under the command of Captain William Bellairs. As the Russians emerged from the fog, driving before them the cartridgeless pickets, a threat developed as grave as any so far in the battle. One breach in the British defences at this point and Soimonoff's left wing followed by Pauloff's right might come surging through the gap, isolating and then sweeping away the entire right flank. It was a crisis which called for the highest degree of aggressive courage and rapid thinking. As Bellairs saw it, to advance firing against such an attacking force would be to advance too slowly. There was only one answer – the bayonet. At no more than 80 yards from the Russians he cried out, 'Fix bayonets – charge!' His men responded with a heartening cheer. It was the Kolivansk regiment who faced them, as brave as any in the Russian army, but this murderous cordon of glittering steel descending upon them, the first they supposed no doubt of many more in the background, was more than their nerves could endure. They wheeled round and fled through the brushwood.

With this rout the attack by Soimonoff's army dissolved and for other reasons than its discomfiture. The first was the death of Soimonoff himself in an attempt (it is believed) to repel Egerton's attack; the second, its shattering loss of officers. Thenceforward the initiative lay for Dannenberg with the still-uncommitted army of Pauloff. Pauloff's troops having farther to travel were a little late in reaching the Heights. The van comprised the Borodino and Tarantine regiments who had already encountered the British at the Alma and could have no illusion about their line or the effectiveness of their Miniés. But they were better troops than Soimonoff's and were to put up a stouter fight. They advanced on three fronts up the Volovia, Quarry and St Clements Ravines.

Between the Barrier athwart the post road and the Sand Bag Battery (concealed one from the other by the spur of the Fore Ridge) lay the gap with its 700 yards of undefended ground. Towards this the Borodino regiment moved with the Tarantine on its left. To support the picket based on the Barrier Pennefather had directed two bodies of 200 men each from the 30th, the first under Major Patullo, the second under their Colonel, Mauleverer. The first, as has been said, soon used up their ammunition and had to fall back, but the second beat the Russians in a race for the Barrier by a small margin. They had just reached its low wall when their densely-packed columns came flooding on to the plateau from the Quarry and St Clements Ravines. Once more there was the same disparity of numbers, but again the same British advantage in extended line over cumbrous slow-moving columns, and disadvantage in rain-soaked Miniés. But Mauleverer was a man as audacious as he was agile (to the end of his service he could vault over a billiard table in the mess). He first caused his men to lie down and next when the Russians – they were two battalions of the Borodino Regiment – were unsuspectingly within a few yards he leapt to his feet, drew his sword and calling on his men to follow, flung himself forward. Once more the speed, the fury and the surprise of this valorous attack by the few against the many (the many being out of breath from their climb and impeded by their ankle-length greatcoats) triumphed. After a brief hand-to-hand encounter, bayonets crossing bayonets, the front Borodino ranks reeled back on those behind, who in turn spread confusion in the rear. In a few moments the two battalions were in retreat, some cascading back down the ravine, others making for Shell Hill on their right and the protection of their guns.

Elsewhere in this sector the position was not so satisfactory. Before Adams could reach it the Sand Bag Battery weakly held by a seven-man picket was overrun by the Tarantine Regiment and for the first of many times passed into Russian hands. Elation at their success, the capture they believed of one of the main features of the British defences, immobilized the Russians as always. They had made no effort to exploit the gain when the 41st, reinforced by Bellairs and his men fresh from their triumph, came over the Fore Ridge and descended on the Kitspur. Spread out in line Adams's men sent volley after volley into the Russians thickly clustered about the battery and followed up with a bayonet charge. This, for a time, swept the enemy off the Kitspur and restored the battery to the British.

Thus far – it may have been about seven o'clock – the Russians had little to show for more than an hour's fighting. Their infantry had not only failed to penetrate the enemy's defences but they had everywhere been repulsed. Their capture of the Sand Bag Battery had been as transient as that of the three guns on the opposite flank. Furthermore the surprise of their attack had worn off and they could reckon on British if not French reinforcements being soon in the field. Against this, however, the fog was lifting, revealing to their men the flimsiness of the defence against 20,000 fresh troops still disposable by Dannenberg. Indeed Adams had hardly got his own men back to the Battery after their pursuit of the Russians than the 'flat-caps' were once more breasting the Heights.

Neither courage nor the penetrating power of a Minié bullet could prevail against such numbers. It seemed to one soldier like firing into a vast grey woolpack and about as useless. A banquette might have done something to help. Without it the battery was becoming a trap every minute more deadly as the Russians began working round the flanks. Once more it was ceded, the 41st making a fighting withdrawal and suffering grievous losses. It was now that Adams, a huge man and a magnificent inspiration to all as he rode up and down on his charger, was mortally wounded; and four young officers in exasperation broke from the ranks and flung themselves to death on the advancing Russians.

At the other end of the Gap there, too, had come a sudden deterioration due to the same cause. Weight of numbers had forced Mauleverer and his men out of the Barrier. The entire British right flank lay open and defenceless to an attack which luckily never came. For once more on the heels of success came that curious lethargy compounded of joy and bewilderment. As always the lull was to the British advantage, bringing with it a precious gain in time. The 500 men of the 95th, held back as reserves, were on the march. The Guards were on the skyline.

When Gortschakoff's army announced its presence on and around the Fedioukine Hills by opening a long-distance bombardment, both Bosquet and the Duke of Cambridge had been put in a quandary. If the Russians meant business they considered they could not quit their station on the Sapouné Heights whatever was happening elsewhere; yet from the sounds coming in the Inkerman direction it was evident to the Duke that it was not the usual case of 'sentries at their old game, blazing at Will o' Wisp'. Hesitation was in consequence inevitable before he felt he might gamble on Gortschakoff's making a feint and dispatch his brigades to the help of the 2nd Division. The first to move were the Grenadiers. They bore their colours – the only Guards regiment to do so that morning – and advanced in line. They were followed at a short distance by the Scots Fusilier Guards and at a very much longer interval by the Coldstream, half of whose men had only just come in from picket duty. Progress through the thick undergrowth was slow and when the Home Ridge was reached it was seen that the 41st were in retreat and the Sand Bag Battery was in Russian hands. 'You must drive them out of it', was all the Duke felt it was necessary to tell Bentinck.

As the Grenadiers went down the slopes towards the battery, they presented as noble a sight as the Highland Brigade at the Alma, their bearskins moving like some continuous black ribbon above the waist-high undergrowth. Those whose rifles were serviceable fired, those whose were not cheered. At their side went the men of the 95th. At about 30 yards from the Battery the order was given to charge. The Russians stayed only to pour 'one murderous volley into us and then scuttled out at the opening on the other side'. They were pursued to the edge of the ravine on which the Grenadiers were halted by the stern commands of the Duke; but the 95th, not subject to his control and led by a giant Irish lance-corporal shouting, 'We're driving them, sir, we're driving them', carried the pursuit far down the slopes from which not all succeeded in climbing back.

On returning to the Battery the Grenadiers adopted a blunted arrowhead formation, one company occupying the redoubt, the others ranged back on either side. A brief lull which ensued enabled them to dry out their Miniés and the Scots Fusilier Guards to draw level. In accordance with orders they were moving to align themselves on the left of the Grenadiers when to their left they saw Russians appearing out of the Quarry Ravine. They were about to charge when the Duke, never at his best in a crisis, furiously ordered them to obey his instructions. Luckily the more level-headed Bentinck saw the danger of the threat and countermanded the Duke's orders. The Russians, who by this time were on the plateau in force, had already seen something of the terrible bearskins at the Alma and what they had seen they had not liked. On receiving a volley at close range, they halted, hesitated and then tumbled back into the ravine before a long line of levelled bayonets. The Scotsmen had hardly disappeared over the edge in pursuit when a further imperious command from the Duke brought them back. In stopping his men from hunting the Russians down into the scrub of the ravines and so from forfeiting the advantage of position the Duke of Cambridge was right up to a point. On the other hand these tactics created a wide area beyond the rim to which the enemy could retreat with safety and where unmolested they could rally their men; and this safety zone began only 100 yards from the right front of the Battery and only 150 from where on the left the St Clements Ravine started. In the fighting of the next two hours as often as the Russians were ejected from the Battery and the Kitspur they were soon back again, having reformed out of sight, and were driving the Guards out by overpowering numbers.

Through the thick mist the yells came loud and long and rushing with a dash and spirit for which we had not given them credit, the enemy threw themselves headlong upon the battery.

After about three minutes to give the men breathing time we charged again but they were too many for us and would not move. Three of us got under the parapet and there they were with the muzzles of their guns close to our heads, but could not depress them sufficiently to shoot us and the moment their heads came over the top we had either a revolver or a sword to receive them with. They then heaved huge stones over upon us.

These two extracts, the first from the report of the *Morning Herald* correspondent, the second from Alfred Tipping, would serve for any one of the numerous attacks and counter-attacks which ensued. It was for the Brigade of Guards their finest hour. 'Never allow anyone to abuse or run down the Guards in your presence [wrote a Highland officer]. They are the finest bravest fellows that ever carried a musket. They fought that day like men fighting for their own firesides.' It was a style of fighting in which they had been particularly drilled. While the Russians had been taught to bring the bayonet down, the Guards had been trained to hold it high in a manner which served them better in close combat. Nor, unlike them, did the Russians ever charge; they came on slowly as they had done at the Alma in their ponderous, unwieldly formations, presenting to agile, aggressive troops an easy, almost static target. Moreover, brave though the Russians were, all who fought against them that day agree in one particular – they never liked the bayonet.

To tell how friend and foe fought would be to repeat the same heroic story over and over again, of a battle line oscillating backwards and forwards as Guardsmen drove the Russians to the lip of the Kitspur only to be thrown back by those columns forever forcing their way up the ravines, of bayonets crossing bayonets, of mounting carnage. Enough that it is the tale of men battling on one side with a determination not to give way and with a discipline second to none, on the other with a fury, fanaticism and confidence enflamed the first by drink, the second by priestly exhortation, the third by consciousness of numerical superiority. Enough to tell of Guardsmen firing while they were able and when ammunition failed ransacking the pouches of the dead and dying or using their rifles as clubs or even hurling them, bayonets first, like spears or in the last resource using their fists and boots, clods of earth and stones; of Russians forcing their way into the twin embrasures until these were choked with bodies, or leaping to certain death on a carpet of bayonets below; of men grappling with each other in the undergrowth and dying in the agony of a throttle, a fractured skull or a bayonet thrust. Finally it is enough to speak of a pandemonium compounded of the raucous shouts of the officers, the cheers of the men, the howls of the Russians, the oaths and the groans, the crashing of artillery and over all the 'song of the bullets' likened by one who fought that day to 'the buzzing of innumerable insects.'

And all the while the level of the floor of the Battery slowly rose till at last a banquette was created out of British and Russian dead lying like sand bags one upon another. In sheer carnage only the blood-soaked hill of Albuera can offer comparison with the Sand Bag Battery on the Heights of Inkerman.

Shortly after the Grenadiers had for the first time reoccupied the Battery and had repulsed at least one counter-attack its uselessness for defence became patent and its abandonment was ordered. But as the Russians moved in with cries of triumph the Scots Fusilier Guards were just returning on the left from another successful charge to the verge of the ravine. To them the sight of a jubilant enemy in a British redoubt was unbearable. Moved by a common impulse they charged the Battery in the flank and drove out the Russians, only themselves to be ejected by a powerful counterthrust. Being even more useless to an attacker, the Battery might now well have been left in Russian hands, had not the Coldstream Guards, 400 strong, appeared at last over the ridge to the accompaniment of cheers. Now between the three Guards regiments there existed wholesome rivalry. Thinking that the Coldstream must immediately attack, the Grenadiers determined that they alone should have the honour of ejecting the Russians and this they did by another furious assault. The Coldstream thereupon aligned themselves to the right of the Grenadiers, facing the valley below.

The fight for the Sand Bag Battery continued. Right and left, as the enemy surged up from the valley or funnelled their way on to the Heights through the Quarry or St Clements Ravines, came the attacks. The defenders took turns to load so as to keep up a continuous fire and even crossed from one side to the other as the occasion required. But with each attack losses were increasing; soon every mounted officer had had his horse killed and was fighting on foot. Though the Miniés were exacting a deadly toll of the Russians, especially of their officers always prominent in advance of their regiment as they waved their swords and encouraged their men, the Russians with their vast reserves could afford their losses. The British could not. Of 1,300 Guardsmen who had set out that morning there were now scarcely more than 700 left and every minute that number was being reduced. As with the Light Division at the Alma, so for them was no relief in sight. 'We were totally unsupported [complained an officer] and put to do what no troops in the world but English would have attempted.'

It need not have been so. The nearest relief should have come from the French troops just beyond the Guards. When the latter had marched off towards Inkerman a message had been sent to Bosquet requesting him to move into the stations thus vacated. Bosquet taking according to Hamley 'too exclusively a French view' and still uncertain regarding Gortschakoff's intentions sent the evasive reply *on verra*. Soon afterwards, however, convinced that the Russians below were staging a feint, he ordered the 6ème de Ligne and 7ème Léger regiments, four companies of the Foot Chasseurs and two batteries to follow him and rode hurriedly off towards the fighting. Somewhere short of the Home Ridge he ran into Sir

George Brown and Sir George Cathcart – the latter well in advance of his division. A more ill-fated meeting was hardly possible. In the breasts of these two veterans of the Peninsular War a Gallophobic spirit still smouldered. When Bosquet offered his help, they regarded as insupportable the idea of British troops being beholden to Frenchmen for succour. Politely but coolly he was told that the reserves on their way up were sufficient to deal with all eventualities. If Bosquet would be so good as to continue to protect the British right that was all that was needed of him. How many lives this foolish answer (which Kinglake foolishly admires without actually approving), made without any knowledge of what was happening ahead, must have cost cannot be estimated. Bosquet turned back to the Sapounè Ridge, but uneasy in mind kept the two regiments ready to move at the shortest notice. He had not long to wait. Soon after reaching the Home Ridge and seeing the task confronting his brigade, the Duke of Cambridge dispatched his Assistant Adjutant-General Colonel Brownrigg back to Bosquet to press this time for immediate support. Brownrigg's arrival coincided with that of Colonel Steele, sent on a similar errand by Raglan himself. 'Ah, I knew it,' exclaimed Bosquet without a trace of pique and instantly ordered the two regiments to the front as well as the two batteries of artillery.

Meanwhile the Duke at his wits' end had gone back in person to 'drag up troops'. As he crossed the Ridge he met the newly-arrived 4th Division. Cathcart had not long received his orders from Pennefather. They were characteristic. In reply to his question where the 4th were required, the reply had been, 'Everywhere.' And everywhere his division had gone, shedding itself piecemeal as it made its way across the Heights. One of these sheddings had been 160 men of the 20th under Major Crofton whom the Duke's ADC had run up against and ordered to the right of the hard-pressed Guards. It was not nearly enough and when the Duke met Cathcart he begged him to send what remained of his division – about 600 men – to his assistance. But Cathcart who by this time had some notion of how the battle was going had other ideas. He had commanded a British army recently in the Kaffir war and no doubt thought he knew better how to employ what men remained to him. This was to make what he felt must be a decisive flank attack on an enemy already shaken by repeated rebuffs. He would descend into the valley of the Tchernaya and work round behind the Russian left. While the Duke and Cathcart argued, Airey arrived from Raglan (who had seen the plight of the Guards) with orders that they be supported. This only made Cathcart the more resolved. He ignored Airey's veto and sent his men led by Brigadier Torrens over the edge and down into the valley, he himself following on horseback. In other words he ordered his men – they were drawn from the 20th, 46th, and 68th – to do what the Duke and others had been at pains to prevent theirs from doing, to abandon the advantages of the high ground for the hazards of the valley.

The men having already been made to jettison their great-coats the more easily to manoeuvre through the brushwood, spread out in extended order once they were on the slopes and swung round to the north. Like the rest of the 4th Division they had not yet been issued with Miniés and were still armed with the old Brown Bess, as much use, said one of them, 'as a broomstick'. Soon they were in difficulties owing to the very heavy going and Torrens fell mortally wounded. Never-theless, with Cathcart prominent upon his horse in the rear encouraging them, they pressed on. 'We killed numbers of Russians [wrote an officer] and as we had no orders to halt we continued keeping along the hillside about halfway down.' Suddenly they realized they were under enfilading fire from the heights to their left and left rear. At first to their fury they believed the firing was from their own men but very soon came the horrible realization that there was no mistake. The Russians were where only a few minutes before the Guards had been. To understand how this came about it is necessary to return to the fighting around the Battery.

To the Guardsmen nothing had been more irksome than the order preventing them from pursuing the enemy over the edge and so allowing them to rally in the dead ground below. Now when they saw and heard Cathcart's men actually down along the slopes nothing could restrain them. Having hurled back one more Russian attack, they poured over the side, shout-ing, cheering, firing, bayoneting. With them went the detachment of the 20th and the 95th, the last as uncontrollable as ever, the only concern in every man's mind being who should get first to Sebastopol, which, mistaking in the mist the quarry workings for walls and houses, they ignorantly imagined lay straight ahead.

It was plain [wrote a Scots Guards officer] that unless the hunters were quickly halted, they hastened to destruction. Therefore shouting, 'Halt, halt', I ran after them. As well might a penny trumpet strive to make its puny voice heard amidst the crash of Costa's orchestra, as my small voice in the mortal uproar. Down the steep we went ... we reached the valley in disorder.

It was what Kinglake, always felicitous in his nomenclature, has called The False Victory. And it brought unrelieved disaster to all.

By shouting themselves hoarse, the officers within the curtilage of the Battery had restrained about 200 men grouped round the colours. Everywhere else, except at the Barrier, the British right was open and destitute of defence, offering an invitation which Dannenberg was quick to seize. Moving strongly up the Quarry Ravine his men, two regiments strong, poured through the Gap and swerved to the left, one, the Okhotsk, more sharply in order to isolate the Battery from the Kitspur, the other, the Jakhutsk, with a scythe-like motion, to sever its garrison from the Home Ridge. It was this regiment which reached the edge of the plateau and started firing down on the conspicuous redcoats below. When Cathcart realized that instead of taking the Russians in the flank his men were themselves being enfiladed and were at a hopeless disadvantage, he exclaimed, 'I fear we are in a mess,' and turning to Dallas of the 46th added, 'We must try the bayonet.' A moment later he fell dead with a bullet in the heart.

The situation of Cathcart's men was now desperate. They were out of breath and out of ammunition; they were being attacked not only from above but, as they halted in dismay, all round them in the undergrowth Russian sharpshooters were springing up. Dallas tried 'to boil up a little charge', but at point-blank range the Russian fire was impassable. It was no longer a question of turning the Russian right but of getting back to the plateau. Led by Dallas, Windham, and other enterprising officers, the men in small groups crouching and threading their way through the scrub made their way back along the face of the hill and finally emerged on the top well in the rear at surprisingly little cost notwithstanding the added fire from Gortschakoff's men across the valley. The Guards found equally cool and resourceful leaders in Captains Percy and Cadogan who led them in Indian file up a bridle path to safety.

How anyone came out of this headlong adventure alive has been likened by a survivor to 'the greatest miracle in the world'. It had been Cathcart's second blunder of the day, but it was an honourable blunder in keeping with one at whose death it was said 'fell all the dash of the army'.

While these events were happening on the slopes below, around the Sand Bag Battery above there was taking place another dramatic episode in the battle. Cut off front and rear by Russians outnumbering them at least ten to one, the little band of about 200 Guardsmen still clustering around the colours of the Grenadiers had fired very nearly their last round. One account speaks of the Russians at no more than 30 yards away to the front and even less to their rear. Nothing, it seemed, could prevent their being overwhelmed and taken. And indeed so they must have been had the enemy followed up their success. But again there was that strange hesitation, that semi-bewilderment, and in it the Guards found their salvation. Splitting, probably unintentionally, into two bodies, one with bayonets fixed and colours held in their midst by Verschoyle and Turner for all to see and rally round set out on its 700-yard journey back to the comparative safety of the Home Ridge. On their left the steep fall into the valley made it difficult for the intervening Russians to outflank them on that side, but on the other they were massed in strength. Now followed an incident curiously reminiscent of the 4th Light Dragoons at Balaclava, except that it was on foot. There the Russian Lancers, here their infantry, seemed too astonished at British daring or too slow-witted to react with any agility. The Guards, like the Dragoons, went past, or rather 'scraped past', so close to the semi-inert Russians that it was possible to smell the peculiarly strong leather-like odour which was always perceptible in their presence.

The second and smaller party, consisting largely of Coldstream men with a few from the 20th and 47th, losing their sense of direction in the mist, very much thickened here by battle smoke, inclined too much to their right and were moving up the slopes of the Fore Ridge when out of the murk at no more than 30 yards' distance appeared a very tight line of Russian skirmishers firing rapidly and completely cutting off further retreat. The crisis, as so often happened at Inkerman, produced the man. There was no Coldstream officer present (most of whom were dead or wounded), indeed no officer at all save a young surgeon named Wolseley. With the courage and promptitude that no professional soldier could have surpassed he immediately yelled, 'Fix bayonets – charge and keep up the hill.' The weary men responded. They threw themselves forward in a wild charge against a body at least twenty times their size. Again the thick-skulled Muscovite appeared dazed by the audacity of his foe. Wolseley and his gallant band came out on the other side, though with heavy losses.

Further to the front Captain Burnaby of the Grenadiers was performing similar prodigies of valour of the true Inkerman type. He had been amongst those who stormed down into the valley and had made the perilous return directly back to the Kitspur. In company with a score of stragglers who had attached themselves to his command, he reached the now-deserted Battery just ahead of the Okhotsk Regiment which was pressing on in order to take the retreating colour-party in the rear. He thus found his little band converted into a rear-guard who could do no more than delay for a very short time the enemy's progress. Gathering his men together he led them at the charge into the Russian column. Only for a moment was it halted by this pin-prick before it resumed its forward drive, leaving in its wake Burnaby and seven men wounded, but that brief halt may have helped to save the colours.

With this retreat of the Guards the position on the British extreme right was nearing collapse. It was not simply that the defenders were reduced from 1,300 to 200 and like everyone were running out of ammunition. Least of all was it that the useless battery was being abandoned. It was that the men were utterly worn out. They had eaten nothing since a sparse supper the night before, and had been fighting desperately for three hours. Nor were there any unexhausted British reserves in sight or to come. The full magnitude of Cathcart's rashness was now apparent. His force which at this moment might have been of incalculable worth was now dead or scattered.

It is not to disparage the heroic fight put up by the British troops during those gruelling hours since dawn to say (as many did who were present) that but for the arrival of the French they would have fought in vain. Yet it was not an honour of which France could be exactly proud. The 6ème de Ligne, advancing on the right of the 7ème Léger, halted when it came under fire, and having no artillery cover declined to go on without orders from a higher source than its Colonel's, de Camas. While the Guards were fighting savagely round the Sand Bag Battery the French half a mile away were squandering precious minutes insensible to the pleas of their officers or the taunts of the British. Not till the arrival of General Bourkabi did they consent to go forward and then it is fair to say they went bravely down the slope at the *pas de charge,* took the Russians in the flank and drove them not only out of the Battery but clean off the Kitspur. By their dash and timely aid they instantly purged themselves in English eyes. 'When I saw them come up [wrote a private] I thought I was seeing my father and mother.'

The Russians had other views. 'The French are saving the English at Inkerman as the Prussians did at Waterloo.' In that bitter outburst by a general is betrayed the depth of Russian chagrin as they heard the shrill notes of the French bugles. The moral effect of the arrival of a new enemy fresh and eager for battle was crippling on men who had fought for hours and at last believed that victory was at hand.

Still, it was premature to speak of saving the English. The Russians who had so lately driven the Guards out of the Battery had been the left wing of a massive force moving against the centre, where the defence was no less inadequate. Beyond a few groups, and some artillery strung out behind Herbert's Folly, there was, as a consequence of Pennefather's policy, nothing. The 4th Division reinforcements had come and had been dispersed; the more distant 3rd had few to spare from the task of protecting the British lines before Sebastopol. There were no others. Indeed, a stranger approaching from the south, if sufficiently deaf not to hear the sound of firing, might never have suspected a battle was in progress a few hundred yards ahead. He would have seen Raglan calm in the midst of a cock-hatted group near the post road, some staff officers riding (but, in obedience to what might be called Raglan's standing orders, never galloping) on various duties or coolly reading their mail from England which an orderly was busily delivering. Except for these and what Kinglake has called 'the spent force', that is a desultory stream of men coming over the crest and out of the battle, either wounded, supporting the wounded, or in search of ammunition, there were few signs of activity and none of the reinforcements. Once Pauloff had breached the Home Ridge there was nothing to prevent him stretching out to the empty Guards camp, spreading confusion far and wide, and above all giving Gortschakoff in the valley below the signal which would convert his feint into a real attack.

The first British troops of the centre to meet the Russian onslaught (in which enemy superiority was never less than five to one) were two detachments which Cathcart had shed in his march to the right flank. They were taken from the 63rd under Colonel Swyny and the right wing of the 21st under Ainslie: 600 men in all posted upon the extreme west of the Home Ridge. As the enemy emerged from the brushwood Pennefather had roared out, 'Let's see what mettle the 63rd are made of.' The answer was a volley, a cheer and a charge. Joined by the 21st they pushed the enemy down the slope and their ensign crying, 'Come on, 63rd', carried on the pursuit till they came under fire from the guns of Shell Hill. 'We routed thousands', reported a private with pardonable exaggeration, 'as fast as we could run and load our pieces so fast they fell, for we could not miss them, they were so thick. We chased them for the best part of a mile.' They were then halted and made to lie down facing north-east.

Further along the Ridge to the right the Russians pressed on with such determination that, assisted by the fog still hugging the Saddleback, they were almost on the crest before being detected. Alone in their path stood 200 men of the 57th, another of Cathcart's sheddings. Forty-three years earlier the regiment had rallied at Albuera to their colonel's cry, '57th, die hard'. This day, in the circumstances no less critical and when some showed signs of wavering, Captain Stanley's voice rang out, 'Men, remember Albuera!' The word had lost none of its magic. Once again the Middlesex men charged, this time driving ten times their number clean off the Saddleback and down into the Quarry Ravine. Just to the right of the 57th, the 30th under Mauleverer, whom we left making a fighting retreat from the Barrier, had reached the Home Ridge under cover of which they sank to the ground so exhausted that despite the din and danger many fell into instant sleep. It was perhaps this overpowering weariness which dulled sense and caused their officers to mistake the grey coats of the Russians emerging from the mist for British. At least it was not until the enemy were close upon them that they were recognized. In a second every man was on his feet and then it was a repetition of the Inkerman story. A small phalanx of determined men flung themselves against a tightly-packed column and by force of their impact drove it back in confusion. It was the same thing with Colonel Horsford and 140 men of the Rifle Brigade, newly arrived and tossed into the fight by Pennefather. A couple of minutes of concentrated fire from the terrible 'Green Flies' and the Russians were in retreat down the Quarry Ravine, their wounded, filled with tales of British brutality, pleading for mercy on bended knees.

Still further to the right 180 men of the 20th led by Colonel Horn did not even choose to await the arrival of the Russians. Instead they marched defiantly in line down from the crest into the Saddle, and as they marched they fired; but because their rifles, like all belonging to the 4th Division, were the old smoothbore musket they had not the same lethal effect as the Miniés. The Russians flinched yet continued to advance, sending out two claws to envelop the British flanks. But if their firepower was weak the 20th enjoyed a secret weapon – the Minden yell, a fearful, almost unearthly cry handed down over the generations. It came now, as with lowered muskets and fixed bayonets, they tore into the ranks of the startled, deafened Russians, drove them out of the Barrier for good and sent them, too, scurrying down the Quarry Ravine in disorder. Then, as was invariably the case, ammunition ran out and men endeavoured to carry on by taking cartridges from the dead who by this time 'lay as thick as sheaves in a rich cornfield'.

On the extreme right the enemy had had a slight success. They had ejected the French from the Sand Bag Battery but were prevented from occupying it through the daring conduct of Boussinière, who despite the killing fire from Shell Hill, advanced his 12 guns along the Fore Ridge from which he commanded the Kitspur. This action converted for a time the Battery and its surrounds into a no-man's-land.

It was now approximately half past ten. The fighting had been in progress for four and a half hours. No penetration of the British defences had been made. The Barrier, temporarily lost, had been retaken and was to remain to the end of the battle a stumbling block in the Russian path. Altogether along the whole line it had been a magnificent defensive action, fought against consistently heavy odds and subject to a gruelling and continuous artillery fire against which our own guns could make no effective reply. Every time the swifter reactions and readier enterprise of the British infantry had triumphed over the stolid, brave, but sluggish Russians. Yet a greater test was still to come.

From his position on Shell Hill Dannenberg was at last ready to launch his massive concentrated attack on the Home Ridge, now visible to him in all its weakness. He had by this time over 100 guns in battery, all more powerful than any the allies had so far mounted. He had at his disposal 10,000 troops with 6,000 in reserve. Timovieff was just about to mount his strong diversionary assault on the French left and so pin down their army directly facing Sebastopol. Gortschakoff, he now hoped, would make something more than a feint and so immobilize the bulk of Bosquet's Army of Observation. Sporadic threats at any moment by the Sebastopol garrison must spread alarm in the British Right and Left Attacks and prevent the sending of supports. To meet this renewed offensive from Dannenberg what had Raglan to put forward? He had 3,000 or so men, scattered in numerous groups, all of them fighting on empty stomachs, many of them

battle-weary and near breaking-point. In addition he had perhaps about three dozen light guns. Two French regiments,
some Chasseurs and Boussinière's two batteries, had indeed
arrived, but this was all that was available to meet a threat
which might extend over a mile in breadth, and if successful
must bring Gortschakoff's 22,000 men into play and inevitable disaster to the allies.

The new phase opened with the Russians advancing in
echelon from the right. Preceded by a shield of skirmishers
they marched up the Volovia and Quarry Ravines protected
by a fierce cannonade from their own guns. They by-passed
the Barrier and spread over the saddleback. The first wave
broke easily over the Western end of the Home Ridge and three
guns, feebly protected, were quickly taken notwithstanding a
heroic fight by Sergeant-Major Henry, who received but survived a dozen bayonet wounds. In this attack the enemy were
described as howling like mad dogs and the simile is not inapt.
By it, indeed, the British here were saved from disaster.
Having seized the guns the Russians behaved as a dog who
has just discovered a bone. They lost interest in everything
else, or, in Kinglake's orotund phrase, 'they disclosed no larger
ambitions'. To them gloating over their easy conquest
appeared suddenly a body of Zouaves who, resenting their
general's caution, had decamped and made for the sound
of firing. Good fortune brought them to this part of the field
just when the enemy were congratulating themselves on their
success. Without awaiting orders they struck at the Russians,
forced them back and recaptured the guns.

Checked at this point the Russians nevertheless had no great
cause for worry. It was the main attack against the centre
which was to count and here things seemed to be progressing
well. Emerging from the mist and brushwood of the Saddleback, the van likewise by-passing the Barrier poured over the
Home Ridge on either side of the post road, took by surprise
100 men of the 55th acting as reserves, drove back some, and
took others prisoner together with six guns, three of which
they spiked. They were the first Russians after more than four
hours' fighting to reach their objective – the south side of the
Home Ridge. Here, as we have learnt, they would have found
a short while earlier a plateau bare of troops as far as the eye

could see, a few guns, some staff officers, the 'spent force' in search of a surgeons's tent or an ammunition wagon, but little else. Even now there was only one organized body visibly capable of putting up a serious defence. The 7ème Léger, 900 strong had not long arrived, having advanced in line four deep – formation unfamiliar to their men.

The Russians halted once more on the threshold of success, irresolute. It was not merely, one suspects, the surprise appearance of the French who for all they knew were the advance guard of an army; it was the losses they were suffering at this moment from their own guns, the Russian bombardment on the Home Ridge, for some reason, not having been lifted when their troops reached the crest. A volley at this unsettling moment from the French, followed by a charge, must have sent them reeling back down into the Saddle and to the cover of their own guns; but there was neither volley nor charge. Like the Russians the 7ème, too, stood irresolute. They were young soldiers and already upset by having to adopt an unwonted formation. Now threatened by heavy fire for the first time, with little supporting artillery apparent on their own side and no commander present more senior than their colonel, they like the 6ème on their right declined to proceed. Their own officers pleaded with them, British officers inquired if they were the same nation who had fought so valorously against their fathers in the Peninsula. The effect of such stimulating oratory was fleeting. They advanced a short distance, but as this brought them under the heavy weight of Russian metal this time they not only halted but turned and retreated. It was the nadir of the allied fortunes. The action of a single French battalion was imperilling the whole allied position. 'I thought it was all up,' wrote an officer of the 30th. 'It was the only time,' remarked Calthorpe, 'that I ever observed Lord Raglan's countenance change.' And no wonder. If the French when they arrived would not fight, where was he to look for supports? Egerton had just appeared with 200 men from the 77th, but these were the scrapings of the barrel.

To the honour of France the officers of the 7ème at last succeeded in their exhortations. The regiment once more advanced, but now in their accustomed columns. It had taken some time to restore their morale and then to reorganize them in their old formation. If during this period the Russians had resumed their march down the southern slope they might well have carried all before them. That they neglected to do so was partly due to their habitual want of enterprise, but much more to a further strange episode in this battle.

Major Daubeney of the 55th had rallied some 30 of his men and had boldly crossed the Ridge. Once on the other side he started to work his way along the flank of the Russian force. When level with the second battalion he turned sharply to the right and struck in. The sequel can best be likened to a pedestrian charge of the Heavy Brigade. Tightly hemmed in, like a spectator in a cup-tie crush, Daubeney was carried forward, his arms pinioned to his side, his feet barely touching the ground. It is said that in his transit of the Russian ranks he passed within a few feet of a Russian officer similarly trussed and the two men exchanged wry greetings. Behind him and supplying the motive force came his little band, amongst whom a giant colour-sergeant named Walker was prominent. Wielding the butt of a rifle as if it had been a sledge-hammer he hacked his way through the Russians and when no longer able to swing this weapon he resorted to an enormous pair of fists and the power behind his ammunition boots. What Daubeney hoped to achieve by this charge is not clear. What he and his band did achieve at the cost of much less than half their number was to disconcert this lumpish forward movement of the enemy. First the battalion into which they had launched themselves halted to deal with the attack, then those in the leading battalion hearing a tumult at their backs halted in like fashion. The pause determined the 7ème. Encouraged by one of their own officers who, cap on the point of an uplifted sword, ran out in front where he was joined by three British officers, all shouting blandishments, they surged forward at the double, to the accompaniment of blowing bugles and beating drums. The 60 free-lance Zouaves went too, but they needed no such promptings.

It was perfect, although unpremeditated, timing. The unwieldy Russian mass heaved like a thing in pain and fell back, those in the rear being propelled down the slope by pressure from those in front who imagined that they were cut off. And as they went some field guns on the right at a range of only a hundred yards tore great lanes into their tumultuous ranks.

With this collapse at last was come the moment for action by the 21st and 63rd, commanded respectively by Colonels Ainslie and Swyny. Ever since their successful charge they had been lying down well forward on the left of the saddleback where they had been under heavy artillery and musketry fire. Now as soon as it was clear that somewhere to their front the main Russian column was in retreat they pleaded to be allowed to charge.

Lieutenant Vaughan Lee, who carried the regimental colours of the 21st, thus narrates the sequel. The colonel having mounted his horse and given the laconic order, 'Fusiliers, prepare to charge':

We all got up and gave a cheer and rushed through the brushwood and down we went with fixed bayonets. ... Stephens was then shot in the arm by grape shot. A sergeant took his colour [*sc* Queen's] from him; I still went on with my sword drawn in one hand and my pistol loosened in my holster. We dashed on, cheered again and gave them the bayonet. They pelted us with stones and rushed off. We went on, men were falling on all sides of me, and we saw the Russians retreating down the hill. We then saw five columns of the beggars advancing upon us, so we retired behind the breastwork.

This breastwork was a mere shallow trench cut athwart the post road in the Quarry Ravine below the Barrier. It soon became untenable and there was a withdrawal to the Barrier, which, not the Sand Bag Battery, was the true symbol of victory. As long as it remained in British hands, hope could not be dead. Goldie, in command of its small mixed garrison now reinforced, had already fallen; Ainslie and Swyny had been killed during the charge. This left Haines of the 21st the senior officer. With a splendid fighting record acquired in India, Haines had never believed that the Russians would not strike again at Inkerman and had made a careful study of the ground. He at once threw out flanking forces to prevent encirclement, extending those on the left as far as the slopes of Shell Hill from which his men began to direct a persistent and harassing fire on the gunners who, unlike the Russian infantry, had been paying special attention to the Barrier. These extensions he had been able to make because his post continued to serve as a rendezvous for waifs and strays of various regiments, notably some riflemen led by Major Horsford and a company of the 49th by Captain Astley, and (there is little doubt) by a few who had been skulking in the undergrowth. His most important acquisition, however, had been a company of the 77th sent to him by Pennefather and commanded by Lieutenant Acton. With such reinforcements and by making use of every scrap of wall, any well-placed rocks or cover, Haines was able not only to enlarge his own private battlefield, but to resist all enemy attempts to get back on to the Saddle by way of the post road.

While Haines was thus engaged in organizing his own sector, independently of what was happening elsewhere and subject to no higher authority, two important developments had been taking place behind the Home Ridge. Together they were to ensure the rout of the Russians. The first was the arrival on the battlefield of something which by the use of common foresight should never have been lacking. Shortly after Raglan's arrival that morning he had detected the weakness of the out-metalled artillery and had inquired if anything could be done. Learning that the siege train had two guns to spare, he sent an order for them to be brought up. Once more a malign fate overtook the commander-in-chief's message. A stupid ADC took it to Colonel Fitzmayer, the officer in charge of the desperately hard-pressed guns of the second division, and was told the order was impossible to perform – for impossible it was for him to leave his guns at such a time and ride down to the siege-gun park. Instead of going there himself the officer returned and repeated Fitzmayer's words to Raglan, who, not realizing his difficulties, expressed annoyance. Only after this unnecessary delay did the order reach the right quarters where it had been eagerly awaited since dawn. Ever since Little Inkerman the gunners, who were of all soldiers the most professional, had foreseen the need for some powerful artillery on Inkerman Heights and had been keeping this pair of 18-pounders ready to be moved off at instant notice. If the guns were so readily available why, it may be asked, had they not been taken up before? Perhaps the staff officer who invented the name Herbert's Folly could supply the answer.

Draught horses not being available, the guns had to be man-handled over about one and a half miles, which included the crossing of a steep ravine. Even with 150 men in harness this took time and it was nearly three hours after Raglan had issued his orders before they arrived on the Home Ridge, three hours during which innumerable lives could have been saved. The immediate success achieved by these guns is the measure of the Staff's wanton negligence in not having them there from the start.

Although throwing only an 18-pound shell, the power and accuracy of these long iron guns was remarkable. It required only two shots to get the range of Shell Hill batteries and then for the first time in the battle the Russian gunners came under damaging artillery fire. The effect was dramatic. First there was a furious and concentrated return of fire from Shell Hill, which resulted in 17 out of 50 in their teams being killed or wounded within fifteen minutes but which never touched the guns. Next, as these two guns sent shells crashing into the batteries, there began a withdrawal out of range. But owing to the superior power of the two 18-pounders the Russians could not do this and at the same time maintain their ability to straddle the Home Ridge. Collingwood Dixon, who for his services in charge of the guns won the Victoria Cross, correctly divined that, the Russians (like the French) being trained to fight under artillery protection, he had only to destroy this to deprive the infantry of confidence.

The second factor was the arrival of Bosquet's main force. Convinced at last that Gortschakoff's demonstration was a blind, he ordered his troops to the Inkerman Heights. And now they came, Autemarre's Zouaves and Algerians in the lead, soldiers of a very different stamp from those of the 6ème and the 7ème Léger, born fighters, agile, fearless, 'bounding like panthers and crying for blood'. They came on to the sound of drums beating out the *pas de charge* and bugles blowing the rousing refrain, *As-tu vu la casquette au Père Bugeaud*. Before them danced a pretty *vivandière*. The exhausted British troops received them with grateful cheers to which the Zouaves with whom they were always on the best of terms (there were a surprising number of British in their ranks) replied with shouts of *Vivent les Anglais ... les plus meilleurs soldats du monde.* In their rear rode the Chasseurs d'Afrique and behind them a pathetic piece of patchwork – the remains of the five regiments of the Light Brigade, 200 men in all.

The screaming Zouaves seemed to skim down the slope. They raced past the gallant Boussinière's battery and over-ran the still-deserted Sand Bag Battery. Here they should have halted, but Bosquet, either out of ignorance of the ground or mistaken zeal, led them on to the tip of the Kitspur. Here, exposed, isolated and useless, they invited and received such a sharp counter-attack as drove them back precipitously with the loss of a field-gun and the near-capture of Bosquet himself. Once more, but now for the last time, the Battery was abandoned to the enemy. Worse still, this retreat infected the 6ème and 7ème regiments which after the retirement of the former Bourkabi had brought together. They too fell back till on the right and centre there was now nothing left in front of the Home Ridge but the indomitable Haines and his men far out in the Barrier. It was a last-minute *bouleversement* which could have led to a resounding Russian victory. If the French failed – and their confidence was badly shaken – their allies were no longer in a position to do more. Behind the Home Ridge there was all that remained of the Guards Brigade, hardly enough to form a company, there were odd groups and fragments of regiments, some of them officerless, all exhausted, and nothing more.

The crisis passed. It did so in a curiously indirect manner, by the arrival in the rear of three more of Bosquet's regiments. These did not go into battle, but their mere presence put heart into his Zouaves. Knowing their character, Bosquet elected to give these temperamental fighters another chance. 'Prove yourselves children of fire!' he cried out as he waved them back into battle. And into battle they went once more, without their *vivandière* who had fallen, but on their left accompanied by a scratch force of the Guards which had managed to make its way up from the valley. This time there was no holding the French. They threw the Russians out of the Battery and shouting and screaming, their rifles held high above their bodies, pursued them down the slopes, killing and shooting and driving them off the last vestiges of the Inkerman massif. It was a sight which few of those who had fought all those hours could witness without a lump in the throat. Even the unemotional Raglan was moved to make a demonstration. He turned to Bosquet and said that he wished he had several hands with which to shake, and to Canrobert added quite simply, '*Au nom d'Angleterre, je vous remercie.*'

The battle was all but over. Before the curtain finally descended there was played out one brilliant little scene entirely in the Inkerman tradition. It concerned Acton's company of the 77th, numbering 50, recently dispatched by Pennefather to the Barrier. To him from across the Saddleback came Lord West whose left wing of the 21st had some time before been directed to the head of the Mikriakoff Ravine where it had remained. As nonchalantly as a cricket captain rearranging his field West told him to take his men, pick up two of his companies which he would find at an indicated spot and advance against a battery on the West Jut. Acton duly complied with the order but it is hardly surprising that after so many hours of fighting without food the two companies of the 21st when reached showed considerable unwillingness for an enterprise which entailed not only extreme physical danger but immense physical exertion. Even his own men hung back when he went on to declare that he would in that case attack with them alone. Shouting, 'Then I'll go by myself', he ran forward some way and paused. As he anticipated first one, then another and finally every man of his detachment took heart and joined him. They had not proceeded far when the 21st, shamed by their example, dashed forward; and the whole lot rushed up the slope in staggered formation. Just as the guns began to send down a rain of canister, the shells from Dixon's two 18-pounders began passing overhead and crashing into the batteries on Shell Hill. The sight of three British companies advancing with a confidence that seemed to the Russians to indicate large forces in the rear, at the same time as British shells were tossing men, horses and tumbrils into the air, was altogether too much for them. The well-instilled fear of never losing a gun led to an immediate limbering-up and withdrawal. When Acton and his men reached the site of the battery there was nothing there but one gun-carriage and two derelict tumbrils.

The moral effect of Acton's charge justified its considerable cost in human life; its practical effect was even greater. Any hopes that the Russians had of digging in on Shell Hill, for which purpose they had brought entrenching tools and cartloads of gabions, were destroyed.

Though the enemy was now everywhere giving way, there was no rout. The Russians showed indeed the greatest reluctance to retire and fought with the utmost courage to cover the withdrawal of their guns. Until the last of these had been removed (in a manner which evoked British admiration) they kept up a persistent fire on the 18-pounders and two ships in the harbour, the *Vladimir* and the *Chersonese*, which had been firing all day, now directed their broadsides on to the slopes of Shell Hill up which the allied infantry were moving. At one point on their proper left they even mounted a counter-attack which the increasing strength of French and British artillery broke up with crippling losses.

By two o'clock the battle of Inkerman was over. As the Russians poured, some across the Tchernaya to the security of Mackenzie's Farm, others into Sebastopol, the bells once more rang out on orders from on high to proclaim a victory.

As after the Alma there was no pursuit. The Russians, whose concern for their guns contrasted strongly with their callous abandonment of their wounded and dying, were permitted to withdraw without interference. Only the French were in a position to follow up their retreat and their failure to do so provoked much criticism at the time. This was understandable but was nevertheless ill-founded. Admittedly absent haversacks could not here serve as an excuse, but French unwillingness was based upon reasons far more solid. The French general staff with its complement of experienced and for the most part battle-trained officers had a very much keener appreciation of what such an operation would have involved than their critics, amongst whom was Lord Raglan. Many years later Sir William Russell in a conversation with Todleben brought forward this very question of failure to pursue. Todleben as a rule is not good evidence but in this instance, where he had no need to romance or exaggerate, his reply is entitled to respect. It is a complete justification of the French attitude.

I would [he said] have desired nothing better. I honestly think you would have incurred disaster. The batteries – our works – the forts – the ships and an army of 40,000 men which though repulsed was not demoralized – would have inflicted tremendous losses on you. A retreat in front of us then might have lost you your trenches. Though Gortschakoff was incompetent, he must have come up from the Tchernaya on your flank with 20,000 excellent troops. No! You did very well – too well. I only wish you had come on.

If there had been little elation after the Alma, there was none after Inkerman. Too many mourned the death of dear friends and relations to rejoice; all that was wanted was food and then sleep. In any case most officers were voiceless from shouting.

So ended the battle of Inkerman, 'this pell mell curiosity of war', as one survivor described it, and likened by another to 'one of our grand football matches at Harrow, the artillery on both sides being the goals'. Indeed the simile of the football match is not inappropriate for a battle which revealed to such an extent the characteristic British refusal to take war seriously, to regard it as anything more than a sport rather more dangerous than football or polo. Typical of this casual approach was the conduct of Captain Peel, RN, who in the deadly fighting which preceded the Guards' final withdrawal from the Battery, strode nonchalantly across to where the Grenadiers were engaged and blandly remarked to Captain Higginson that as things were dull up at the naval battery on Victoria Hill he was 'come to have a look at you fellows'. Another 'sporting occasion' had Robert Lindsay for principal actor. Somewhere in the wilderness of scrub and boulders he came upon five Guardsmen attempting to bayonet a Russian officer not for his resistance, because he was making none, but for a purse of gold he was carrying round his neck. Considering 'the idea of killing a man for his money' to be 'outside the scope of warfare' Lindsay threw up their muskets with his sword, thus enabling the Russian to escape into the mist, but not before he had turned to and saluted his deliverer. There was the nervous young officer who seeking help for his hard-pressed men ran into another in charge of a small detachment. 'My men', he pleaded, 'can hardly stand their ground. Would you object to bringing yours into line with ours? I had the pleasure of being introduced to you at Lady Palmerston's last summer.' There was the superb composure of the white-haired General Strangways, the chief artillery officer and a veteran of Leipzig and Waterloo, who while riding with Raglan in the rear of the Home Ridge was struck by a cannon ball which shattered the leg beneath the knee. Turning to one of his staff he said, in the tone of a man asking for a match, 'Would someone have the kindness to help me off my horse?' When carried to the surgeon's tent and told he was too old to stand the shock of an operation his only remark was, 'Then let me die among my gunners' – a prayer that was answered two hours later. Finally there was the case of Private Bancroft of the Grenadier Guards who, while battling for life with two Russians, lashed out with his boot at one of them who from the ground was trying to seize him by the leg while the other was attempting to bayonet him, and received the stern command from his sergeant, 'Don't kick a man when he's down.'

To comprehend the nature of Inkerman it has to be regarded less as a battle won than as an attack defeated. Its character was negative. It destroyed the Russian plan to overwhelm and roll up the British right wing; it destroyed allied hopes of an immediate assault upon Sebastopol. It was positive only to the extent of giving the Russians time, or putting it in another way, of condemning the allies to a Crimean winter.

Inkerman has been described as 'rather a gigantic instance of heroism by which we saved ourselves from impending destruction than a victory over the enemy'. Yet even this heroism, equalled perhaps but never surpassed in British military history, would have been insufficient but for the fog and Soimonoff's mistake. It was the compressing of two large armies under conditions of poor visibility on a battlefield where only one could have manoeuvred with any freedom which doomed the Russian offensive. 'We only succeeded in beating the Russians', a survivor told his son, 'because of their failure to coordinate their attacks. Huge columns came up the three ravines in *succession* and we just managed to drive each attack back before the other developed. . . . If they had arrived together we should have been swamped.'

The cost of human life of this heroic defence – 'John Bull's butcher's bill' – was awesome. At the Sand Bag Battery alone where the battle-hardened Bosquet uttered those fearful words, '*Quel abbatoir!*', a man might reconstruct its history from the layers of British, Russian and French dead, as a geologist the past from the strata of rocks. Before the Home Ridge and along the sides of the ravines bodies lay in ranks as canister and Minié had mowed them down. All over the battlefield men could be found in every possible contorted attitude, sometimes in couples who, with bayonet in hand, had simultaneously transfixed each other. Even a year later they were still being discovered in the thick brushwood or in the rock crannies, either having been killed outright or having crawled into some rude shelter, there to die in agony. Six months after the battle Sir John McNeil rode one Sunday morning over the Inkerman Heights with its dozen or more cemeteries and was moved to write: 'It has been said that there are sermons in stones, but I have heard few sermons that filled me with thoughts so solemn and so little connected with the amenities of life as that ride over the field of Inkerman.' To Lord George Paget that field was worse than anything he had ever seen at Balaclava. 'O, war, war! How one has read and heard about it without realizing all its horrors.' 'This is what's called glory!' remarked Sir Thomas Troubridge to Hugh Hibbert of the same regiment as he lay with two stumps thrust (to staunch the bleeding) into two barrels of gunpowder.

The British dead numbered 632, of whom 43 were officers and of these eight were from the Coldstream Guards, the wounded 1,873.

Seven weeks had passed since the Alma, enough it might be thought to have done something to improve the sufferings of the stricken. Nothing had been done.

'The unfortunate disabled [wrote Colonel Bell, a Peninsular veteran in command of the Royal Regiment] were day and night exposed to cold without any covering, nothing to lie on but the wet sod, groaning, yelling, agonized, and dying. . . . I have never witnessed in all my days such a frightful scene of human misery.'

Of these wounded many of those who lived to be borne off the battlefield died on board ship or in the wards of

Scutari. The French casualties were 1,726 killed and wounded, the Russian no fewer than 12,000.

Among the several features which distinguished Inkerman amongst modern battles one requires special mention. It was – even more than the Alma – fought without directives. On this every combatant was agreed. Of these few were more qualified to speak than Patullo of the 30th and he writes: 'No orders were given from first to last but to advance. No attempts to reform shattered battalions, no plan of operations.' Robert Lindsay, giving the Guards' point of view, is not less trenchant: 'No divisional brigade or even regimental order was given.' In the absence of direction everything came to depend upon local leadership, upon officers in charge of companies, even half companies. In this the British were at an advantage over the Russians. Though no braver individually their background of the public school, the hunting and football field, of steeplechases and all forms of sport rendered them, for all their professional shortcomings, better leaders of men in an emergency, more resourceful, more active, more enterprising. No Russian officer showed such daring initiative as Clifford, Burnaby or Bellairs.

Nevertheless without the rank and file the British officers could have achieved no more than the Russian.

I feel gratitude [again to quote Patullo] to the courageous British soldier who fought all day, replenishing his ammunition from his wounded comrade's pouch without a direction or hint from superior authority, only the example of his officer who was left equally without guidance, not to the generals who in my opinion have not distinguished themselves.

Opinions such as this make a mockery of the dispatches and later the honours which succeeded the battle. To Raglan, whose presence on or off the battlefield would have made little or no difference, came the baton of a Field-Marshal. This brought the caustic remark from Clifford that he had more reason to thank the army for the honour than the army had to thank him for his services; and James Williams wrote equally sarcastically that 'future historians will be rather inclined to award him a cypress than a laurel'; while Brooksbank supposed 'he will be made Duke of Inkerman next'. All members of his staff, whether or not they had come within the range

of Russian gunfire, received a step in brevet-rank. In his dispatch every divisional commander was fulsomely mentioned.
The Duke of Cambridge certainly deserved to be and the
wound that Sir George Brown received might be regarded
as cancelling his snubbing of Bosquet. But few of Sir Richard
England's men would have endorsed Raglan's reference to 'the
excellent disposition he made of his [the 4th] division'. This
many felt had been made from that abundance of caution
which had earned for him the nickname, 'Old Woman'. When
he gave orders that his division was to remain strictly in reserve, old George Bell cried out 'No . . . no . . . no! No more
reserves for me. We had enough of that at Alma', and followed by the 50th he moved the Royals forward as near as he
could get to the fighting.

The moral of Inkerman is expressible in a sentence: big
battalions count less in battle than superior enterprise, mobility
and intelligence; and courage which is not aggressive is not
enough. Of course not every British soldier who fought that
day disclosed these high qualities; not everyone fought as a
hero. The broken ground gave ample scope for the skulker. 'I,
in common with other officers,' wrote a Captain in the 49th
of one episode, 'did all in my power to make the men stand
but failed.' As there were many brave deeds done that day
and many that went unseen and unrecorded, so there were
men who acquired an Inkerman clasp to their Crimean medal
who had spent much of the battle hidden or feigning death
behind a boulder.

Inkerman has rightly been called a Soldiers' Battle and for
that reason its laurels belong to no single man. Except for the
few shirkers, all fought and all won. But if any single name
deserves to be mentioned, it is that of John Lysaght Pennefather. Whatever there was of leadership and inspiration came
from him as he untiringly rode from one end of the Home
Ridge to the other, for ever exhorting and encouraging in his
rich and expressive vocabulary. From him, in justice, shall
come the last words on Inkerman. 'I tell you, we gave 'em a
hell of a towelling.'

5

Winter

'How patient those men of mine; how admirably they behave. In silence they bear with all privations; away they go to their daily bread, ankle deep in mud, and wet to the skin, down to the trenches. Thus is the British soldier most to be admired. This is discipline; here he is in all his glory.'

— *Colonel George Bell*

'The best general is he who best feeds his soldiers.'

— *Marshal Saxe*

ONLY METAPHORICALLY was the Crimean Winter a battle, but in that sense it was a very real battle. It was waged against misery and want, disease and wet, fatigue and cold, shortsightedness and inefficiency, red-tape and mismanagement; and by the British army it was a battle lost. It is a familiar story and it is considered here only in so far as it occasioned the weaknesses, which in turn decided the fortunes of that army in the last battles of the campaign.

Geography had determined the division of the British army on the Heights before Sebastopol into two unequal portions, known as the Right Attack and the Left Attack. The first spanned a spur of the plateau which lay between the Woronzoff and Dockyard Ravines, a distance of rather more than half a mile. Except for one important rise some distance ahead of the British lines this spur fell away to end in the Karabelnaya, the eastern suburb of the town. Once this was in allied hands, Sebastopol across the Dockyard Creek would lie defenceless. Of this danger Todleben had naturally been aware and had evolved a powerful defence to the suburb based on two strong points or forts, the first on the above-mentioned rise, and called the Redan, the other farther to the east on the Victoria Ridge between the Dockyard and Careening Ravines and known as the Malakoff. The latter originally came within the British sector, but when after Inkerman Canrobert at last agreed to take over part of their siege works the Victoria Ridge as well as the Inkerman Heights became the concern of the French army. The British Right Attack had thus for its sole objective the Redan. Its base was Gordon's Battery of 21 guns in front of which as the months passed parallel after parallel was thrown forward, connected one with the other by 'zigzags' or to use the language of the First World War, communication trenches. It came within the purview of the Light, the 4th and, after the French had taken over the Inkerman Heights, the 2nd Division.

The Left Attack extended from the west side of the Woronzoff Ravine to the Picket House Ravine and was likewise just over half a mile in length. Its base was Chapman's or Greenhill Battery, and its trench system and defences were in charge of the 3rd Division with the Guards Brigade in their rear. The Left Attack so far as concerned the infantry was hardly more than a token attack. It had nothing before it to assault, its spur, shaped like a tongue, falling away with steep sides before ending at the head of the Dockyard Creek. Equally it was secure from any large-scale assault by the Russians. On the other hand its guns were capable of playing upon the Redan and its adjacent batteries, thus giving it particular importance in any scheme of attack. In the course of the siege it was to receive much punishment.

None of the divisions taking part in these two Attacks was less than seven miles from Balaclava.

In confident anticipation of the fall of Sebastopol after the opening bombardment in October no provision had been made for wintering on the plateau because such a necessity was not contemplated. It was not till Inkerman had indefinitely postponed the assault that the problem became urgent. By then it was late but not (as the French found) too late to make tolerable arrangements.

Any authority on the Crimea must have underlined the variability of its climate in winter and that of the 1854-5 winter was to be no exception. It was to be cold all over Europe that year and it was to be cold in the Crimea – so cold that ink froze in bottles, toothbrushes had to be thawed before use and a private who overnight put two shirts to soak found them next morning so unthawably embedded in ice that for some days he had to parade complete with wash-tub at kit inspection. On a night working-party icicles 4 inches long and as thick as his little finger formed themselves on the moustaches of Elton's commanding officer. We learn, too, from Hugh Hibbert how his men on duty dropped off to sleep through sheer fatigue and on being woken were perfectly stiff from head to foot. But such spells of very cold weather were rarely prolonged; the wind would change and even in January it would become sunny and mild overnight. A few days later above the mountains to the north clouds of a blackness one writer averred he had never seen in his life would be massing and rain, sleet and snow would follow. Provided the authorities had taken reasonable measures, had they made the utmost use of the finer spells, the sufferings of the army could have been very much reduced. Given the minimum of comforts, Earle maintained that the army could have wintered on the Sebastopol Heights with very little more hardship than on the Malvern Hills. 'I never felt better in my life'; 'I never had a cold or chilblain' are recurrent remarks in Crimean letters, but always from those who had the means and prevision to keep themselves warm and to sleep between dry blankets. It was ignorance, neglect, officialdom, and absence of foresight which made the Crimean winter cruel and killing. From these shortcomings resulted much of the chaos down at Balaclava where food and stores of all variety accumulated and for lack of storage space rotted in the open, where bales of warm clothing, bags of biscuits, and trusses of hay were flung into the harbour to provide additional landing stages, which no one thought of building till January. Departmental frontiers and jealousies cut across the path of efficiency.* Problems were

* Even when the appalling state of the army was common knowledge the Treasury still lived in a world apart. The Government sent out a Colonel MacMurdo with independent purchasing powers to form a much-needed transport corps. It was a costly undertaking and when MacMurdo sent in his requisitions Sir Charles Trevelyan, Secretary to the Treasury, replied saying, 'Colonel MacMurdo must limit his expenditure', to which MacMurdo riposted neatly, 'When Sir Charles Trevelyan limits the war I will limit my expenditure.'

tackled as they arose and consequently not always with success; they were rarely anticipated. 'No preparations are ever made [Windham told his wife] for what is to happen five days in advance.' 'There is a general fear of taking responsibility', a Member of Parliament informed the Commons on his return from a visit to the front. 'Everyone is afraid to act with vigour.' It was the set-up of an incurably unmilitary-minded nation gone to war.

Excuses were found and made in plenty. The terrible storm of November 14th which sent the *Prince* and its shipload of warm clothing to the bottom; the lack of transport; the congestion in Balaclava harbour; the shortage of labour; the recent occupation by the Russians of the Turkish redoubts which deprived the army of the only metalled road up the Sapounè Ridge and confined it to a country road over the Col which in the worst of the winter became almost impassable.

There is some substance but not as much as the authorities claimed in all but the last. In this, the inability to use the Woronzoff road, there is no substance at all, although eagerly seized upon as the principal reason for the breakdown in supplies. What is surprising is that its adoption as an excuse should have been sanctioned by all who, with the advantage of official maps, have written since then on the Crimea. These maps will show the Woronzoff road running three miles to the north of Balaclava with nothing directly joining the two. When Russell, who should have known better, repeated this convenient excuse for the benefit of *The Times*' readers, Captain Montgomery who, stationed with the 42nd down at Kadekoi, was much better qualified to speak, told a correspondent to pay no attention.

He is perfectly wrong and does not know what he is talking about. The Woronzoff road ... does not lead to Balaclava and was never used for the transport of guns. The guns go up by the same route as they did at first. A part of the Woronzoff road was used for about a mile for ammunition but we had to cross the mud in the open country to get to this mile of road. ... In fact if we chose we would use it still if it was an advantage to do so.

The road over the Col continued to be used because, there is little doubt, it was the road which from the time of their arrival soldiers and drivers had used. What made nonsense of the official excuse was the abandoning by the Russians on December 6th, not six weeks later and before the worst of winter had begun, of the entire Balaclava position and their retreating under a smoke-screen across the Tchernaya river. It made no difference. Men and horses, able thereafter, if they reached it, to use the Woronzoff road, still went slithering and stumbling up the muddy road over the Col.

Admitting that road conditions became deplorable, that labour, even Turkish labour, presented a problem, the effect on the army need not have been to create more than temporary hardships. What killed more men than Russian bullets, what made life miserable, what sent men by the hundreds to the hospital tents or the grave – they were frequently synonymous – was the want of firewood. Without it not only were men never warm, not only could they never cook their ration of 'cold grunter', but they were never dry. 'They go down to the trenches wet [wrote Colonel Bell], come back wet, go into hospital wet, die the same night and are buried in their wet blankets next morning.'* 'I never thought [declared a surgeon] the human subject would endure so much privation and suffering.' Yet two or three vessels sent across the Black Sea could have loaded up enough cordwood from the forests of Anatolia to have kept every camp fire burning throughout the winter. Instead men already exhausted by 24 hours' continuous duty either in the trenches or digging new parallels and soaked to the skin were compelled to go ever farther and farther afield, as the meagre supply failed, to grub up first the brushwood and when that petered out their sodden roots.

But it was not only the damp from the air which undermined vitality, it was the damp from below. When men, wet, shivering, hungry and worn-out, lay down to sleep on the bare damp earth then was the harm done which even liberal tots of rum could not prevent. A soldier's bed was often nothing better than 'wet blankets and mud'. Though it might have

* By January even the wet blanket acquired survival value and to Corporal Dolton's indignation could no longer be spared. 'They bury our men quite naked and throw him [sic] into the grave like a dog. I wonder what the people of England would think if they were to see it.'

been impossible to get the army hutted by winter, the tents could have been rendered endurable, even though made of material likened by one officer to a cambric handkerchief and by another to tin-foil. Flooring, roughly shaped to fit the base of a bell tent, would have kept out the rising damp, and should have been quickly obtainable from the Turks, that 'nation of carpenters'. If Raglan had encountered any difficulty he had only to apply to our ambassador, Lord Stratford de Redcliffe, who enjoyed more authority at Constantinople than any minister, European or Turkish. Though the suggestion, which might have saved hundreds of lives, was put forward by Sir John Burgoyne himself, nothing was done. Even the so-called hospital tents were lacking the simplest comforts. In that of the 4th, James Paton tells how 'there was not even a bed, a table, or a chair – men lay on the bare grass and died'.

Major Campbell of the 46th who wrote, 'I don't think the fault lies with the men so much as with the system, but that we are mere infants in the art of war', and the correspondent of the *Morning Advertiser* who declared that 'those fearful sufferings and privations are the result of official system entirely independent of individual omission or commission' both penetrate to the heart of the trouble. A review of all who worked in the various departments from William Filder, the 66-year-old Commissary-General and Peninsular veteran, down to the rawest clerk would have revealed men overworked, well-intentioned, zealous, conscientious, but entangled in a bureaucratic mesh out of which none had the ability or the courage to cut his way. When, as the sickening toll of human lives mounted daily, it was asked why that system was permitted to continue, why there was no one big enough to act, eyes were inevitably directed to a farmhouse on the plateau where bowed over his desk for hours on end sat a kindly, sensitive sexagenarian writing laboriously with his left hand endless letters or poring over the contents of his heavy mailbag.

The British army has never been led by a greater gentleman than Lord Raglan. His high sense of honour, scrupulous conduct, perfect manners, kindness of heart and unselfish devotion to duty have never been surpassed by any commander-in-chief. In a single sentence the Duke of Wellington had epitomized his character: 'Raglan is the sort of man who would die rather than tell a lie.'

But Raglan was more than a gentleman. He was a patrician with roots in the eighteenth century. Proud, reserved, completely master of his emotions, remote from the rough and tumble of everyday life, Raglan was an aristocrat to his fingertips. Nothing was more disagreeable to him than to be under an obligation, to ask of anyone a favour. Nothing is more characteristic than his loathing the idea of employing spies.

The tragedy of Raglan is that these fine qualities unfitted him for command of an army in the Crimea after 40 years of peace. That army, shivering on the Heights, did not want the perfect gentleman, the disinterested aristocrat. They did not want, as Layard informed the House of Commons, to be commanded by 'a mild, good-tempered old gentleman'. They needed a younger man, or, as Captain Higginson declared, 'an iron-fisted general who will stand no nonsense', someone who was less of the gentleman and more of the cad; someone who was ruthless, emphatic, energetic, imperious, a slave-driver if necessary, who to feed and clothe and warm his men and keep them in good fettle, would threaten, storm, abuse, act and in the last resource dismiss his dearest friend from office. Raglan at 67 was not and never could be that type of man. He was incapable of thumping the desk or shouting, like Pélissier when told that some order was impossible, 'Let it be done, sir, within an hour – or look out!' Except after the Light Brigade charge there is no record of his ever having raised his voice, of his having whipped himself into a fury. It is perhaps significant that the only two occasions when a trace of anger passed over that serene countenance had French implications. The first was when after the Alma he was told of a French attempt to appropriate one of the two captured guns; the second, as we have seen, when the 7ème Léger retreated at Inkerman. Even when he is known to have felt angry, as when two surgeons were detected in gross neglect of the wounded, for fear it seems of undermining the respect he felt due to officers, he declined to mention their names.

Nor was it only character that unfitted Raglan for command. His training for nearly 40 years in the capacity of what

Robert Portal scornfully called 'Wellington's head clerk' had converted the dashing young soldier into the Whitehall warrior, the complete civil servant, patient, urbane, tactful, conciliatory and loyal to his subordinates. Called, as it might be said, out of retirement to command an army debilitated by 40 years of peace, or rather by 40 annual Army Estimates pared to the bone by those who wanted an Empire on the cheap, he, who had never commanded a company let alone a regiment, was out of his depth. Raglan had all the High Tory's allergy to change, fortified in his case by the conviction that what had been good enough for his master, the Duke, was good enough for himself. To Palmerston, rarely a bad judge of character, he was 'a creature of habit' and to Windham (who saw him in the field) he was 'a good red-tapist but no general'. He possessed to perfection the Englishman's mastery of the understatement, or, in the words of his biographer, he showed 'a profound distrust of emphasis both in speech and writing'. It would be impossible to deduce the full sufferings of his army from his letters to the Government, either official or private. 'The silence of Lord Raglan [complained the Lord Privy Seal] was positively excruciating. Nothing came from him but the driest facts.' The Government, blameworthy in many directions, had at least this excuse that they were never really made aware of the true conditions obtaining in the Crimea till informed by Russell's articles in *The Times*.

Akin to the propensity for understatement went the civil servant's instinctive dislike to committing himself. 'I have never heard him give any [opinion] at any time [said a French General]. If he would state his opinion I think his rank and experience would ensure respect and probably acquiescence from our generals.' Rightly or wrongly this buttoned-up manner created an impression of indifference. 'Lord Raglan takes things very coolly', wrote Captain Heath, the hard-pressed harbour-master at Balaclava. Hamley was more critical. 'He never appeared to be a commander who took his responsibilities anxiously; indeed to some observers it seemed that they scarcely impressed him in due proportion to their gravity.' It was not true, nor was it consistent with the 'anxious face' which Clifford saw out of the corner of his eye as he sat by permission sketching Raglan's room at Headquarters in February. It was his unfortunate manner and habits which gave the impression of unconcern. Raglan was the English country gentleman before he was the serving soldier; the grand seigneur before he was the commander-in-chief. He dressed habitually in civilian clothes and when he moved through the camps it was in a pea-coat with a muffler round his ears and throat. Detesting any sort of demonstration on the part of others, he made none himself. Unlike Canrobert who rode about in pomp with a glittering retinue Raglan was accompanied by an ADC and a single orderly. He never sought popularity. Limelight was odious to him. In his relations with all except his Staff he was distant and formal, though always courteous. His rare conversations with the rank and file were stilted and lacking in warmth. He was not a good mixer. There was nothing of the Petit Caporal about Raglan. A visit to the Light Brigade lines shortly after the Charge, an occasion which Napoleon would have embraced to make some emotional speech or gesture, brought from him no comment, no word of appreciation. He would have hated to have received praise had he been in the Charge and so he gave none to the survivors.

He who in everything else tried to model himself upon the Duke failed in one respect. Whether from pressure of paperwork or whether from fear of being embarrassed by a few cheers he never moved about the camps as Wellington did in the Peninsula. To many a soldier he was no more than a name. 'Is that old gentleman with one arm the General?' Russell was asked by a sergeant of the 23rd. 'We never see him, which I think makes him very unpopular', wrote William Pechell at the end of November. Two months later he returns to the subject. 'We all complain very much of Lord Raglan whom we never see. . . . We therefore conclude that he does not know or care what goes on.' More ill-natured is the Hon. Strange Jocelyn's outburst: 'He lives in a comfortable farmhouse from which he never stirs and knows but little of the misery his officers and men are living in.' Of greater worth is the opinion of Earle, who in his letters home having constantly defended the commander-in-chief from attacks, had to confess that 'Lord Raglan does not make himself acquainted with the misery of his troops.' When at last stung by articles in *The Times* and prodded by the Cabinet Raglan started to show himself more often about the camps his visits, according to Richards, were never more than once a week, and not so often if the weather was bad. The general feeling was expressed by George Higginson in a sentence: 'The whole thing is resolved into one grand fault – we literally have no commander-in-chief'; and by Colonel Windham in five words: 'Lord Raglan does not command'.

It has been said in extenuation that, due to the army's un-professional organization, Raglan was compelled to spend long hours every day doing paperwork, especially exhausting for a one-armed man. Yet when urged by the Queen, the Prince and the Secretary of War to take on a *chancellerie militaire* on continental lines and relieve himself of much drudgery, Raglan demurred. It was something presumably never employed by the Duke.

Living though he might in his neat little house with a plenti-ful table prepared by a continental chef, 'Old Raggles', despite what Pechell and others might say, knew that his army suffered from long wet hours in the trenches, that having taken over too much ground for its size it was grossly overworked, that it was ravaged by sickness and debilitated by want and the knowledge deepened the lines on that pale, sensitive face. Yet it is hard to believe that a man of Raglan's profound compassion really knew the extent of these sufferings and still made no violent or dramatic gesture to end them. Again an officer not habitually ill-disposed towards him found him-self compelled to write: 'It is quite impossible he *can know* the sufferings of his men or he would never have allowed it to get to the pitch it has without attempting to stop the evil.' The true picture he could only learn from his Staff, and that Staff either did not know it themselves or if they did, they con-tinued to keep all unpleasant facts from their beloved chief.

A poor commander-in-chief can have a good Staff, but a good commander-in-chief cannot have a poor Staff. If Rag-lan's Staff, 'that nest of noodles', had been based on anything better than interest and nepotism (five members were related to him by blood), had it possessed what can only come from genius, training or experience, that is, some inkling of the art of war, a capacity to anticipate problems before they arose, it might have discounted some of the weaknesses of its chief. If he was confined to his Headquarters by work or inclination, his Staff should have been his eyes and ears. But when they went on their rounds it was not to look for trouble. One illustration reveals their apathy. An army of sutlers before long descended on Balaclava, 'brutes of Maltese, and Jews, Turks, infidels, and heretics', and set up booths in which everything in the way of food and clothing was sold at 300 to 500 per cent above the retail price. They had also gone to Kamiesh, but there the active French authorities instantly confronted them with a tight schedule of prices and a threat of expulsion for any overcharge. The British Quartermaster-General's staff merely shrugged their shoulders and lifted no finger to prevent the exploitation of the army. As a result Balaclava became a racketeer's paradise while Kamiesh developed into a bustling little town complete with restaurant and a madame behind the *caisse*.

The unvaried criticism of the Staff, the obloquy with which they are mentioned in letters – 'the greatest set of muffs possible', 'a parcel of lazy, idle, drinking, and swearing fellows', 'comfortable, easy set of do-nothings, who are only fit to scribble a dispatch to the Secretary at War' (the last two from Guards officers of birth and 'interest' themselves) – cannot simply be attributed to jealousy or the contempt of the front-line soldier for the men at Headquarters. It is too general not to be based on solid reasoning, and this was briefly that the Staff were a blend of incompetence, indifference, and ignorance. They did not know because they did not see or want to see what the common soldier was suffering, or if they saw they seemed to have considered such conditions to be unavoidable, irremediable and, above all, uncommunicable to Raglan. One of them when confronted with Russell's accusatory articles replied that the men were no worse off than they would have been in their own homes and, as regarded food, rather better off. They judged others by themselves, who quite rightly were immune from problems of food and warmth. It was because those others considered that in return for those amenities they did so little that their name stank throughout the army. Had they been men dedicated to their profession, like those on the French Staff, trained, efficient, energetic, none would have grudged them their comforts.

Before considering more closely the effects of the Crimean winter on the army it is necessary to guard against making any sweeping generalizations. One man's hardship could be another's luxury. There were differences in character and upbringing. There were, as Hume tells us, the 'Mark Tapleys, cheerful under any circumstances', there were those (and they formed a substantial percentage) who having been brought up in an Irish cabin in the 'Forties and lived through the Potato Famine would hardly grumble at a diet of salt pork, biscuit, green coffee, berries and rum, however monotonous. There was also a difference of location. Those in the Highland Brigade and cavalry down near Balaclava lived better than those on the Heights because they were nearer to the source of supplies, had no trench duty and suffered less from the weather. The artillery as a rule fared better than the infantry because they had more horses to make the terrible journey down to Balaclava. In the infantry some regiments lived better than others, depending on the ability, resourcefulness, and energy of their colonels or surgeons. Where there was an officer like Lacy Yea, whose life was wrapped up in his regiment, the men benefited, or where there was a surgeon of the calibre of Blake of the 55th the men when they went sick had a chance of surviving. Officers as a whole lived better than their men: they had ampler opportunity of getting dry and longer purses to pay the high prices of Balaclava or had more scope to keep hens, goats and in at least one case a milk-giving camel. The Guards and cavalry were better off than the line regimental officers. There could have been few among the latter comparable with Captain Brigstock of the 4th Dragoon Guards who wearying of the war sold out in disgust and by auction disposed of no fewer than 197 pots of preserved meat and more than a dozen hampers of food; or with Colonel Darby Griffith of the Scots Greys who arrived with a magnificent stock of provisions put up by Fortnum and Mason and a French cook.

It was on the whole upon the long-service soldier, the backbone of the Crimean army, that the winter fell most hardly.

The admirable sangfroid of the old campaigners soon puts the new troops at their ease and a man goes with as little unconcern to the dark night and the unseen missile as he could to his bed.

So the extremely literate Private Cormack told his brother. But as one winter's night succeeded another, those old campaigners, with their ability to set a fine example, became fewer. It was of these that Earle wrote:

The resignation of the British soldier is noble. He performs the harassing duties imposed on him without a complaint, he bears fatigue and illness without a murmur and finally leaves the busy scene without a sigh.

In the whole campaign there is nothing more tragic than the deaths from cholera, scurvy, gangrene, fevers, frost-bite, dysentery – all brought about largely through departmental incompetence – of men who had stormed the Heights of the Alma and had almost incredibly survived those battling hours in the fog of Inkerman. This, of course, is not intended to imply that there was no tragedy in the holocaust of eager young recruits who arrived with the drafts and were dead in a fortnight – at least they died quickly and without prolonged disillusionment.

Only the Highland Regiments down at Balaclava retained their original complements more or less intact. It was those on the Heights who melted away. What could be expected of regiments which like the 63rd came off duty in the trenches, where, we are told,

they had been all night exposed to bitter rain and snow, their clothing was drenched through; the rain continued all day and there being no fire in the camp their clothing remained in this dreadful wet state. Yet these same men were ordered to the trenches again at three o'clock next morning.

Was it to be wondered that some weeks later the regiment consisted of 20 men, most of them bandsmen, and ceased for a period to form part of the army? Conditions were no better in the 4th. James Paton writes:

For seventy-two hours I have been on duty with only twelve hours rest and that in daytime. Two nights running I was in the trenches and the one next on guard laying on hard ground.

It was a vicious circle. The damp and the cold, shivering

maybe all night on sentry-go out in no-man's-land, caused gums to become so inflamed that men could not eat their stand-by, the biscuit. Hence for lack of nourishment they were less capable of resisting the cold. In December the 7th paraded 350 men and four officers out of 1,000 and 24 respectively. Early in January the Grenadier Guards had only 128 men fit for duty. When a month later Lord Rokeby arrived to take over the Guards Brigade from Bentinck he burst into tears on seeing it parade no more than 300.* A fortnight later it would have been 225. The 4th Division could muster only 2,500 out of 6,800 and those 2,500 'absolutely crying with cold and discomfort'. What was left of the gallant 95th with its magnificent record at Alma and Inkerman was marching to a new camp when someone shouted out, 'Here comes the advance party!', but another replied, 'It can't be, for two officers are carrying the colours.'

As the winter wore on it became increasingly true that 'the finest army that had ever left our shores' was nothing more than 'a contingent of the French'. At the end of January it was only 11,000 strong, its sick and wounded totalling 23,000. The wounded were a concomitant of war, but the sick?

Il me semble que vos soldats ne sont pas accommodés comme il faut [said a horrified French officer to a friend of Alfred Tipping]. *Ils méritent de vos mains les soins à tout prix. Si nous avions de tels soldats nous les garderions comme nos yeux.*

It gave him and other officers no satisfaction to hear in one breath their men generously acclaimed the finest fighters in the world and in the next as 'an army of lions commanded by asses'. What rebuttal could they make? The richest country in the world had been at war for nine months, yet, with its vast Empire from which to draw supplies and its incomparable fleet to carry them, medicine chests were so bare and hospital tents so ill-provided that old George Bell declared that surgeons possessed little more than their 'carving knives'. At one time there was no quinine in the whole army. Even the supply of laudanum failed. Reference has already been made to

* He also arrived with a patent water closet which was promptly stolen by those engaging thieves, the Zouaves, in order to make soup in, according to Clifford.

medical tents. As regards medical comforts, Bell, well knowing the answer, once asked a medical orderly what rations the sick had. 'Salt pork and green coffee berry, sir.' As late as February surgeons were still finding their sick lying on bare ground, ten or twelve to a tent like spokes with their feet to the centre-pole. For transporting the invalids down to Balaclava there was nothing. 'If it were not for the "French ambulance" [wrote a surgeon] not a single man could be moved from the camp.' What infuriated Hugh Hibbert was that 'by common forethought all this might have been avoided'.

With such sickness and misery coupled with the inability to bring up heavy ammunition in sufficient quantities – some shells weighed 200 lb – the siege of Sebastopol became nominal. Batteries lapsed into silence, having orders only to fire when fired upon. When in February Gordon's battery chose to send out a round or two, it was answered punitively from 52 Russian guns and at once desisted. Infantry fighting in the British attacks became purely defensive, limited to repelling occasional Russian sorties. These were confined, incidentally, to moonless nights, especially when, as Tinley tells us, there was plenty of wind and rain 'the first to deaden sound, the second to drive, as they hope, our men under cover and once under cover soon asleep'. But the Russians too became distressed during the very severe spells, contrary to the belief that they were inured to cold, and showed little inclination to fight. Then would develop an unofficial truce. Such a one was described by Hibbert. The date was January 21st and the snow lay two feet deep.

We have come to a kind of understanding now with the Russians as the cold has forced us all out of our holes, to walk about without molestation, so we now perambulate within 150 yards looking daggers at each other through the sleet.

Moreover sentries in their struggles to keep warm and alive reverted instinctively to a custom once obtaining in the Peninsula and ceased worrying about each other's presence.* At such

* The habit once acquired persisted when warmer nights arrived. As late as June Charles Elton told his father: 'The night before last I was on a covering party and the Russian sentries were lying all night within ten yards of ours but of course it is against the rules of war to annoy sentries unless you intend an attack or something serious.'

a time, lying out in no-man's-land under a full moon with
nothing to break the silence but the crying of plovers and
the flighting of geese overhead, more than one peacetime
sportsman had little difficulty in imagining himself back in
England.

Surprisingly enough soldiers living in such unspeakable conditions and yet doing no fighting rarely descended to crime.

Surely there is nothing in history grander than the enduring
courage and discipline of the British soldier as shown in the
winter of 1854–5. There was practically no crime.

This testimony from Sir Evelyn Wood is confirmed without exception by all letter-writers from the Crimea. Though in
too many respects the French army was superior to the British
their own officers freely admitted that their men would never
have endured such conditions with such resignation, not to say
docility.

Nevertheless the high morale of the army after the Alma
had sagged steadily since Inkerman. Desertions became frequent – no fewer than 24 in January – although mostly by
the newly arrived or those who had undergone punishment. In
step with declining morale went a falling-off in appearance.
'The Crimea will take the pride out of any man or men',
lamented an officer. Fighting more for life and less for
country, the army steadily shed conventions and any regard
for polish. Slept in, worked in, fought in, never taken off,
the once-bright scarlet tunic had become a blotchy purple,
its gold trimming torn and tarnished. As trouser ends frayed
and rotted with wet and mud, legs became encased with
sleeves made out of dead men's greatcoats, strips of old haversacks, odd bits of Russian leather and always stuffed with hay
and straw. 'You would laugh to see what queer figures we cut
on parade', wrote an officer of the 38th. But for epaulets it was
impossible to distinguish a private from an officer, but for
numbers one regiment from another. Only the Rifle Brigade
retained their unmistakably soldierly appearance. Nor did it
make conditions more endurable to see the French moving
about with beards neatly trimmed and looking, wrote Pechell
enviously, 'as clean and regular as if they were at Paris'. For
with a dire scarcity of water all ideas of cleanliness had long

been discarded. A subaltern thus wrote to his young brother: 'Mama asked if I ever took my clothes off. Ans. Never. If I ever washed. Ans. Never.' In the circumstances it was not long before all were verminous. 'The Duke of Cambridge is covered with them, sir,' the Scots Fusilier Guards surgeon was assured by his servant when complaining about the state of his shirt. When a freshly-landed officer saw a party of the 28th go by, he was heard to say, 'D'you call those dirty fellows soldiers? They look more like Cossacks.' The reply evoked from an old soldier was unoriginal but obvious: 'You'll look a bloody sight more like a Cossack when you've been here half as long.' By the end of the year soldiers were described as 'looking like old men twice their age'. And the worst of winter was still to come.

'You might pass me twenty times in the street and not know me', Alfred Tipping told his parents. Inevitably when one walking scarecrow, whatever his rank, hardly differed from another, respect for officers as a class apart declined. Boredom accelerated the process. During those long winter months in the trenches officers played cards and smoked by day and by night wrapped themselves in their greatcoats and slept, setting an example which some NCOs, the backbone of every regiment, were not slow in following.

The effect on the private soldier of this winter in the trenches was more serious. Instead of fighting he was endlessly and uncongenially digging trenches and outworks in rocky, unyielding soil and all the while being reminded of the need to keep the head down; for if the guns were asleep the sniper's rifle was very much awake. In time the lesson was taken so much to heart that – conduct unheard of in the earlier days of the siege – men would refuse to expose themselves in order to bring in the body of a dead comrade. In the trench duty men became laxer. They were more easily surprised in night sorties when it was not uncommon for pickets to be bayoneted in their sleep or to make a panicky retreat.

Yet at heart the army was sound. Humour and cheerfulness were never deeply overlaid by suffering. The sun had only to break through and laughter would be heard. Indeed, it needed pathetically little to revive the Crimean soldier, patient, uncomplaining and enduring. As the spring advanced, slowly

and with many disheartening false starts, so did the army regain its spirits. By the end of March the railway from Balaclava, begun by imported British navvies two months earlier,
had reached the plateau, thus not only putting an end to those
exhausting fatigue parties sent for supplies down to the port
but ensuring a speedy and ampler delivery of all the warm
clothing and prodigal stocks of food which patriotic subscrip-
tions as well as the more war-minded Government of Lord
Palmerston were pouring into the Crimea by every ship.
Appearances improved, officers again looked like officers and
men less like tramps. Belts were ordered to be pipe-clayed and
boots blackened. Colonies of hutments were spreading over
the Heights and dawns were heralded by crowing cocks from
innumerable poultry runs. 'Worse than drum and fifes',
grumbled Brooksbank. By March it was regarded as an in-
fallible sign of returning life when men were known to be
swearing again. Soon a song or two was heard about the
camps and there was some recreational activity, which, in
default of any equipment, took the form of throwing cannon
balls about. March 5th saw the first 'Spring Meeting' with four
races, when Tinley heard one man say to another, 'Blow me,
Bill, if I ever saw sich a crowd o' men without a single petticoat
among 'em.' Thereafter racing became a regular feature of
camp life together with football and cricket. When a Russian
officer asked sarcastically during a truce when we were going
to attack, he was told it could not possibly be the next day or
the day after that as 'we have two race meetings to come off'.

The Russians, too, were gaining confidence. The recent
death of the Czar brought to power a son who as yet lacked
the prestige to be able to come to terms with the Allies without loss of face. Fresh efforts, on the contrary, were put in
hand. There was a steady stream of troops marching across
Russia and every week the armies of Prince Gortschakoff, who
had succeeded Menschikoff, grew in size. Before long the
Russians had become aggressive again. The comparative peace
of the trenches was now over and men going into them were
likened by Hibbert to sheep en route for the slaughter-house,
everyone 'not knowing when it will come to one's own turn
to receive an ounce of lead for breakfast or about six pounds
of iron in the stomach as a cure for the cholera'. In the middle

of March the Russians scored an important tactical success by seizing and fortifying the Mamelon, a mound roughly midway between the Malakoff and the most advanced French parallel.

Twelve days later they mounted powerful night sorties against numerous points in the British and French lines. In the end after bitter fighting they all failed, but there had been a disturbing lack of vigilance on the part of both Allies. Clifford was probably right when he felt that all had been looking at Sebastopol too long to have the same zest they had had after the Alma. When the French, outraged by the Russian occupation of the Mamelon, attempted an ejectment and failed our officers (he went on) 'spoke very lightly of our Allies' and one suggested that Canrobert's name should be transposed to Robert Cant.

On April 9th, Easter Monday, at dawn and in heavy rain and a high wind blowing into Russian faces, 520 guns, including some powerful 13-inch mortars, opened the second bombardment of Sebastopol. Though the railway this time ensured ample supplies of ammunition – 1,000 rounds to every British and 5,000 to every French gun – this bombardment, mightier and more punishing than the first, was at heart a spurious affair. The French, now the senior partner in the alliance, never seriously contemplated an assault to follow. The Emperor's orders to Canrobert envisaged something very different – a complete investment of the city from the north as well as the south. Sebastopol was to be starved into submission, so rendering a costly assault unnecessary. After ten days during which remarkably little damage was done, especially to the Redan fortifications, stagnation returned to the battlefield. Throughout the British army, which did not know how Raglan's hands were tied, there was anger, mystification and a widespread feeling of having been let down by the French. 'They are tremendous fellows to talk about assaults and going in [Goodlake complained to his mother], but there they stop. Their generals can't trust them.'

Early in May depression was lifted by the dispatch of an expedition to capture Kertch at the eastern end of the Crimea and so cut one of the main Russian supply routes. It consisted of French, Turkish and British troops, the last from the Highland Brigade, and by a gracious gesture on the part of Canrobert the choice of its commander was vested in Raglan. His choice, perhaps naturally, was his old Peninsular friend, the buckram Sir George Brown. Unfortunately just one week before the expedition sailed the Crimea became connected by telegraph with the outside world and in that fact lay its miscarriage. When within two hours of its destination it was recalled the reason was not, as one wag said, that Sir George had left his stock behind (which another declared was impossible as he invariably slept in it), but because Napoleon wished everything to give place to his own grandiose ideas and required the French transports for the conveyance of fresh troops awaiting embarkation at Constantinople. Though the recall only applied to the French it was obviously impossible for the British contingent to continue. The choleric Sir George had to restrain himself from knocking down the innocent French general in his fury, and Anglo-French relations, already strained over the recent futile bombardment, became tense. The Prince Consort wrote furiously on hearing the news: 'Who will rekindle the spirit of the French army which has been dashed by Canrobert's irresolution and want of firmness?' And in the British army the further indignation felt by all towards the French surpassed, as he confessed, Calthorpe's powers of description. Neither the Prince nor the Crimean army could appreciate poor Canrobert's position now that his Emperor was at the other end of a telegraph wire, peppering him with instructions at all hours. On May 16th, overwrought by his anxieties, he resigned and asked to be demoted to the command of his old division. His request was granted and he was succeeded by Pélissier, a man of a very different stamp, a Norman, a fire-eater, who was energetic, ruthless and foul-mouthed – he was known to refer to himself as 'that bastard Pélissier'. But he was – and it counted for much – a devoted admirer of Raglan. Within a week in defiance of the Emperor's veto the Kertch expedition was on its way again. Its subsequent outstanding success achieved with the loss in the British forces of only one man (and he by an accident) removed the last traces of winter discontents and provided a happy augury for operations which would obviously follow the succession to supreme command of this passionate man of action.

T—G

6

The Redan

'British pluck is very much like any other pluck, and
British soldiers will be found to resemble others most
uncommonly, if they are badly managed.'

– *'Redan' Windham*

By the end of May the siege had lasted for eight
months and except at one point on the French left and at
another (some rifle pits) on the British Right Attack the Allies
were no nearer Sebastopol than they had been in September.
Not only was any destruction caused by their guns repaired
during the night, but with ample willing labour at his command Todleben had strengthened the defences by every device
of which his genius was capable. There were secure bomb-
proof messes and sleeping-quarters for officers and men constructed of old ships' timbers, some over two feet in diameter.
Nearly every magazine was wired so as to be capable of being
exploded electrically if required. Secure sick-bays had been
excavated complete with fireplaces and chimneys. In the
Malakoff there was even a patented water-closet of English
manufacture for the use of its commander. Camouflage of
the twentieth century had been anticipated in the painting of
a formidable work to represent a dwelling-house. A successful assault would clearly be very much more costly in men
and materials than after the Flank March. Manpower, however, no longer presented a problem despite the hideous losses
of the winter. Sardinia had joined the Allies at the end of
January and her efficient little army had taken over the defence
of the Balaclava plain and the line of the Tchernaya; the
French army had expanded to 90,000 and Pélissier was ready
to use it without regard to cost. Named *l'homme brutal* from
his ruthlessness in Algerian wars, he had been heard to

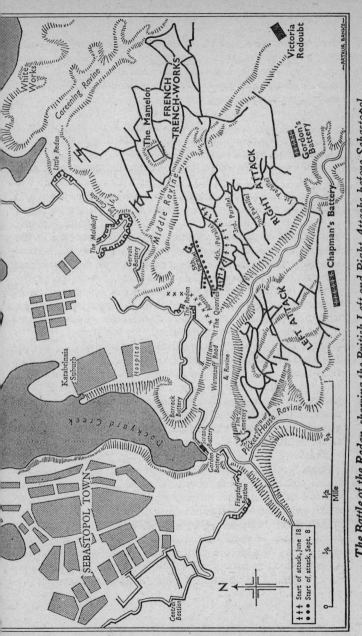

The Battle of the Redan, showing the British Left and Right Attacks before Sebastopol

declare that omelettes could not be made without breaking eggs and that war could not be waged *à la Monsieur Cobden,* that is without losses. As for materials, an ample flow should now be guaranteed not only through the coming of the railway but through the efficient reorganization of Balaclava harbour by the energetic and unfairly-maligned Admiral-Superintendent, Edward Boxer. All that was required was a carefully worked-out plan of attack, based on exact timing and thorough preparation.

Nothing that the Allies or Todleben had done could alter the fact, apparent from the first days, that the Malakoff was the key to Sebastopol. Once in Allied hands the Redan and the entire quadrant from the Point Battery on the harbour's edge to the north-east round to the Barrack Battery to the south could be taken in reverse. The main anchorage in the harbour from which it was only 2,000 yards would become unusable. The Karabelnaya must be abandoned and that meant Sebastopol. Todleben had done his best, but he could not remove hills or level valleys. Nevertheless he had strengthened the Whiteworks on the edge of the Inkerman Heights, and the subsequent seizure of the Mamelon under the eyes of the French had vastly increased the Malakoff's ability to resist assault. Finally between the Redan and the British Right Attack some diggings named by us the Quarries had been occupied and the foreground liberally planted with fougasses, the Crimean equivalent of a land mine. The Quarries not only provided a vantage point from which sharpshooters could harass the British trenches and batteries but served as a buffer to the Redan. Before any attempt could be made on this or the Malakoff the Quarries and the Mamelon respectively had to be stormed. By the last days of May Raglan, working with Pélissier in greater accord than he had found possible with Canrobert, had agreed to combine operations to capture these twin strongpoints as a preliminary to a grand assault on Sebastapol.

At the first camp 'shave' of impending action at last, excitement already aroused by the success of the Kertch expedition swept through the two armies. Some opposition to a scheme which so blatantly conflicted with the Emperor's pet idea, naturally came from certain of Pélissier's own staff, notably General Niel, but this was rudely shouted down with the words: 'Lord Raglan and I have decided it', to which in reference to the Mamelon was added, '*si ça coute dix ou dix millions, nous le prenons*'.

At three o'clock on the afternoon of June 6th an avalanche of metal broke from the mouths of nearly 550 allied guns, half of them concentrated on the Karabelnaya's defences. Firing less impulsively than the French but with greater accuracy the British gunners produced results qualified by Todleben as 'terrible, violent, murderous'. Soon all batteries were blanketed with smoke. When night fell the guns ceased, but against a background of a mighty thunderstorm rolling and flashing to the north-east, 13-inch mortars continued the bombardment. As their shells curved through the night sky, shedding tiny sparks from their burning fuses they looked like so many fireflies, whose journey's end was indicated by a great flash which threw the Russian earthworks into sharp silhouette. At dawn the guns began again on the tortured defences, which despite the mortar shells the Russians had none the less repaired under cover of a short summer's night. But to replenish ammunition had not been possible and soon the batteries which the day before had replied with remarkable rapidity and warmth started to flag, some firing only once to every 20 or 30 allied rounds.

After this there was no question of a surprise attack. The Russians no less than the French and British knew that this could not long be delayed. Indeed as the afternoon wore on the Heights behind the allied batteries began to take on a 'going to the Derby scene'. Wives, 'Travelling Gentlemen' (or more briefly TGs), newspaper correspondents, all who were not on duty (and some who were) began to assemble as for a spectacle. To pass the time of waiting the band of the Rifle Brigade considerately played light airs. Below these gathering crowds the troops detailed for the capture of the Quarries began filing into the trenches. With his immense confidence in the prowess of the British fighting man Raglan chose to use only a small but select force. While the French (admittedly for a rather more extensive operation) were employing more than four brigades, the number of British troops was only 400, drawn from the Light and 2nd Divisions and commanded by

Colonel Shirley of the 88th, reserves to be provided by the 62nd. Nevertheless everywhere confidence was supreme. As for excitement, this was so great that Pennefather had to go through the parallels urging the men not to shout and betray their presence.

Shortly after six o'clock a rocket shot into the air and the firing which had somewhat eased off thundered into life. Roger Fenton, the photographer, watching with the crowd, thought that nothing more terrific had ever been seen or heard in battle. The furious cannonade lasted for 15 minutes and then three rockets went up. In an instant the French guns ceased and their troops, looking from a distance like 'so many little rats', shot out from their trenches and led far in advance by the brave Colonel Brancion, scrambled across the 500 yards which separated them from the Mamelon. Up its now silent sides they swarmed and all at once a tricolor was waving from the parapet and Brancion lying dead at its foot. Unfortunately the Zouaves, whose courage hardly required the stimulus of a pint of wine recently issued to each man, were so carried away that they charged on towards the Malakoff itself, from which they were not only repelled with great ease and loss but were pursued by the Russians back through the Mamelon to their own lines. This was, however, a contingency for which Bosquet in charge of this operation had provided. He at once ordered out the ample reserves he had been withholding. These drove back the Russians, re-entered the Mamelon and held it this time for good.

On seeing the Zouaves for the first time surging into the Mamelon, Raglan had given his signal. The artillery lifted from the Quarries and cheering loudly the 400 stormers dashed forward. Divided into two equal bodies led by Colonel Campbell of the 90th and Major Armstrong of the 49th, they advanced not directly but on either flank of their objective, thus to a great extent avoiding the fougasses. The swiftness of the attack took the Russians by surprise for all their awareness. In a very short while they had fallen precipitously back on the Redan with the loss of over 100 officers and men. The main body of stormers, after pursuing them for some distance, was ordered to lie down and open fire on the embrasures so as to keep down gunfire on the 62nd, who had arrived in the

Quarries on their heels and were busily engaged in reversing the fortifications and incorporating them into the British works. A few bolder spirits disregarding orders had in Zouave fashion pressed on as far as the Redan itself which some actually claim to have entered till driven back, having suffered some losses which included Lieutenant Webb, whose body was later found close to the parapet.

A comparatively easy conquest was followed by a night of heroic defence as the Russians fought desperately to regain this important strong point. Shot and shell from the Redan and Barrack batteries crashed into the Quarries, lifting only to allow their infantry to attack. This they did six times in the course of the night, flinging themselves against the inadequate and uncompleted defences. As the fighting swayed backwards and forwards across the no-man's-land occasionally someone would tread on a fougasse and in the darkness there would be a blinding but rarely fatal flash. More often ammunition would run dry and as at Inkerman there would be recourse to fists and stones. Frederick Elton, who was attached to the working party, tells how because of the inadequate number of men and the thinness of the supports:

We were ordered to throw down our tools and form a support instead of a working party which we did and shortly afterwards advanced to where the others were fighting and joined them.

Between alternately fighting and struggling to fill gabions and reconstruct defences out of the rocky, scanty soil men became utterly exhausted before the final attack which might be expected before dawn. They had even dropped to the ground, asleep in an instant and snoring away above the din. When at length the attack came, preceded by what Captain Garnet Wolseley called 'that horrible jackal sort of rasping screeching discordant yell which with the Russians takes the place of our manly telling British cheers', a hundred stout-hearted enemy could have retaken the Quarries with more ease than they had been overrun. But (Wolseley goes on) no soldier fights his best at night, whatever his courage by day. He attributes to the enemy unwarranted superiority in strength and a more madcap eagerness to engage in battle. To those fears the hard-pressed British garrison of the Quarries owe their survival. Accompanied by Wolseley, Colonel Campbell mounted the tumbledown makeshift parapet in order to give the men confidence. While a bugler of the 90th was ordered to blow every regimental call he knew, officers fired off their revolvers recklessly and the men thus encouraged cheered with all their remaining breath.

Before this pandemonium the Russians, although not a dozen paces away, hesitated, imagining the worst. In the dim half-light of the dawn officers could be seen vainly pulling at their men, belabouring their backs with the flat of their swords. The attack aborted and morning found the Quarries firmly held, its parapets built up of gabions, stones and dead Russians. There were no further attempts at recapture.

The cost of the Quarries had not been light for so limited an operation. The killed and wounded amounted to 671 or nearly half the number engaged, but it was not the sum so much as the ratio of officer casualties which was significant. With these totalling 47 the percentage was higher than ever before and provoked such comment as 'It makes one think that there has been some occasion for the officers to expose themselves to get the men on, though when once they are at it, they always fight.' Nevertheless the operation sent a wave of optimism through the camps. 'Johnny Russ is done for', Hibbert told his sister. The conquest of the Redan now began to be talked about with as much unconcern and confidence as if it was to provide 'a day's rabbit shooting'. It was not appreciated that the capture of the Quarries had been glorious only when related to the drab background of the past six months. To astute observers there were other disturbing features besides the high officers' casualty rate. The affair could so easily have ended in disaster. Staff work had been wretched. Orders received had been confused and sometimes contradictory. Headquarters who did the planning had miscalculated not merely the strength needed to occupy the Quarries but also to repel counter-attacks. Reserves had been too few and too distant. Little intelligence had been shown in selecting the right quality of the troops to be employed. The proportion of veterans was low. Many of the officers, although unquestionably brave, were absurdly young and inexperienced. The 7th Fusiliers, one of the regiments chosen, is described by Hibbert as 'full of Sandhurst boys; such little rascals I never saw, mere children'. That a working party should have been required to put down their tools to fight 300 or 400 yards in advance of our parallels indicated mismanagement somewhere. Yet what lay ahead would require very much greater care and more inspired planning. How far these were to be found in the attacks on the Redan will now be seen.

Had there been a single command of an integrated army there would have been no need for anything more than a feint or diversion against the Redan. To capture it without the Malakoff would be to waste lives – in such circumstances it could not be held. On the other hand to require the British army after eight months of frustration and inactivity to remain spectators while the French gained the glory and renown of taking the Malakoff and through it the right to claim all honour for the fall of Sebastopol was out of the question. The idea was never even considered. The Redan presented to the British army a challenge which had to be met, which pride would never allow to be shirked. Any French assault on the Malakoff had to be accompanied by a British assault on the Redan.

Built on what had been a vineyard, 306 feet above sea-level, the Redan as its name denoted had two faces, each 70 yards long, meeting at an angle of 65 degrees. The base from which it jutted out was a fortified line of earthwork spanning the ridge. In front of it had been dug a ditch roughly 20 feet in width and 14 in depth. Above this the Redan rose to a height of 15 feet, making its escarpment from top to bottom nearly 30 feet. Between it and the new parallels, advanced as a result of the Quarries success, there were about 450 yards of ground, much of it uphill and all of it exposed either to the Barrack and even the Garden batteries on the left or the Gervais or Malakoff guns on the right. The Redan itself abounded in guns (some in two tiers) behind embrasures across which hung rope mantelets shielding the gunners from rifle fire, while well constructed traverses to their rear protected them and their guns from everything but a direct hit. Unlike the Malakoff it had no 'Gorge' which an enemy once in possession of the fort could use to defend themselves against counter-attacks. But more effective than any gorge was a broad road running up from the last houses in the suburb. There, where incidentally a concealed battery was sited, troops could be collected unseen and rushed forward to defend the Redan from any assaults. Finally, about 50 yards in advance of its ditch an abattis had been made out of a tangle of branches some six or eight feet in height and many more in depth.

Though neither the secrets of the Redan's great strength nor the magnitude of the defences to protect its garrison and magazines were known, it was confidently predicted that nothing could resist the pulverizing bombardment which the Allies were now able to mount. When this had reduced the Redan, the Malakoff and all other fortifications to rubble then there should be a combined assault extending from the French right, where the Whiteworks on Inkerman had been captured at the same time as the Mamelon, to the British Left Attack. In addition the French left facing the city should make a diversionary demonstration and those on the Tchernaya, in association with the Sardinians, threaten a feint attack on the Mackenzie Heights. The date chosen was June 18th, the fortieth anniversary of Waterloo. In the success which must attend such an overwhelming offensive, a day and a memory so inconvenient to an Anglo-French alliance would be gloriously buried. The time was fixed for five or six in the morning so as to allow at least two hours for the guns and mortars to destroy the inevitable repairs of the previous night. It remained only for each army to organize its own method of attack.

Once again Raglan, either through pride or ignorance, was to use far fewer troops than Pélissier – 8,000 to his 25,000. Nine months earlier there might have been no comment, but to those who now realized the extent to which the old army of Alma and Inkerman days had disappeared the numbers seemed perilously small for the tremendous tasks to be undertaken.

There were to be two British offensives. The first was against the Redan by three columns attacking its right and left face and its salient angle. The composition of each was identical. First, there were 100 skirmishers provided by the Rifle Brigade, closely followed by ten sappers, a ladder party (half of them sailors) and 50 men carrying woolbags for filling the ditch. Behind these were to go the storming party, 400 strong, then the reserves numbering 800. The command of the left column was given to Sir John Campbell, one of the most popular men in the army, that of the right to that fine veteran of the Alma, Lacy Yea. The centre column intended to assault the salient angle can be ignored, as it was destined to play no part in the day's tragic proceedings. The men for all columns were to be drawn from the Light, 2nd and 4th Divisions.

The second offensive was to be carried out by the Left Attack which meant the 3rd Division and its purpose was at once diversionary and contingent. Eyre's brigade was to move down the Picket-House Ravine between the French and British armies and attack various works at the head of the Dockyard Creek. The other brigade, commanded by General Barnard, was to assemble in the Woronzoff Ravine and wait till a signal indicated that the Redan had been carried. It was then to sweep round to its right by the head of the Creek and take the Barrack Battery in reverse.

Precisely at four o'clock on the morning of June 17th 800 allied guns flashed into life and there began a cannonade the like of which the world had never seen or heard before. To Sergeant Gowing, 'The very ground seemed to shake beneath the crash of guns.' Nevertheless the Russians were neither daunted nor backward in retaliating, which they did with only 50 fewer pieces of artillery. But as the day wore on this spirited reply notably weakened. Some batteries fired only fitfully, some like the Malakoff became quite silent. As the British gleefully watched embrasures crumbling, guns disappearing and parapets disintegrating, the outcome of the morrow was assured. Wagons seen that afternoon carrying straw into Sebastopol, presumably for the firing of the city, seemed to confirm its doom. Goodlake was enthusiastic. 'You cannot conceive the excitement. We are all the world like tigers. I believe the men would go in without arms.' Roger Fenton was being strongly urged by his friends 'to stop over tomorrow and you will at last see the inside of Sebastopol'. By nightfall they confidently reckoned to be dining in what remained of the town's restaurants. What no one either in the camps or at Headquarters realized was that the weakening of Russian fire was only partly due to destruction: the other factors were the need to conserve ammunition and cunning. When a gun vanished from an embrasure it was not necessarily shattered; it could just as well have been withdrawn for safety's sake or to deceive the enemy.

In a chain of events leading to an operation of this magnitude an item of no great significance at the time can have far-reaching consequences. A map of the Malakoff found on a dead Russian in the Mamelon had been brought to Bosquet and retained instead of being passed on to Headquarters. This irregular behaviour decided the fiery Pélissier, whose relations with him had been strained for some weeks. Bosquet was removed from the division facing the Malakoff and sent down to take charge of the troops on the Tchernaya. To succeed him came General St Jean d'Angely, whose credentials as commander of the Imperial Guard were unimpeachable, but who was unfamiliar with Bosquet's old division and, which mattered more, with the terrain before the Malakoff. It seemed to him to be impossible to conceal his men for two hours of daylight preceding the attack and to protect them from Russian fire. He accordingly made representations to Pélissier, who without consulting Raglan advanced the hour of attack by two hours to dawn. His reasons, in the message which he sent through an ADC, were tersely described as *'incontestables'*. But the idea that after a 24-hour bombardment the Russians could be taken by surprise at dawn, of all times, was ingenuous, and from a man who professed to care nothing for the 'butcher's bill' so long as he achieved his purpose, surprising. It was more important to reduce as much as possible the fire against men crossing open cannon-swept ground, even if this entailed incurring casualties in the parallels while awaiting zero hour. Such reduction could be obtained only by a resumption of bombardment in the morning.

Lord Raglan did not receive Pélissier's message till he had returned late at night from a round of his divisions. Then in Goodlake's scornful words, 'he gave way *as usual*'. Knowing, as he did instinctively, that the change of time was wrong and must imperil the attack of his army, it may well be asked if he ought not to have resisted. Was concurrence here not the paying of too high a price for allied harmony? Hamley believed that he 'would have done well in declining to cooperate except on the jointly agreed plan'. On the other hand if he did agree to the alteration he still retained one powerful trump card: he had all along (knowing the Redan to be untenable without the Malakoff) reserved to himself the timing of the British assault. If all went well with the French, what reason was there to suppose the British would not succeed? If the French failed, a British attack would be quixotic and useless. Unhappily it was a card Raglan was too much of a gentleman to play.

Having decided to agree to the change of time, Raglan sent word to Sir George Brown in command of the whole operation and by him it was relayed to the various subordinates. Received only a short time before the attack was due to start, it added to the confusion which obscure and imprecise orders from Headquarters had already caused. It had not, for example, been made clear beyond all doubt whether the centre column was to advance in step with the others or wait till they had made a lodgement on the two faces of the Redan. There was no proper arrangement for getting the troops into the parallels in the right order or keeping our truants from other regiments who long before the attack came crowding into the trenches 'to see the fun'. Nor once in the trenches was there any method devised for getting the men out together and in line by building a banquette. All this was hardly surprising when, according to Patullo, 'many of the details were made out and superintended by staff men who (you will hardly believe it) had never been in the trenches before and I need hardly tell you that it needs considerable experience of the trenches to move men in and about them; the dullest subaltern who daily does duty there would have made a better commander than the shrewdest staff man without experience of the ground'. And if Ensign Maule were asked why this was so, he had his reply, 'They seldom or never come down.'

The effects of the imperfect knowledge in addition to those consequent upon the change of hour were very soon evident. Dawn found the columns (again to quote Patullo)

far from being prepared for the attack for want of previous

arrangement and an ignorance of whom we were immediately acting under; each brigadier seemed to have a different vague idea of the general operation. We were told off as a working party to enter immediately a footing had been made in the enemy's works but by some mistake we were pushed on next to the storming parties and between them and their supports, effectually blocking the trenches.

Daniel Lysons having been briefed to command a storming party was at the last minute switched over to supports. Tinley in command of the 39th was without positive orders.

But it was not only in the British sectors that the full effects of Pélissier's misguided action were felt. For it a terrible price in French blood was to be exacted. Brunet, whose Brigade was to assault the face of the Malakoff, was to find the advance trenches not yet vacated by Autemarre's men who were to attack the Gervais battery on the left. Unlike the British, the French command had no idea of sending men into battle on empty stomachs and the cooks had not cleared away their paraphernalia when Brunet's men arrived. Worse than the confusion which this caused was the late starting from their distant lines of two brigades ordered to act as reserves.

With generals, both French and English, unsettled and worried by the change of hour, only a slight mischance was needed to throw everything out of gear. It came in the form of a mortar shell fired from the Mamelon. General Mayran, who was in charge of the French right attack on the Point Battery and Little Redan, had recently been publicly reprimanded for not obeying orders on the 7th and was overwrought. When he saw this trailing light, although it wanted 30 minutes to zero hour, he took it for the signal rocket and ordered his men to attack. The other columns were not ready and the planned synchronized assault from three points never materialized. Forewarned by Mayran's move, which collapsed before the fire of the two batteries, and by the flanking fire of ships in the harbour, the Russians were fully prepared at the Malakoff by the time Brunet's men began to advance. Those who survived the searing blasts of grapeshot from guns, which far from having been destroyed had been raised during the night *en barbette* (that is, able to fire down at a steep angle), were met when they reached the surrounding ditch by the bullets from riflemen ranged two deep along the parapet. So far had these progressed from the technique of Alma days that those in the front rank having discharged their muskets passed them over their left shoulder to receive instantly from the right another loaded and at full cock, thus enabling a constant fire to be maintained on the enemy below. Not a Frenchman crossed the ditch. To Hume watching from the British lines they seemed to beat like waves helplessly against the rocks. Brunet was killed and his men fell back in disorder. At first Autemarre's division looked like succeeding. Hurrying down the Dockyard Ravine where they were out of sight of the Russian guns, they cut into and overran the Gervais Battery. However, without the reserves which had been late in starting out, it was impossible to consolidate their gains and after a brief occupation they had to withdraw, having suffered severely.

In what was now daylight with visibility extending to half a mile Raglan from his position in the third parallel of the Right Attack could see that the French were failing to carry the Malakoff. With his men still in the parallels the realistic course would have been to reopen the bombardment and so revert to the original plan. Two hours later or less, the Russian batteries having been silenced and the infantry dispersed or driven under cover, his men would have gone forward with some chance of succeeding. By that time the French should have recovered their breath and have resumed their share of the attack. Such a course a hard-headed, practical general would have taken. In Raglan the gentleman took precedence over the opportunist, honour outweighed policy. He believed that the fair name of England was at stake. To stand by, whatever the ultimate advantages, even for two hours, while the guns roared, would be to incur obloquy in the eyes of the French. He was too far from Pélissier to confer with him. Instead he turned to Sir George, who strongly advised an immediate attack. The order was thereupon given and the British army was sent forward into an infantry Balaclava.

Synchronizing with the deployment of troops into the trenches there had been taking place that assembling of spectators without which no Crimean battle save Inkerman had been fought. This time, as befitted the occasion, the audience had been vastly increased in size. There were captains of merchant-men, civilian clerks and navvies, all hotfoot from Balaclava in addition to the TGs and off-duty officers and war correspondents. Foreigners were present in such force that Portal believed the North American Indian was the only race not represented. Moreover this time the ladies were much in evidence. There was Mrs Duberly, wife of the paymaster in the 8th Hussars, who has recorded her impressions, Mrs Escourt, wife of the Adjutant-General, the ravishing Lady George Paget, the 'belle of the camp'. Near at hand was her husband, Lord George, in command of the cavalry now by drafts and reinforcements 800 strong. This time his orders were not to make a desperate charge or even to give his 'best support' but to function 'as special constables . . . as if it were a review'. So complete had been Raglan's confidence that he intended Paget's duties to be to stop a rush of souvenir-hunting civilians into the conquered city. There was to be no such rush and those eager spectators were to be treated to a rare show which ought for ever to have weaned them of morbid curiosity.

As they thronged the hill the audience heard bugle calls sounding from the town, but in their excitement they paid no attention. Later on their significance was to be realized. Ten thousand men were being alerted for the defence of the threatened Redan.

The signal for the attack was a rocket and the waving of a flag three times from where Raglan had stationed himself. The next moment the skirmishers, ladder parties and woolbag men on the left and right columns were scrambling out of the parallels as best they could. The commander of the centre column, wrongly it seems, interpreted his equivocal orders as not to advance till a lodgement had been made in the Redan, and his men remained behind.

Now, if ever, was the moment when every available British gun should have been turned on to the Redan and its adjacent works and batteries, stripping the bastions of riflemen and driving the gunners under cover. By what Tinley justly calls 'some unaccountable stupid blunder' the artillery

received order to cease firing. The consequences can be left
to the imagination. As the men came out of the parallels into
the long, rank grass pitted with shell holes, the guns of the
Redan crossed by those of the Gervais and Barrack batteries
and supplemented by a long-distance shelling from ships in the
harbour opened such a *feu d'enfer* as moved Raglan to write,
'I never before witnessed such a continued and heavy fire of
grape combined with musketry from the enemy's works which
appeared to be fully manned.' Its swish and roar as it raced
through the air reminded Midshipman Wood of the simulated
rainstorms heard in the wings of a theatre, only greatly
exaggerated. To those waiting their turn in the advance
trenches it seemed to pronounce their death warrant. 'As soon
as the guns of the Redan opened upon us [confessed Captain
Hibbert of the 7th] we all knew that it could end in nothing
but butchery for us without the slightest hope of success.'

And it was not only from the guns that death threatened.
Along the earthworks, all fully repaired after the previous
day's bombardment, and behind the parapets, Russian soldiers
stood four deep, awaiting the appearance of the first redcoat
above the fifth parallel. Sergeant Gowing went so far as to
affirm that 'we were sold that morning by traitors from our
own ranks', adding that he knew one of those who had deserted carrying with him the date and time of the attack. As
the hour had been so recently changed his information would
have been valueless; as regards date, even if the Russians had
not learnt this from their spies it was an easy deduction that
the anniversary of Waterloo would be the chosen day. Whether
their knowledge was deduced or acquired, the Russians were
ready to deal with an attack across 450 yards of rising ground.
Men later remembered that, as they made their way to the
advance parallels, there had been an unwonted ominous
silence on the part of the enemy as if they were determined
to conserve everything they had for the moment of the assault.

It was a massacre from the start. The skirmishers from the
Rifle Brigade cutting their way through a curtain of lead lost
heavily. On the left they were brought to a halt while still a
long way from the Redan. On their right, where because the
French were still in the Gervais battery and the Malakoff was
engaged in its own defence, the flanking fire was less severe,

they reached the neighbourhood of the abattis in the branches of which (largely undamaged by artillery fire) the body of Captain Forman was found next day. Unable to advance further they halted, took cover in shell holes or behind boulders and opened fire, but as the gunners and riflemen were well protected behind the embrasures and gabions, repaired during the night, their shooting had little effect upon the fire now directed upon the ladder parties and woolbag men. Moving more slowly because of their loads and bunched together, these were moved down as they toiled up the slope. As each member of the ladder party dropped dead or wounded the weight of the 18-foot ladder grew heavier for the survivors until it became unbearable and what was left of them sank to the ground, hoping somehow to escape destruction. Those who had made slower progress, seeing what was happening to their comrades in front, either took cover or retreated. The men of the Naval Brigade carried on the furthest but even they collapsed long before reaching the abattis.

Meanwhile the two storming columns were out of their parallels and advancing across the uphill 450 yards to the Redan. To deal first with those on the left. Campbell's men ran into trouble even before they encountered the Russian fire and blame for this rested squarely on the shoulders of the staff. The congestion in the trenches and lack of a banquette resulted in men's scrambling out anyhow here and there in ragged files instead of in line. In a moment they were a rabble. The 57th on the left flank found it simpler to edge still further away to the left to where the press was thinner and to emerge as a narrow column near the rim of the Woronzoff Ravine.

Here the slope of the ground certainly gave some protection but this splitting of the storming party into two rendered each too weak to make any impression. Seeing the danger, Sir John Campbell attempted to coordinate his attack and with sword drawn ran out in front of his men and was shot dead. 'Was he mad?' asked an astonished Russian officer next day. Almost at the same moment Colonel Shadforth of the 57th was killed and the command of the left column devolved upon Lord West of Inkerman renown. West was in the rear in charge of the reserves and by the time he had shouldered his way to the front the heart had gone out of the young soldiers who formed the majority of stormers. With their lessons on the need to keep well under cover given practical illustration by the fate overtaking their comrades exposed on that murderous grape-drenched glacis they had fallen back on the fifth parallel from which neither threats nor blandishments would move them. Seeing the staggering losses – the 57th had lost 113 killed and wounded out of 400 – Lord West sent back to Sir George an urgent message for fresh troops. He received the bleak, unhelpful answer, 'Reform your attacking column'. As this was no longer possible Lord West ordered a withdrawal. What remained of the advance parties had already retreated, leaving here and there dour pockets of resistance.

The right attack fared little better. Here, as we have seen, the fire was slightly less intense but because of the same congestion and lack of a banquette the men, drawn from the 34th, went over in driblets of twos and threes. Nor, thought Lord Wantage as he watched, was there any dash about them. Such an irregular, hesitant advance, so different from the impressive determined march up Kourgane, appalled Colonel Yea. 'This won't do,' he roared. 'Where's the bugler to call them back?' But there was no bugler and before the blasts of grape and canister the orderless 34th was brought to a standstill with a loss of more than 200. Yea thereupon called up his supports which included his beloved Royal Fusiliers, the 23rd and 33rd, all commanded by Dan Lysons. Putting himself at their head Yea strode on, roaring out encouragements, and had reached the abattis where he was discussing the next move with an officer of the Engineers when he was struck in the head. He fell forward, crawled a few yards, his sword upraised in front of him as if pointing the way, and then fell dead.

With the death of Yea, who represented the finest type of British officer, brave, inspiring, efficient, dedicated to his profession, all fire went out of the attack. Once the men had halted or dived for shelter nothing, now he was gone, could get them to move. Battle-hardened sergeants, veterans of the Alma, were seen to be threatening them with death by shooting if they refused to advance; but it was generally the sergeants who perished as they exposed themselves fearlessly. The utmost the men could be induced to do was to fire wildly in the direction of the Redan. Hugh Hibbert, by now the only survivor but two of the 23 officers of the 7th Fusiliers who had landed in the Crimea, came up at this moment and has recorded his impressions.

We had some hundred yards to advance across an open plain with guns loaded with grape and canister shot blazing away into us. As I advanced I thought every second would be my last. I could hardly see for the dust that the grape shot made in plough-ing up the ground all around us – before – behind – and on each side – shells bursting over my head and fellows rolling over right and left. I seemed to bear a charmed life for nothing would hit me! My haversack was covered with blood from men who were shot near me and so was my sword. When we got to the abattis which is at least 50 yards from the Redan the fire was so heavy that no mortals could stand it and there was nothing for it but to retreat as rapidly as possible. ... In fact we were regularly beaten back and I saw the rascally Russians taking off their caps and jeering at us.

Lysons's account is largely confirmatory. After describing how he led 'all that could follow' of his supports past the 34th, 'halted from the severity of the fire', as far as the abattis, he found he had not enough with which to make a charge, and ordered them to lie down until further supports arrived. But when it became clear that there would be no further supports and his little force was reduced to about half a dozen men, then (he says) 'I thought it high time to be off; we were the last to go in. They fired at us all the way back. The Russians were perfectly prepared for us'. They even shouted derisively, 'Come on, Ingliski.'

With disaster on their right and left the centre storming party was very wisely held back and further useless carnage was avoided. Only then did Raglan order the artillery to re-open fire. This they did with appalling effect upon the parapets crowded with hurriedly-summoned Russian reserves.

Later in the day the wind freshened and blew up a blanket of dust over the battlefield. Under its cover a number of wounded men and others who had remained out in front worked their way back. These included the indomitable Cap-tain Forsyth of the 57th who, refusing to retreat with his men, had ensconced himself in a shell hole round which he constructed a parapet of dead bodies (from the pouches of

whom he supplied himself with ammunition) and had kept
up a harassing fire upon the embrasures of the Redan.

Only a lacklustre gleam filtered through the gloom
brought about by these failures. A very modest success had
been scored by Eyre's Brigade in the diversionary operation on
the left extremity of the line. The 3rd Division had been
excited the day before by the issue of the New Enfield Rifle
in place of the Minié. Moreover Eyre that morning had
further whipped up the enthusiasm of the 18th, the premier
Irish regiment, by an address (said to have been delivered in
Erse) in which he told them that he hoped their exploits
that morning would make every Irish cabin ring. When on
getting Raglan's signal he gave the word, his three regiments,
the 18th, 38th and 44th, pressed down the Picket House
Ravine which separated the Left Attack from the French in
front of the city. Nicknamed Eyre's Greyhounds from their
custom of being exercised at the double, they took the Russians by surprise and threw them out of a cemetery they had
been holding near the end of the spur overlooking the Dockyard Creek. From here they fanned out and pressed on with
such zeal and speed that they actually reached and occupied
the outlying houses of Sebastopol. In them terrified women
and children were quickly reassured by signs that they had
nothing to fear.

Although most of the houses were too low to be attacked
by the guns of the Garden Battery ahead, they were defenceless against those of the Strand and (after the collapse of the
Redan assault) the Barrack Batteries. Only splendid service
with the New Enfields, directed into the embrasures, kept
down the fire. When nettled at last by this resistance the
Russians brought into the creek some warships, no effective
return fire was possible. It was now that Eyre himself was
severely wounded in the head.

While this gruelling defence was being fought out, those not
at the moment employed were diverting themselves in a
manner undreamed of during the previous nine months.
Officers and men sat about drinking coffee which the women
were induced to make and eating their pork rations off books
in lieu of plates. Some houses contained a piano, the tinkling
of which with or without the accompaniment of songs could

be heard above the rattle of the musketry. The Irishmen were quick to unearth a store of wine and cherry brandy and many were soon reeling about, dressing themselves in women's clothes, dancing and pirouetting in bonnets and shawls on a plot of grass, regardless of the firing. In this strange oasis of junketing there was a positive indifference to all that was happening elsewhere. Once when two Irishmen quarrelled over some booty, a ring was formed in the open and they fought it out with bare fists.

With his communication cut off by the fury of the Russian fire, Eyre did not for some hours learn of the failure against the Redan and despite mounting casualties there was no alternative but to hold on until nightfall. At five o'clock Eyre's wound compelled him to hand over to Colonel Adams of the 28th (which had been in reserve) and it was he who after dark, with very little interference from the enemy, brought back the Brigade, using doors torn from their hinges as stretchers. All conquests except the cemetery were abandoned and this was not worth the price paid – 31 officers, 44 sergeants and 487 rank and files, killed or wounded.

No one sought to minimize the disaster. The British soldier had been defeated but not disgraced. He had been defeated because of him it was possible to ask too much. British pluck would do a great deal, but not, Windham protested, 'everything'. He goes on: 'British pluck is very much like any other pluck and British soldiers will be found to resemble others most uncommonly, if they are badly managed.' And it was the opinion of everyone who fought and watched that day that they had been disgracefully managed. 'The officers behaved most gallantly but not with judgement; the supports did not come up in time: in fact the whole thing was a botch.' 'Sir George Brown inflated by the bloodless conquest of Kertch directed the operations as if the garrison of Sebastopol were a body of serfs.' Nevertheless James Williams considered that the army though humiliated was not, strange to say, disheartened, regarding the whole thing 'as such a bungling disgracefully childish failure that it was rather laughed at as a joke'. Earle, slightly wounded in the fighting, declared angrily that 'we are prepared to try it again provided Sir G. Brown has nothing to do with it'. Failure was the more galling because

of the general cocksureness which had preceded the attack and
had received the official *imprimatur*.

'We had been told from Headquarters and other high
authority that success was certain; that the arrangements for
the plan of attack were so perfect that they must succeed;
whereas when put to the test they turned out to be so
execrably bad that failure was inevitable.'

With that indictment written by a Staff officer no one who
fought that day would have disagreed. Words such as 'mis-
managed', 'bad business', 'feeble and ill-conducted', 'botched',
'bungled' figure in nearly every letter. It seemed as if by no
possibility could Headquarters ever reach a correct decision
or dispatch an order that was not liable to misinterpretation.
'The batteries, instead of shelling the Redan and Malakoff
so as to render it impossible for a Russian to exist in either,
by some unaccountable blunder received an order to cease
firing so our fellows were exposed to a most dreadful galling
fire the whole way.' There was no feint attack by the French
(as had been stipulated) against the Russians defending the city
to our left. Their failure to make this together with the change
in the hour of assault Raglan was to put forward as the two
main reasons for the fiasco; yet he never at the time, or as a
condition of the British attack, insisted upon its being carried
out.

Nor was it only a question of defective tactics. At Headquarters there was not merely ignorance but entire lack of
perspicacity. How was it possible that Raglan and those about
him, knowing as they ought by this time the remarkable
Russian ability to repair damage overnight, could believe that
2,000 soldiers would be able to advance over a shell-swept
glacis 450 yards in length, thread their way through an un-
destroyed abattis, cross a ditch 20 foot wide and then assail
an escarpment, all without preliminary bombardment? 'You
can ask too much from even British soldiers' (wrote Lord
Wolseley, drawing on the experiences of half a century.) 'Upon
this occasion what we asked from them was beyond the power
of men to give. Our plan for the attack was simply idiotic and
was bound to fail.' To send 1,500 men, the majority being
young soldiers straight from England, whose only training had
been in trench work and in learning the virtues of cover, on

such a journey was murder. Colonel Froissart of the French army and our own Colonel Dacres had pointed out at the preliminary Staff conference the immense distance to be crossed in the open, but their objections had been overruled. Raglan's error was the more surprising because (as Palmerston later reminded his Secretary of War) Wellington had failed in his first attempt against Bajadoz through attacking a fortified wall protected by a ditch without first silencing the guns. Once again the high ratio of officers killed or wounded – 93 out of 1,473 – indicated that they had exposed themselves more than they should have been required to do in an endeavour to urge their men on, even allowing for their conspicuous uniforms.

The fact is only the officers and the best men ever reached the battle; a good many of the men did not behave well at all. The army does not consist of anything like so fine a set of men as those that fought at Alma and Inkerman.

What a lot of funkers they are making in our army; we have lost so many men and so many are wounded that they are always looking out for cover. They are quite right to do so, but what an effect it has on them. When they are wanted to storm they hang back a bit. Look at the officers' butcher's bill – that will show you that they were well forward. There will never be any mistake about them. I am sure that if our army were to take the field and had to storm a position like the Alma there would not be one officer left ... there is not that idea (among the men) that they never could be licked and did not know when they were licked.

The truth of these criticisms, the first by Campbell of the 46th and the other by Gerald Goodlake, is incontrovertible, but its implications may be doubted. Not even the men of Alma or Inkerman could have succeeded if the abattis had not been destroyed or the batteries and parapets not been silenced. They would not have halted, perhaps turned or sought shelter, but they would have died caught up in the branches or helplessly struggling in the ditch.

So profound was the depression following the disaster that to Goodlake's certain knowledge there were 50 officers who had sworn not to spend another winter in the Crimea and to sell out if need be. On the generals the débâcle of the

18th acted like an emetic. Sir George Brown and Pennefather went home; Escourt died of cholera, even the younger and haler Codrington went sick for a time before returning to take over from Brown. But the most tragic victim was Lord Raglan. On none had the bitterness of the 18th weighed more heavily. As Private McAusland of the 42nd passed him that afternoon he seemed 'very downcast and crestfallen'. Some months earlier he had declared that if he went home he would be stoned to death before he reached his town house in Stanhope Street. Yet then at least he could trail some of the glory of Alma and Inkerman. Now he was only the commander-in-chief of an army which had suffered an ignominious reverse. He started to age rapidly; his bodily resistance weakened. When he entertained Lord and Lady Paget to dinner on the 24th he did not look well. A day or two later he was in the grip of cholera and able to put up no fight. On June 28th, ten days after the ineffectual assault, he was dead.

Raglan was regretted, but, by the army, not greatly missed. Pélissier stood over his bedside for an hour crying like a child, but from what Goodlake overheard he thought the men 'were glad he is out of the way. They fancied that because he was not often seen he did not care about them enough.' The funeral was impressive. The cortège moved in solemn and stately pomp down to Kamiesh en route for England while the Russians everywhere chivalrously ceased firing. And then at Headquarters the page was hastily turned. To the rank and file, to the hard-working regimental officer, Raglan had been hardly more than a name, a figure slightly more familiar recently than in the dark winter months, but still an unfamiliar figure. Even that name was rarely mentioned and after the failure on the 18th only, James Paton tells us, abusively. 'His greatest fault was his excessive good nature and his wish to please everybody who was in personal communication with him; he was no doubt a man of considerable talent but his proper sphere was an office.' To this epitaph from the pen of Captain Campbell might be added one brief sentence from that of Arthur Brooksbank, 'He was distinguished for nothing but his amiable qualities.'

The clear choice of a successor was Sir Colin Campbell. He was peppery, without Raglan's urbanity; he was said to be cool towards the French and unable to speak their language, but there was probably no commander-in-chief who would have been more widely acclaimed by the army. Unhappily, except by Raglan, who had recognized his merits, he had never had a following either at the Horse Guards or at Headquarters, where his contempt for the Staff was notorious. 'God help the Staff officers who are not up to their work if he gets to the top', wrote his brigade-major Anthony Sterling.* They need have had no fear. The Government hastened to give the command to General James Simpson, who had recently been sent out to act as Chief of Staff. He was 63 and what young Pechell called 'a very good old man'. Like Raglan he was a Peninsular veteran, unlike him he had seen a little active service under Napier in India; but years and experience had done nothing to improve his mediocre talents. He was frequently prostrated with gout.

His methods were very much simpler than Raglan's. He gave no orders, he devised no plan, he left everything to the Staff. In other words, as Colonel Windham put it bluntly, 'he did not command the army'. On the day of his promotion he is credited with saying, 'They must indeed be hard up when they appointed an old man like me'; and being an honest man, he meant it.

With the British army under such a commander-in-chief and the French army after their terrible losses beginning to 'se lasser de telle charcuterie' the height of the campaigning season passed with little incident and the thoughts of many were already turning with dismay to the prospect of passing another winter on the Chersonese uplands.

---

* Ever since the beginning of April when it had become the practice to appoint a general for the day instead of the week to supervise trench duties, Campbell, although divisional generals were exempted, put himself down on the roster, the better to gain knowledge of the ground and to enforce discipline. After Raglan's death, for no reason assigned, he was ordered to discontinue the practice.

II

AUGUST found the Allies, according to Campbell, like Micawber, waiting for something to turn up. The Russians, disheartened by their own losses, appeared to be alternating between despair at ever being able to drive the invader into the sea and resolve to defend Sebastopol to the last man. It was significant, however, that early in the month they began to build a bridge of boats joining the north with the south side of the harbour. Furthermore during the truce for burying the dead of June 18th it was remarked that they were 'sad and sombre' and very different from the jaunty and confident air they had sported during the earlier truces. When Calthorpe referred in conversation with a young officer to the grievous British losses, the Russian had turned to him and, choking with emotion, cried: 'Losses? You don't know what the word means. You should see our batteries; the dead lie there in heaps and heaps. Troops can't live under such a fire of hell as you poured on us.' Already, he could have added, some 150,000 had been killed or wounded and possibly double that number had perished during the winter of hardship and disease on the bitterly cold marches to the Crimea. Yet all the while transports streaming across the Black Sea were week by week enlarging the allied forces with men, fit and well, with guns and ammunition and supplies. There seemed no end to Russian sufferings. In Sebastopol gloom and despair were spreading. 'Not a woman left, not a restaurant', Tolstoy (who was there) makes Semyonitch tell the elder Kozeltsof, 'no music; the last brothel went yesterday. It's melancholy.'

The daily losses, however, of the French as they sapped nearer and nearer the Malakoff were mounting and it may have seemed to Gortschakoff that there was still a chance, although a tenuous one, if all were staked on one epic battle. With everything he could spare he decided to fling himself on the extreme left of the allied front resting on the

Tchernaya river. As this was defended by the French, it became entirely a matter for them, assisted by some Sardinian troops. On August 16th the Russians, coming down in great strength from the Mackenzie Heights, fought their way across the Tchernaya. Had they succeeded in driving on, overrunning the French position on the Fedioukines and threatening the allies' right flank, 40,000 men from the city and Karabelnaya would have struck at the besiegers. Instead, in what Fortescue airily called 'a little affair', but which was in fact one of the most important engagements of the campaign, the Russians after some initial success were repelled with fearful losses. The gamble had failed and the fall of Sebastopol was now assured. Further positive action by the allies was no longer necessary. Only patience was needed. The bridge of boats was completed before the end of the month and every day streams of traffic could be seen transporting effects to the northern bank. All wagons entering Sebastopol were empty. One day very soon, it was clear, the Allies would wake up and find the enemy gone.

So tame a conclusion, so undramatic a climax, to an eleven-month siege did not suit the ambitions of Napoleon III who wanted something more creative of *la gloire*, so necessary for his Second Empire. Nor would it have been welcomed either in Whitehall or at Simpson's Headquarters. A second attack upon the Karabelnaya was an inevitability; and with the French army now outnumbering the British by three to one it followed that the chief responsibility for its planning rested with Pélissier. Certainly nothing very constructive came from Simpson, who at the council of war convened to arrange particulars, dozed much of the time, the mechanical nodding of his head being the only indication that life was not extinct. He returned (it is alleged) momentarily to consciousness to veto a sane suggestion that volunteers should be enrolled for the British assault on the Redan.

The plan agreed upon provided for an all-out offensive against the city and suburb at a number of points on a front of over six miles. The French were to start by rushing the Malakoff from which, at great daily cost and in loamier soil than existed before the Redan, they had sapped to within 25 yards. The hour chosen was midday, a time of garrison deadwater when (they learnt from a deserter) the old relief had marched out but, in order to avoid possible losses from congestion, the new relief had not marched in. For this important operation the resourceful Bosquet had been restored to his old command. Under him MacMahon's Division was to lead the attack directly against the Malakoff, to his right La Motte's was to advance against the Curtain and beyond him Dulac's against the Little Redan. The Central Bastion before the city was committed to Levaillant's Division, assisted by a Sardinian brigade, who when this was overrun were to wheel to the right and take the Flagstaff bastion in the flank. It will be noticed that no direct attack was contemplated upon the last-named and what lay behind it and particularly concerned the British army, the Garden Battery.

Having learnt from experience the difficulty of bringing up supports, the French had built before the Malakoff a broad road 50 yards wide and cutting straight through the parallels. Its existence was disguised from the Russians by lightly replacing the gabions where these should be.

The British arrangements were not so elaborate or extensive. Nor were the numbers to be employed, though greater than in June, more than a fraction of what the French were throwing in. But more dubious than the quantitative was the qualitative factor. With cruel kindness Simpson elected to give to Codrington's bled-white and used-up Light Division and the much-buffeted 2nd Division 'the honour of the assault, from the circumstances of their having defended the batteries and the approaches against the Redan for so many months'. Whether he did this on his own responsibility or (as some alleged) under pressure from an ambitious Codrington, it was a mistake. By a recognized maxim of war troops who had been roughly handled should go to reserve for a considerable time and not be used again in the identical operations. Nevertheless there might have been some justification for Simpson's ignoring this rule if both these divisions had contained a high proportion of veterans who had fought at Alma and Inkerman and had survived the winter. But the veterans numbered no more than 15 per cent in the 2nd Division and much less in the Light Division, which with its large intake of very young soldiers and 'weedy boys' was hardly more

than in name that which had landed at Old Fort. As for knowledge of the ground (reduced after painful weeks of sapping
in rocky soil to 250 yards) and of its hazards, there were
those who maintained that this was a positive disadvantage.
Whether it was so or not, it was inexcusable in Simpson to pass
over for this crowning exploit the claims of the unimpaired
Highland Division and of the comparatively unimpaired 3rd
Division.

The plan for attack provided for a covering party of 200,
a ladder party of 320, a storming party of 1,000 and 1,500
supporting troops, all to be supplied in equal numbers by the
Light and 2nd Divisions. What was left over in either division
was to form a reserve based on the third parallel. The only role
marked out for the Highlanders and the 3rd Division was to
act as second line of reserves with no method of being brought
forward except through several thousand yards of zigzags.
The entire enterprise was committed to Codrington and
Markham, an 'Indian' officer with an impressive record, who
had succeeded Pennefather to the 2nd Division.

While on this occasion the covering party and laddermen
from both divisions were to advance abreast, the storming
parties were to go one ahead of the other. Which this should be
Colonels Unett and Windham, who commanded the stormers
of the Light and 2nd Divisions respectively, put to the toss of a
gold Napoleon. It was won by Unett. 'My choice is made,' he
said, adding with no premonition of death, 'I shall be the first
man to enter the Redan.'

The date of the attack having been fixed for September 8th,
at dawn on the 5th the final bombardment opened with a
mighty roar. Like every one of its predecessors it reached a
new degree of intensity. During the next three days 13,000
shells and 90,000 round shot pounded the fortifications from
the muzzles of 800 guns. A new technique, too, of frightful-
ness had been developed by the French. From 250 of their
guns at the same instant would come a salvo creating terrible
losses and havoc in the Russian lines and filling the spectators
with awe. On the first night a shell, naturally claimed by them,
fired the *Beresina,* a two-decker moored in the harbour, and its
flames roaring up into the sky were a sight which Earle believed
any man at home would have paid £100 to see. Two

days later another man-of-war was hit and as it burned fiercely that night – the night before the assault – it was received as a happy omen of disaster for the enemy and further raised the excitement of the troops. They had just been issued with ten extra rounds of ammunition, two days' rations with orders to cook them and fill their water-bottles – sure indications of a battle on the morrow.

Indeed, hardly had darkness fallen on the evening of September 7th than troops started to parade and to move off, going from parallel to parallel to their allotted positions. Though a fault on the right side (as Windham was to acknowledge), there was no need for such an early start, which meant a long nerve-racking wait for the young untried soldiers, 'mere boys without a whisker'. Nor to the few who considered the preliminary deployments dispassionately did they appear to offer the best guarantee of success. Instead of arranging to send over the storming parties from the fifth parallel and so enabling them to advance, strung out across the whole spur in an extended and consequently less vulnerable line, they were ordered to follow the covering and ladder parties into and out of two *boyaux* or saps running forward at an angle from the fifth parallel and capable of accommodating only 20 files at a time. By this plan the distance to be covered was indeed reduced but the columns as they emerged from the *boyaux* one behind the other presented a perfect target for flanking fire from the Barrack and Garden Batteries. Even more open to criticism was the concentration upon so narrow an objective – the salient angle only of the Redan. To the more discerning the consequences of this restricted goal were only too vivid. 'This looks like another 18th of June', more than one officer was heard to prophesy gloomily. Unhappily it was to be an understatement.

September 8th dawned with a strong wind blowing straight from the north and driving eddies of stinging dust into the eyes of the men, though it helped to conceal them from the enemy. The batteries on the slopes behind were now firing vigorously and receiving in return only a feeble and desultory reply. Still further to the rear the off-duty military men and all amateurs and wives who had succeeded in piercing the military cordon, assembled to applaud, this time with complete confidence, the final act in the Sebastopol drama.

On this occasion there was to be no repetition of the Mayran miscalculation to upset the time-table. Pélissier would have no flag waved or rocket fired. Anticipating by 60 years procedure on the Western front his generals carefully synchronized their watches. As the hands reached 12 and the batteries relaxed their fire, a bugle call rang out. MacMahon's Zouaves sprang from the foremost sap, bounded across the intervening 25 yards 'like a lot of cats', and without firing a shot were into the Malakoff. A movable bridge on rollers, of a kind never thought of by our own Engineers, was run across the ditch, and racing three abreast the men went into the assault. As Pélissier had hoped, the Russians, not expecting an attack at that hour, were taken by surprise; their commander was actually sitting down to a plate of soup when the French burst into his dug-out. A few seconds later the tricolor was floating from the ramparts. Much hard fighting followed as the enemy fought desperately to regain this key fortress, but the gabions having been thrown down more and more French troops followed by artillery poured along the broad prepared way. In vain the Russians threw in a forlorn hope consisting chiefly of officers and cadets. The French hold on the Malakoff was never shaken.

For the British the hoisting of the tricolor was to serve as an alert only; the signal for attack was to be the firing of four rockets from Simpson's temporary Headquarters. Unfortunately on seeing the French flag flying from the Malakoff there broke from the impatient, excited troops shouts of 'Forward! ... Come on!' Over the parapets they went, which but for a last-minute insistence by Windham would have still been without any kind of banquette despite the lessons of June. They went, too, in headlong disorder, only the few older hands moving unhurriedly, some even pausing to light their pipes. The confusion brought about by this crazy, unregulated rush was instant and lasting and it permeated the entire operation. The ladder parties – each eight men this time to a 24-foot ladder – were not ready and in the rush some ladders were left behind. Those who eventually got away were not able to advance as planned abreast of the covering party, but went stumbling along in their rear.

As on June 18th the Russians were ready. The guns in the Salient had indeed been crushed and abandoned, but those in the earthworks to its right and left and especially those in the Barrack and Garden Batteries were in place and fully loaded. The instant the covering parties, laddermen, and stormers came into the open, one after the other, they were raked by such a fire of grape, canister, round shot, and musketry that it seemed later to survivors a miracle how anyone escaped. Particularly deadly was the enfilading fire from the Barrack and Garden batteries. A British battery recently built to hold three guns for the very purpose of countering such a threat had through someone's negligence been mounted with one only and was useless. By the time the abattis (on this occasion effectively shattered by artillery fire) had been passed and the ditch reached, great rents were visible in the columns. Everywhere redcoated soldiers could be seen from the rear lying like poppies dead on the ground or making their way back wounded. Only about six of the Light Division's 20 ladders ever got into the ditch, but here so crumbling were the sides (first dried out by the hot summer's sun and then pulverized by the guns) that they were hardly needed. The storming parties, the Light Division's on the left, the 2nd Division's on the right, were soon across the ditch and clambering up the escarpment, extending on either side to about the third gun embrasure. The Russian garrison estimated at more than 150 had meantime retreated behind the traverse running across the base of the triangle.

So far, notwithstanding the ragged formation and the severe losses suffered, the operation had gone more or less according to plan. Had the storming parties on both faces now pressed on through the embrasures it was, in the opinion of Hamley and others qualified to speak, not unlikely that the Redan might have been captured. But to George Ranken, a very intelligent Royal Engineer trying to do his best to construct a ramp across the ditch, the men coming up in driblets showed no sign of pressing on. They seemed to him 'stunned and paralysed – there was little of that dash and enthusiasm which might have been looked for from British soldiers in an assault.' And indeed what ensued was a repetition in a much aggravated form of what had happened in front of the Great Redoubt of

Kourgane, except that now most of the soldiers were mere boys who, Sergeant Gowing, looking back on that day, declared, 'had no learnt how to die, but who knew how to run'. Some of them confessed to be unable to use a rifle. Only two nights before there had been a disgraceful panic by these very troops during a Russian sortie on an advanced post and they scurried back, abandoning their officer. That morning, responding to the general excitement, they had quitted the *boyaux* bravely enough, but what courage they possessed (and according to Lord Moran courage is a capital sum reducible by expenditure) had progressively oozed away as they crossed those terrible 250 yards of fire and fury and saw comrades falling on every side, till when they reached the comparative safety of the salient parapet there was little left. Some indeed got no further than the edge of the ditch, where, finding shelter behind a rock or in a shell hole, they started to blaze away uselessly. Others seized the excuse to get back by offering to support a wounded comrade. Those, however, who crossed the ditch and scaled the escarpment pulled up as they reached the embrasures and saw through them the Russians lining the base of the Redan in ever-increasing numbers. Safe where they were, provided they kept their heads down, but their *élan* expended, they had time to remember having heard how the place was heavily mined. For all this, it is possible that they might have still obeyed the commands of their leaders and gone in. But there were no field officers left of the Light Division storming party, which had been the first to arrive. Colonel Unett was dead and Colonel Handcock of the 97th, whose young wife was watching with the other spectators, had fallen mortally wounded, both before reaching the abattis. Major Welsford, of the same regiment, who led the ladder party up the escarpment, had his head blown off as he entered an embrasure. The authority and even the example of the younger officers was insufficient to overcome their men's fears, now increased by the loss of their leaders. Captain Chippindall of the 19th might stand exposed on the parapet, forage cap on the point of his sword and urge his men on; Lieutenant Molesworth, scarcely more than a boy, might coolly light a cigar till it was knocked out of his mouth by a shell splinter; the men clinging to the outside of the Redan parapet and there for a time fairly immune from harm, refused to advance farther. A very long siege (as Sir Evelyn Wood has pointed out) 'is destructive of that discipline which is so essential to success in all operations requiring reckless daring but especially so in assaults of places.' To go forward in the face of such a storm of iron, increasing every moment as Russian reinforcements hurried up the broad strategic road from the rear and lined the traverses, seemed to them not only madness but contrary to the precepts they had imbibed and the practice of 'gabion-dodging' they had developed during their comparatively brief time in the Crimea. Now, in this crisis on the Redan they reacted, perhaps instinctively, to their training by sheltering in small groups behind the various screens, traverses and parapets skirting the Salient, whence those in the front ranks started to fire while those lower down the escarpment passed up their pouches. There ceased to be any consciousness of mutual support, which alone might have revived their courage and sent them forward to conquer or to die. From the moment that file firing began the rhythm of the attack was destroyed, a concerted assault on the second line of defences became impossible. As more and more men arrived the position grew worse instead of better. Even if eager to do so they could not break the human cordon stretched along the escarpment, composed, as Nathaniel Steevens arriving with the 88th found, of broken companies, regiments and even brigades. When enthusiastic young officers flourished their swords and dashed into the enceinte, when valorous buglers like Doyle of the 55th leapt on to the parapet and sounded the advance, there came no response. They would not take orders from officers they did not know. Only here and there a few stout-hearted, such as the giant Dan Mahoney, were prepared to follow some inspiring leader. But they were never enough to make an effective charge and their falling dead or wounded further reduced the morale of those crouching behind the gabions.

The fears and inertia of the first comers very naturally infected the reserves as they arrived. Thus when Hume coming up with the 55th of Inkerman fame but no longer composed of Inkerman veterans offered to lead a charge and only three men stepped forward he had to abandon the idea as useless and suicidal. Anthony Sterling, incensed at the choice of these

'pumped-out' troops', nevertheless as he watched from the
third parallel was not surprised. 'Some martinets, who have
seen nothing but parades in England, imagine that a boy put in
a red coat becomes wood or iron. There is as much art in
maintaining the courage of a soldier as in preserving their
health.' 'The heart was out of them', wrote another. In vain
Windham, who had arrived on the proper left of the salient
leading the stormers of the 2nd Division, crossed from one side
to the other, coaxing the men, patting them (in one case hitting
out with his fist), adopting 'the most approved theatrical atti-
tudes and *strong* language'. Clustering like bees round the
escarpment, men from at least ten different regiments, all
hopelessly intermingled, were too scared either to advance or
retreat. 'Oh England! Oh England!' apostrophized Earle, now
acting as Windham's ADC. 'Must it be said that not a man
moved, not a man would go backwards or forwards.' It was
only pressure from behind, thought Wolseley, that could have
given the men confidence and this for reasons soon to be
apparent was not forthcoming.

The only troops to advance with any semblance of homo-
geneity and discipline were the men of the 23rd. Acting as part
of the Light Division's reserves under the command of that
splendid soldier Dan Lysons it was in due course, but too late,
ordered by Codrington to assault the left of the Redan near its
re-entering angle with the bastions. Lysons, no doubt
remembering the lessons of the Alma, formed up his men, five
and a half companies in strength, not in the advanced *boyau*
but in the extended fifth parallel. Only when they had been
deployed in line and he was satisfied that what constituted a
banquette was in order (planks hastily laid across upright
barrels) did he give the order, 'Line will advance – quick
march.' Then (as he told his sister) 'over they came, the smooth-
faced boys of officers waving their swords – it was a fine sight'.
One of these, Boscawen Griffith, has written his impressions of
the next half an hour; 'I never expected to get to the Redan
alive; men were falling all round me. When I got to the head of
the Redan ditch I found men of different regiments all huddled
together in a vast mass but keeping up a good fire.' Dropping
into the ditch, he and his men fought their way up the escarpment where amidst 'the appalling confusion and noise', he

cannoned into another youthful officer named Deane of the
30th who like him was cheering on his men. 'We had not seen
each other for a long time. We shook hands. A moment
afterwards we separated and he was shot through the
heart.'

It was probably about this time that Windham on the
opposite face was taking a decision which was to have an
important bearing on the last tragic minutes of the attack.
Whether the initial surprise having failed the Redan could ever
have been carried by the arrival of reserves in considerable
strength and in good formation is doubtful. Unlike the Malakoff, where all-round defensive works turned to its undoing,
the Redan's great strength lay in its open rear, through which
the defenders could pour in reinforcements. Nevertheless,
Windham felt at the time (though he was not so sure later)
that the attack might still succeed if sufficient troops could
be thrown against the right face of the works. Three times he
sent back officers pleading for 'soldiers in formation and under
obedience' but received only penny-packets useless for his purpose. For this, the fault lay not with Codrington nor Markham
but with the master strategists at Headquarters whose plans
had required the reserves to be so far in the rear, but had provided no means of bringing them to the front with speed. Dis-
daining to copy the French, they left them to move by Indian
file through the thousands of yards of zigzags. Nor had they
foreseen the likelihood of these trenches becoming congested
with the wounded and dying from the preliminary assault and
with the improvised dressing-stations which harassed surgeons
were compelled to set up anywhere. 'How any man [declared
Lord Wolseley on looking back] who knew our narrow
trenches could have hoped that supports and reserves could be
led through them in time to be of any use to the troops is
beyond my conception.'

Unaware of these causes of delay Windham adopted the
well-intentioned but highly equivocal step of going back himself. Calling to a young subaltern named Crealock he said,
'Bear witness that I am not in a funk but I will now go back
and try what I can do.' He went and left in the Redan no officer
of higher rank than a captain. Colonel Cuddy of the 55th had
been shot dead, Eman of the 41st and the tall handsome

Patullo now in command of the 30th had been mortally, and Gough and Tyler of the 33rd and 62nd severely, wounded. On reaching the fifth parallel he met an extremely worried Codrington who after urging him to jump down out of the line of fire replied in answer to his request for men: 'Why, my good fellow, they won't go. And I've no number to send.' Daringly Windham ran across to try his luck with Markham. 'Only give me a battalion,' he cried, 'and help me out with it and I'll carry the work at once.' 'Can you?' said Markham coolly. 'Then take the Royals.' But it was too late. The men were already in retreat.

Reasons given for the final breakdown of the assault differ according to the exact position of the writer. To Griffith on the left face it was the moment when the ammunition failed. Then it was, he records with sorrow, 'that a general panic seized our men and they rushed suddenly out of the ditch and back across the open towards our lines, although the officers remained as long as they could and tried to rally the men in every possible way, but it was of no avail'.

Ranken's version (he was below the right face) is more dramatic:

I heard directly after I had regained our trenches that three officers of the 41st after vainly striving to induce the men to advance rushed forward together and were all three shot down like one man by the cross fire of the Russians behind their parados. This was the turning point according to this account of the men's indecision – they wavered and fled. I was near the counterscarp when I saw the whole living mass on the salient begin reeling and swaying to and fro.

In front of them, as the British fire weakened, the Russians started to move forward like a solid wedge forcing themselves inexorably into the narrowing area of the salient. Through the air came hurtling hand-grenades and the fire from their serried ranks converged on to the apex-shaped target like 'a storm of iron'. Confronted by such a threat, seeing ahead of them the interior of the Redan strewn with their dead, behind them not a shadow of support, with no high-ranking officer left, no ammunition in their pouches, it is not surprising that the nerves of these youthful soldiers collapsed. To the cry of

'The Russians are coming!', they leapt and slithered and tumbled from the two faces of the Redan like flies treated with insecticide. A moment later the dried-out escarpment subjected to the sudden pressure of men in a panic gave way in great segments, hurling them into the ditch below. There amidst a hell of broken ladders, smashed gabions, dead bodies and protruding bayonets (on which some falling men were impaled) soldiers struggled for breath and survival, yelling, kicking, swearing, groaning, some in their death agony, others as heavy boots tore into their lacerated limbs.

In a moment [continues Ranken] I found myself knocked down and lying on my face, with a number of men scrambling over me – their bayonets running through my clothes. I expected to have been stunned and bayoneted and to have been left insensible in the ditch, or shot by the enemy before I could drag myself out of it.

As the last soldiers jumped from the Redan the Russians surged forward lining the parapet and to the accompaniment of jeers and abuse fired down into the tortured, writhing mob below, or for lack of ammunition hurled stones, twisted pieces of iron, anything that came to hand. There was nothing in the whole campaign with the exception of the Sand Bag Battery at Inkerman to compare with this closing scene in the last of the Crimean battles. And nothing more ignominious. 'It almost broke my heart', wrote Clifford sadly, 'and drove me mad to see our soldiers, our British soldiers, that I was so proud of, run away.'

With shattered limbs, or blinded with blood and stricken with panic, men were crawling or staggering or running across those 250 yards. Caught in great eddies of grape shot they were seen to roll over and over like rabbits; those who survived the ordeal tumbled exhausted, sometimes as many as four deep, into the nearest trench. Even here their agony did not end. Vertical fire directed by the Russian guns into the seething parallels provided the final contribution to the day's carnage.

When the cost was counted it was found that this had been nearly as great in the two hours of fighting as in the whole eight hours of Inkerman. The killed amounted to 385, the wounded 1,886, the missing 176, in all 2,447, of whom 156 were officers.*

Once again letters describing the second débâcle, so much more mortifying than the first, are bestrewed with words and phrases imputing to Headquarters botchery, mismanagement, obtuseness, inability to profit from experience, and wilful refusal to learn from the French.

Was it prudent [asks Henry Clifford] to send these two divisions that had never for a moment been out of the trenches to take the Redan? Second was it right to send any men two hundred yards in the open against a place like the Redan with guns vomiting forth grape, and when hundreds of their comrades fell long before they ever got to the Ditch? The French, with older and more tried troops, would not assault the Malakoff again till they had silenced the fire of the guns and brought their trenches within twenty yards of the Ditch.

The inability to sap as close as the French was unavoidable in view of the rocky ground; the failure to silence the batteries and to foresee the hopelessness of the attack as planned was inexcusable. On this point Sir Colin Campbell had no doubt.

Was it supposed that such a work, defended by Russian soldiers, could be carried by 40 men, presenting themselves on the ramparts from 40 ladders, even allowing that we had succeeded in bringing the whole 40 to the scarp of the work and placing them against it? – a most impossible event under the fire of artillery and musketry to which our troops would be exposed in passing over the distance of upwards of 200 yards.

'As faulty in every detail as it was puerile in conception.' No one who fought that day has been found to disagree with this severe summing-up by Lord Wolseley. To direct 3,000 men (assuming all reserves came up on time) into a powerfully-defended triangular space of only 2,500 square yards – further reduced by traverses and barriers – with no gorge in the rear to give defence against counter-attacks and no provision made for the arrival of a constant stream of supports was imbecile planning. The only chance of taking the Redan – and

* The total of Inkerman was 2,573, but to the Redan casualties should be added 24 of the Naval Brigade.

it was never more than a chance as long as our nearest sap was
250 yards away – was to employ at least twice the number of
troops, preferably seasoned troops and send them forward on
a wide front, having previously silenced or crippled all flanking batteries and above all having made possible the swift and
continuous arrival of supports.

Naturally Simpson as commander-in-chief came in for most
of the blame. He and his Staff were without question responsible for the plan of attack and for the excluding of the Highland Brigade, Eyre's division with its first brigade which had
fought so spiritedly on June 18th and its second which had so
far never been given a chance, and a reconstituted Guards Brigade, who instead of fighting 'watched [wrote Paymaster
Dixon indignantly] from a distant hill as safe and useful as if
they had been in Regent Street'. His leadership had been consistently pedestrian and uninspiring. But it is unfair to criticize
him (as has been done) for consenting to attack the Redan
instead of confining the British contribution to bombardment
or feints, on the grounds that once the Malakoff was in French
hands it could only be a matter of time before the Russians
were compelled to abandon it. As in June, the prestige of his
country, if not respect for the feelings of his army, required an
assault upon the challenging Redan. Where Simpson himself
failed was in not insisting that Pélissier, as a price of British
support, should launch a simultaneous offensive against the
Bastion du Mât and the Garden Battery.

Next after Simpson and his Staff, critics fastened upon Codrington. Anthony Sterling saw him standing in the fifth parallel

with all his Staff, about 250 yards from the angle of the Redan,
with his men clustered on its ramparts neither advancing nor
retiring for three-quarters of an hour. . . . If ever a General should
have played the part of a grenadier that was the time. If he had
rushed up he might have failed in getting the men to move on;
but he should have tried and died there.

This censure, like much that comes from Anthony Sterling's
gall-dipped pen, is not altogether just. Codrington was called
upon to carry through an operation not of his planning, an
operation likened at the time to that of a fireman being ordered
to extinguish a vast blaze equipped with nothing better than a

garden syringe. Nevertheless he did show less enterprise than was expected for one of his years (he was only 51), he failed to ensure the speedy arrival of his supports and in general did not live up to his Alma reputation for coolness and resolution. Certainly he showed none of the spirit of Vinoy, who when beating off attempts to retake the Malakoff drove his sword into the ground, drew his revolver and threatened anyone who retreated beyond it with death.

Cynically it has been said that no matter what mistakes a general makes the pluck of the British soldier will usually see him through. It did so at the Alma and again at Inkerman, it nearly did so at Balaclava; it had no chance to do so in the June and failed utterly in the September attack on the Redan. Though Windham, out of loyalty, sought to stifle any inquiry into the conduct of the troops, in his private conversation and correspondence he was less reticent. To Mrs Duberly he said: 'the moment they saw a gabion they ran to it as they would to their wives and would not leave its shelter'; and to Campbell: 'I could have forgiven them if they had been beaten out of it, but they would not go in. . . . All dash seems to have gone out of them.' He told Clarke Jervoise that of the 2nd Division those who really entered the Redan were nine-tenths officers 'who failed by example or encouragement to get their men on'. In a letter to his close friend Charles Greville he wrote: 'There was a great deal of individual pluck particularly in the officers, and many of the old soldiers behaved well; but there was no "united pluck" and without that how can you act against numbers?' The emphasis laid upon the *old* soldier needs no comment. It was not he but the young soldier that Maule had in mind when he gave his impressions of that he saw as he watched the attack from the 3rd Division across the Woronzoff Ravine.

I am sorry to say our infantry did not do as well as [*sic*] ought but the fact is that our men were stale in the trenches having been down so often, together with the distance from the Redan as well as the capital flanking defence they have got.

It almost makes me think [wrote Clarke Jervoise] that true courage is not found in every hedge and ditch in England or in every alley from which we recruit our army.

Lieutenant Fletcher, RN, who was a closer spectator, is even more candid.

> I am sorry to say the men behaved in a most cowardly and rascally manner, left their officers to be killed and failed entirely. I was in the trenches and a fearful sight it was, one body of men were in the advance and the wounded were brought back and killed in as large a body as those advancing to the attack. We were entirely repulsed ... and disgracefully repulsed. ... The men held back or ran, the officers were all obliged to go to the front and were shot like dogs, not being able to get the men to advance.

These things could not have happened had there been more men of the calibre of Colour-Sergeant McAlister who, when grievously wounded and ordered to retire, attempted to carry on, crying 'I've done nothing for old England yet.' But soldiers like him were by now (as one writer wrote) 'underground'.

It was no doubt natural that, incensed by the humiliating failure, those who dashed off their comments were unreasonably harsh. The young soldier may not have distinguished himself, but he was called upon to perform what in like circumstances it is by no means certain Sir Colin Campbell's veteran Highlander could have done. Moreover, it must be remembered that though successful at the Malakoff, whence came MacMahon's heroic affirmation *J'y suis, j'y reste*, the French were twice repelled with tremendous losses from the Little Redan (which like the Great Redan had no gorge to protect its assailants once in possession) and altogether failed in their attack upon the Central Bastion.

Humiliated by this staggering reverse Simpson would have at once flung in the Highland Brigade and the 3rd Division, but that the chaos and congestion obtaining in the parallels made it impossible to move them forwards in time. Instead Sir Colin Campbell was ordered to make the attack on the following morning. Even so it was not till late that night that his men had replaced the shattered divisions in the front parallels.

In this way it came about that in the early hours Private McAusland was lying in advance of the trenches within 50 yards of the ditch when a sergeant of the Rifle Brigade crawled up to him with the news that the Russians were leaving the

Redan. A few moments later one explosion after another burst from the Redan, the town and the Karabelnaya. In the light of brilliant flashes, to be followed by a dull roar, huge blocks of masonry were seen tosssed in the air like so many pebbles. Jagged tongues of flame illuminated the ruined empty buildings which had been set alight. All along the bastions where Russians had died in their thousands spread a coruscation of fire as magazines went up one after another. Ships in the harbour, similarly fired, floated like so many flaming torches, only to be extinguished when the flames reached water-level or the magazine, in which case the vessel disintegrated in a treendous explosion and 'you saw the great masts flying in the air like arrows'. Soon the city, the bastions, the harbour were lost in an enormous cloud of smoke made incandescent by the raging fires beneath. Under its cover the Queen of the Euxine was abandoned to its besiegers.

It will never be known who was the first to step across its shattered fortifications into a silent deserted Redan. Some time before dawn an NCO of the Royal Engineers is said to have reported it to be empty. Robert Lindsay, leading a burying part at 5 AM, may, as he believed, have been the first to enter. Within nothing was to be heard but the 'painful breathing and moans of the wounded who lay there amongst the dead. There were no living creatures, besides the poor shattered soldiers.' Close under the Russian breastwork, furthest in of all, lay the body of James Swift, the youngest ensign in the 90th Regiment of Foot. As daylight came and smoke cleared, the bridge of boats over which the Russians had retreated was seen to be destroyed. With this final retreat Tolstoy closes his *Sebastopol* in words of unforgettable pathos:

On reaching the north side and on leaving the bridge almost every man took off his cap and crossed himself. But behind this feeling was another, a sad, gnawing and deeper feeling which seemed like remorse, shame and anger. Almost every soldier, looking back from the north side of the abandoned town, sighed with inexpressible bitterness in his heart and menaced the enemy.

For almost exactly a year the Russians – 'What plucky troops they were', ejaculated the future General Gordon – had put forth a defence which evoked the admiration not only of their enemies but of the whole world. And now they were gone, with dignity and with honour, having tended our wounded as they lay in the Redan and put water within their reach.

'It was a great occasion. I could na' resist', said Simpson as he recounted Pélissier's kiss of victory upon his cheeks. But there was little joy in the minds and hearts of his soldiers that morning or, if there was, its roots were shallow. Hugh Clifford is not likely to have been out of the ordinary when he put his feelings into these words:

If a few days before I had been told 'on the morning of the 9th September at five o'clock Sebastopol will be in the hands of the Allies and you will stand in the Redan held by the English', I should have said, 'Oh! that will be a proud and happy moment that will repay us for all we have gone through, even the loss of so many lives, so much suffering and hardship will not have been thrown away in vain.' But no, I stood in the Redan more humble, more dejected and with a heavier heart that I have yet felt since I left home.

I looked towards the Malakoff and there was the French flag, the Tricolor planted on its parapet. Yes, the French had taken the Malakoff, but the English had not taken the Redan. No flag floated on the Parapet on which I stood and if it had I could have seized it and dashed it into the ditch we could not pass, or hid it in the bosom of the young officer, dead at my feet inside the Redan. I could not stand it long. The Redan was ours because the French had taken the Malakoff which commanded it and we have lost a great number of brave officers and some brave men and some that were not so . . . to no purpose.

The absence of exhilaration which normally succeeds achievement was not only due to failure at the Redan. Twelve months on the Chersonese upland, seeing death daily in many forms and circumstances, had not sufficiently hardened stomachs for the sight that awaited British troops as they penetrated the hospital wards and cellars of Sebastopol with their scores of unburied dead and saw the maggot-infested wounds of those who were still living and smelt a stench so terrible that it defied description.

It is quite useless [Clifford told his father] my trying to give you any idea of the awful spectacle. Some had died from bad wounds, but the greater part, only slightly wounded, had died from exhaustion, hunger, thirst, and want of common care. Every possible attitude of agony was depicted there and I did not see one that looked as if he had died quietly and without great pain. They were almost naked and had crawled about the room. Some had been dead for days and their flesh was falling off them, some looked like Negroes, so black and almost all were swollen to an enormous size.

In one large hospital every bed contained a corpse.

No battle followed the fall of Sebastopol. Nor was there much heart left for fighting. Palmerston, raised to power in order to produce a victorious peace, might deplore the ending of the war with such a lamentable British '*fait d'armes*'. The fighting man saw it in another light. 'I am tired of war and should not care if I never heard another shot fired in anger in my life.' These sentiments of Frederick Elton, shortly to be decorated with the Victoria Cross, have a very different ring from those of Private Dempsey of the 33rd when writing home a year before: 'I am very proud of my position as I hope to be one of the number that will muzzle the Russian bear and revenge the wrongs of the weak on the tyrant's head.'

In conditions very much changed from those a year before the army, well-hutted, well-fed, dry and warm, spent another winter on the Chersonese upland. There were races and sporting events, entertainments, private theatricals, lectures for those with a more serious turn of mind, and drinking for all, especially for those in receipt of more than £2 of back pay. In February a Peace conference met in Paris, four days later an armistice was proclaimed and a month later peace was signed. On April 17th there was a grand military review of the Allied armies by the Russian General Luders. The British troops numbered 31,000 and were acclaimed by him to be 'magnificent'.

*   *   *

Sixty years later another British Expeditionary Army was making its way through the Aegean Sea bound for the coasts of the Sultan's dominions. Ahead of it past the Dardanelles on the shores of the Bosphorus lay the bones of 10,000 British soldiers. Three hundred miles farther to the north-east reposed 10,000 more scattered through the 130 cemeteries of the Crimea. Twenty thousand men who had fought and died (the majority by disease) to preserve from the imperial ambitions of Russia the integrity of the Porte which a third generation of Britons had come, as allies of Imperial Russia, to destroy. . . .

Appendix

The modern designation of Regiments mention in the text

The 1st: The Royal Scots
The 3rd: The Buffs (East Kent Regiment)
The 4th: The King's Own (Royal Lancaster Regiment)
The 7th: The Royal Fusiliers (City of London Regiment)
The 18th: The Royal Irish Regiment (*Disbanded 1922*)
The 19th: The Green Howards
The 20th: The Lancashire Fusiliers
The 21st: The Royal Scots Fusiliers
The 23rd: The Royal Welch Fusiliers
The 28th: The Gloucestershire Regiment
The 30th: The East Lancashire Regiment
The 33rd: The Duke of Wellington's (West Riding Regiment)
The 34th: The Border Regiment (*1st Battalion*)
The 38th: The South Staffordshire Regiment
The 39th: The Dorsetshire Regiment
The 41st: The Welch Regiment
The 42nd: The Black Watch (Royal Highlanders)
The 44th: The Essex Regiment
The 45th: The Sherwood Foresters (*1st Battalion*)
The 47th: The Loyal North Lancashire Regiment
The 49th: The Royal Berkshire Regiment
The 50th: The Queen's Own (Royal West Kent Regiment)
The 55th: The Border Regiment (*2nd Battalion*)
The 57th: The Middlesex Regiment (*1st Battalion*)
The 62nd: The Wiltshire Regiment
The 63rd: The Manchester Regiment
The 68th: The Durham Light Infantry
The 77th: The Middlesex Regiment (*2nd Battalion*)
The 79th: The Cameron Highlanders
The 88th: The Connaught Rangers (*Disbanded 1922*)
The 91st: The Argyll and Sutherland Highlanders
The 95th: The Sherwood Foresters (*2nd Battalion*)
The 97th: The Royal West Kent Regiment

Bibliography

MANUSCRIPT SOURCES (LL = Letters; D = Diary)

Colonel Frank Adams, 28th Foot (LL); Cornet George Clowes, 8th Hussars (LL); Corporal Dolton, Scots Fusilier Guards (D); Lieut A. M. Earle, 57th Foot (LL); Captain F. C. Elton, 55th Foot (LL); Lieut W. A. Godfrey, Rifle Brigade (D); Captain G. L. Goodlake, Coldstream Guards (LL); Ensign Boscawen Griffith, 23rd Foot (LL & D); Captain F. Haygarth, Scots Fusilier Guards (D); Lieut Michael Heneage, Coldstream Guards (LL); Captain Hugh Hibbert, 7th Foot (LL); Colonel J. Hunter Blair, Scots Fusilier Guards (LL & D); Captain J. C. Jervoise, 23rd Foot (LL); Lieut V. H. Lee, 21st Foot (LL); Captain F. Maxse, 13th Light Dragoons (LL); Captain G. A. Maude, RA (LL & D); Private McAusland, 42nd Foot (D); Corporal T. Mitchell, RA (LL); Captain H. Montgomery, 42nd Foot (LL); Lieut J. Paton, 4th Foot (LL); Major J. B. Patullo, 30th Foot (LL); Captain W. Pechell, 77th Foot (LL); Lieut. E. Phillips, 8th Hussars (LL); Lieut W. P. Richards, RA (LL); Lieut P. Robertson, 4th Foot (D); Private C. Smith, 7th Foot (D); Lieuts William and Charles Stirling, RA (LL); Lieut Francis Stirling, RA (LL); Surgeon A. H. Taylor, RA (LL); Major R. Tinley, 39th Foot (LL).

PRIVATELY PRINTED

Letters of Lieut Brooksbank (38th); Lieut Rowe Fisher (4th Dragoon Guards); Captain G. A. Maude (RA); Edward Portal (4th Light Dragoons); Sergeant A. Mitchell (13th Hussars), *Recollections of the Light Brigade*.

PUBLISHED SOURCES

Adye, J., *Review of the Crimean War* (1860)
— *Recollections of Military Life* (1895)
Airlie, Countess of, 'With the Guards We shall go' (1933)
Atkinson, C. T., *History of the Royals*
Aubrey-Fletcher, H. L., *History of the Foot Guards* (1927)

Army List, 1855

Annual Registers, 1854/5

Bannantyne, N., *History of the 30th Regiment* (1923)

Bostock, Surgeon-Gen. A. B., *Letters from India and the Crimea* (1896)

Brunon, J., 'Balaclava, la Charge de la Brigade Légère'
— *Revue Historique de l'Armée* (1954)

Burgoyne, Sir John, *Military Opinions* (1859)

Calthorpe, S. J. G., *Letters from Headquarters*, 2 vols. (1856)

Campbell, Colin F., *Letters from Camp* (1894)

Campbell, Sir Colin, *Life by Shadwell*, vol. I (1881)

Clifford, Henry, *Letters and Sketches from the Crimea* (1956)

Colebrooke, Sir E., *Journal of Two Visits to the Crimea* (1856)

Duberly, Mrs Henry, *Journal kept during Russian War* (1855)

Evelyn, G. P., *Diary of Crimea,* edited by Cyril Falls (1954)

Farquharson, K. S., *Reminiscences of Crimea,* etc. (1883)

Ferrar, M. L., *History of the 19th Regiment* (1911)

Forbes, A., *The Black Watch*

Fortescue, J. W., *History of the British Army*, vol. XII (1930)

Franks, Sergt-major, 'Leaves from a Soldier's Note-Book' (1904)

Gadsby, J., 'A Trip to Sebastopol' (1884)

Gernsheim, H. and A., *Roger Fenton, Photographer of the Crimean War* (1955)

Gooch, B. D., *The New Bonapartist Generals in the Crimean War* (1954)

Gordon, General, *Letters* (1884)

Gowing, T., 'Voice from the Ranks' (1954)

Hamilton, F. W., *History of the Grenadier Guards,* vol. III (1874)

Hamley, E., *The Campaign of Sebastopol* (1885)
— *The War in the Crimea* (1891)

Heath, L. G., *Letters from the Black Sea* (1897)

Hibbert, C., *Destruction of Lord Raglan*

Higginson, G., 'Seventy-one Years of a Guardsman's Life' (1916)

Hodasevich, R. A., 'A Voice from within the Walls of Sebastopol' (1856)

Hume, J. R., *Reminiscences of the Crimea with the 55th* (1894)

Illustrated London News 1854/5

Jowett, Sergt W., *Diary* (1856)

Kinglake, A. W., *The Invasion of the Crimea,* 9 vols., 6th edit. (1887)

Kingsford, C. L., *Story of the Middlesex Regiment*

Lysons, Sir D., *Crimean War from First to Last* (1895)

Maurice, Sir F., *History of the Scots Guards*, vol. III (1931)

Maxwell, E. H., *With the Connaught Rangers* (1883)

Money, A. and G. H., 'Sebastopol', *etc.* (1856)

Munro, Surgeon-Gen. W., *Reminiscences of Military Service with the 93rd* (1883)

Nolan, E. H., *The War against Russia*

Pack, C., *Sebastopol Trenches* (1878)

Paget, Lord G., *The Light Cavalry in the Crimea* (1881)

Panmure Papers, 2 vols. (1908)

Parry, D. H., 'Death and Glory Boys', *the Story of the 17th Lancers* (1899)

Peard, G. S., *Campaign in the Crimea* (1855)

Porter, W., *Life in the Trenches before Sebastopol* (1856)

Ranken, G., *Six Months at Sebastopol* (1857)

Reid, D. A., *Memories of the Crimean War* (1911)

Robinson, F. *Diary of the Crimean War* (1856)

Ross-of-Bladensburg, *The Coldstream Guards in the Crimea* (1897)

Russell, W. H., *Life by J. B. Atkins* (1911)

Russell, W. H., *The War in the Crimea* (1855)

— *The British Expedition to the Crimea* (1858)

— *The Great War with Russia* (1895)

Ryan, G., *Our Heroes of the Crimea* (1855)

Sayer, H., *Crimea Dispatches* (1857)

Skene, J. H., *With Lord Stratford in the Crimean War* (1883)

Slack, J., *History of the 63rd Regiment* (1884)

Steevens, N., *The Crimean Campaign with the Connaught Rangers* (1878)

Stephenson, F. C. A., *At Home and on the Battlefield* (1915)

Sterling, A., *The Story of the Highland Brigade in the Crimea* (1895)

Stuart, B., 'Soldier's Glory', *being Rough Notes of an Old Soldier* (Sir George Bell)

Thomson, Anstruther, *Eighty Years' Reminiscences*, vol. I (1904)

Taylor, G. Cavendish, *Adventures with the Army*, 2 vols. (1856)

Tyrrell, H., *The War with Russia*, 3 vols.

Vieth, F. H. D., *Recollections of the Crimean Campaign* (1907)

Vulliamy, C. E., *Crimea* (1939)

Walker, General B., *Diary of a Soldier's Life* (1924)

Wantage, Lord, *A Memoir* (1904)

Whinyates, F. A., *From Coruna to Sebastopol* (1893)

Whom Shall We Hang (Sir P. B. Maxwell) (1855)

Wightman, J. W., *One of the Six Hundred* (1892)

Williams, G. T., *The Eleventh Hussars* (1908)

Willy, H. C., *The 95th in the Crimean* (1899)

Wolseley, Viscount, *The Story of a soldier's Life*, vol. I (1903)

Wood, Sir E., 'The Crimea in 1854 & 1894' (1895)

Woodham-Smith, C., *The Reason Why* (1954)

Wrottesley, G., *Life of Sir John Burgoyne* (1873)

Windham, C. A., *Crimean Diary and Letters* (1897)

Index

ILLUSTRATED **BRITISH BATTLES SERIES**

BATTLES OF THE CRIMEAN WAR 6/-
W. BARING PEMBERTON

'The best Crimean "primer" ever ... engagingly written and goes at a rollicking pace' *The Daily Telegraph*

THE BATTLE OF MATAPAN 6/-
S. W. C. PACK

'Told with a skill and vividness which recreate the picture in all its gallant and striking colours' *The Times*

THE BATTLE FOR NORMANDY 6/-
EVERSLEY BELFIELD and H. ESSAME

'Clear, vivid account of what the authors describe as "the last great set-piece battle of the Western World".' *The Observer*

THE SOMME 5/-
A. H. FARRAR-HOCKLEY

'A model military history, unsplashed with rhetoric' *The Observer*

CORONEL AND THE FALKLANDS 6/-
GEOFFREY BENNETT

The story of the first major sea battles of World War 1. 'An excellent account, notable for its insight and its commendable freedom from hindsight.' *Royal United Services Institution Journa*

CORUNNA 6/-
CHRISTOPHER HIBBERT

The battle in the Peninsular War which saved a British Army from annihilation. 'Fast-flowing, taut and economical ... the pithy thumb-nail sketches are masterly, the account of the battle superb.' *The Times Literary Supplement*

These and other advertised PAN books are obtainable from all booksellers and news-agents. If you have any difficulty please send purchase price plus 6d. postage to PO Box 11, Falmouth, Cornwall.

BRITISH ILLUSTRATED BATTLES SERIES

WATERLOO 6/-
JOHN NAYLOR

'No commanders were ever better served by their men, British, French and Prussian ... graphic descriptions present a moving story of courage, devotion and endurance.'
British Army Review

AGINCOURT 6/-
CHRISTOPHER HIBBERT

'A straightforward and absorbing account of this astounding battle and the campaign that so improbably led up to it.'
The Observer

BATTLES OF THE '45 6/-
KATHERINE TOMASSON and FRANCIS BUIST

The story of the fiercely fought engagements which took place between the royal army and the Jacobites, led by Prince Charles Edward. 'History as it should be written ... infinite research and highly entertaining.' *Books and Bookmen*

THE SPANISH ARMADA 5/-
MICHAEL LEWIS

'A brilliantly clear picture of the campaign.
British Book News

TRAFALGAR 5/-
OLIVER WARNER

'A stirring picture of the battle in which Nelson died destroying Napoleon's power at sea.' *New York Times*

THE ENGLISH CIVIL WAR 5/-
AUSTIN WOOLRYCH

'An excellent book. Covers the three decisive engagements which sealed the fate of King Charles I: Marston Moor which lost him the North, Naseby which lost him most of his army, and Preston which lost him his head.' *The Daily Telegraph*